# Trinity Methodist Church, Penarth: A Portrait

by

## John and Sheila Gibbs

ISBN 1 85852 015 0

Published for Trinity Methodist Church, Penarth

by Methodist Publishing House

1994

The cover makes use of a painting 'Pentecost' by Dennis Hawkins. The intense circle of white on an old school desk suggests the way in which the Spirit can transform the ordinary, the familiar, the patently blemished. The original is part of 'The Church and Artist' Collection.

# CONTENTS

2

# FOREWORD

## by Rupert Davies

If you pick up a history of a local church of any denomination, you will expect to find, and usually will find, a straightforward description of its buildings and a narrative of the chief events of its life, with a list of the clergy or ministers who have served it. You will not often find much about the community in which the particular church is located, or even the larger church of which this local church is a part.

This book is of a different sort. Trinity Methodist Church, Penarth – often thought of as a suburb of Cardiff, but actually a town in its own right, like other churches has seen many social and economic changes in its own neighbourhood and in the country at large, and each of these has affected all its members in one way or another. So also with the numerous developments in the Methodist Church in England and Wales: every change has affected the corporate worship and the individual lives of everyone connected with Trinity Church.

So John and Sheila Gibbs have decided to see and describe Trinity Church in its local and national context, to show how such events as two world wars, and the aftermath of each, the change of Penarth from a shipping centre to a middle class stronghold, the Great Depression, periods of severe unemployment and occasional bouts of prosperity, have made their impact on the church community and its members. And at the same time, and at rather greater length, to measure the impact of Methodist Union, the arguments about pacifism, the pioneering youth work of James Butterworth in London, the foundation of the Methodist Association of Youth Clubs, the revision of the liturgy, the formulation of the Anglican-Methodist Union Scheme – and its disastrous rejection by the Anglicans in England, and the ordination of women.

As we see the life of Trinity Church evolving in this context, we realize that we are being asked to look at a mirror of modern Methodism in its twentieth century setting. This is one great merit of the book.

But it does not mean that the inner life of the church and its members, or its problems and disputes, are neglected. Quite the contrary. The chapters are mostly arranged under the names of successive ministers down to the present day; and each of them is duly appreciated. The

3

benign influence of certain families is brought to our notice, notably that of the Morels – in earlier days, and of the Gibbs and others in the more recent past – one may suspect that the influence of the Gibbs family is somewhat understated for reasons of modesty. The foundation and history of the Methodist International House of South Wales – now closed after twenty-one years' invaluable service, and of the Penarth Methodist Home for the Aged – both closely connected with Trinity, are fully chronicled. Distinguished Methodist leaders such as Scott Lidgett, Russell Maltby – one of whose sermons is here printed, and Robert Bond, mingle with other people of light and leading, but of local rather than national importance. And Anne Knighton, a native of Penarth, who made a deep impression on the whole of Methodism until her sudden death, has a chapter to herself.

Not the least fascinating feature is the account of the Drama Group which performed plays of many kinds for thirty years in many other places as well as in Penarth, and set a high standard for others to follow.

You might think that the story told is now complete. But it is not; for Trinity Church goes on. This is a remarkable record of the progress made so far.

# LIST OF ILLUSTRATIONS

# ACKNOWLEDGEMENTS

We would like to express our appreciation to all those members of Trinity who have contributed to the life of the church and to the bringing together of this account of its history. We hope that they find within these pages a recognisable portrait of the community of which they are a part.

We are very grateful to the Rev'd Dr. John Newton for giving permission for the inclusion of his Address at the Service of Celebration and Thanksgiving for the life and witness of Anne Knighton, with which we close this history, and to the Rev'd Arnold Morris for giving his permission for the inclusion of the text of his Televised Sermon from the B.B.C. Service in April 1970.

No one can write on Methodism without borrowing from the Rev'd Dr. Rupert Davies' book of that name and from his other writings in the *Proceedings* of the Wesley Historical Society. Sometimes the borrowing is conscious and can be precisely acknowledged; often it lies below the surface in the writers' subconscious.

The late Rev'd Kenneth Garlick's help was invaluable; he provided details of the lives of Trinity Ministers from the earliest times. Sadly, later compilations of Methodist history will miss the help and enthusiasm with which he joined in the writing. His *Registry*, the Methodist Crockford, was invaluable in supplying facts about the lives of living Ministers.

The Rev'd George Thompson Brake's large and detailed *Policy and Politics in British Methodism 1932-1982* was extremely helpful. By encompassing in one volume the background and the detail of what was happening on the larger map of Methodism, it complements the task we set ourselves.

Dr. John Vickers seems able to provide the answer to almost any question that can be asked about Methodism. Whether, for example, Pew Rents were collected quarterly or annually, or who was the fine looking Churchman in the photograph of a stone-laying in 1899; the answer being Hugh Price Hughes.

We took full advantage of the recollections of Kathleen Ede, nee Bond, our oldest living source, for the events of her father's two terms of

Ministry at Trinity. We thank Beth Sloan, now of Blackheath, for material on Russell Maltby – she was one of his Deaconesses – and for the copy of one of his sermons which she had fortunately preserved.

Patricia Moore, in the last days of her service as Glamorgan County Archivist, made material available to us, particularly the 1891 Census, and copies of the *Circuit Record* deposited there. In our first Chapter on Penarth we used material from her long essay on *South Glamorgan: A County History*.

We thank Jean Good, a volunteer in the Archives Service and a member of one of the Trinity families which go back to the 1900s, for the research she did on the addresses of the Trinity members in the Census of 1891 and in the Street Directories.

The other copies of the *Circuit Record* are in the National Library of Wales at Aberystwyth, deposited there by a member of the Porthkerry Road Church, Barry, and we thank the library for being given access to them.

We are grateful to Jean Pullin, a member of Albert Road Church, who, fortunately for us has taken early retirement, for typing the later chapters and putting them on disc for collation into the final form, which here appears.

Our thanks to Simon Gibbs for maps, to Susanna Gibbs for drawings of hands, to Kelvin Johns for photographs of Trinity in 1993, to George Best for photographs of Penarth in 1903, to the Methodist Department of Education and Youth for permission to reproduce the painting on the cover, and to the Editor of the *Methodist Recorder* for permission to reproduce the photographs of Dr Russell Maltby and Dr Robert Bond.

Finally, we thank our son, James Morel Gibbs, for his typing of the earlier chapters and for putting the whole of 'The Story of Trinity' on disc. He has made felicitous suggestions for the text and has overseen the publication of the book. He has been a great Encourager.

John and Sheila Gibbs.

**Here is the church.**

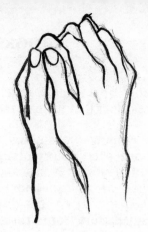

**And here is the steeple.**

**Open the doors and here are the people.**

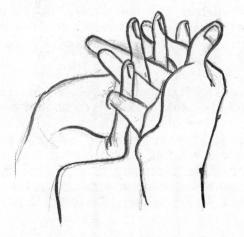

# AUTHORS' PREFACE

The children's finger game about the Church and the steeple and the people makes clear that without the people there can be no Church.

If in the beginning the authors had intended to make this story an impersonal one – the history of a particular Methodist Church against a back drop of national events and Methodist history, as set down in Rupert Davies' *Methodism* and Thompson Brake's *Policy and Politics of the Methodist Church*, the discovery of the Testimonial to Robert Bond on his departure from Trinity in 1905 put an end to that idea.

The Testimonial itself came to light in 1992 in the possession of John Ede, grandson of Robert Bond and one-time master at Kingswood School. A list of the signatories is included in the Note to Chapter Two and provided a fund of information.

It was obvious that as many of the signatories as possible must be followed up. Where had they come from – and why? Why did they found a Methodist Church in which to worship God the Father, God the Son, and God the Holy Ghost – the Trinity?

So the character of the book changed.

The practice grew of including in later chapters, experiences and memories alongside the development of the Society, as it is shaken by national events and reflects the wider Methodism as it tries to carry out Conference resolutions. The result is like a piece of Indian material which has glass stitched into the weave; the stories light up the narrative. The fact that the authors have spent a very large part of their 160 years as members of Trinity sometimes seemed an advantage – sometimes a disadvantage.

The history of any Church is about the people who make it up, and the way in which God has worked through them. Invidious it may be to have mentioned some people by name and omitted others, 'of whom there is no memorial'; and we are sorry that some people on looking through the index will not find their names or those of their families. Selection was inevitable, especially in the later chapters. We pay tribute to the present Membership in whose hands lies the future of that small part of the Church Universal – Trinity Methodist Church in Penarth.

Within the Methodist pattern, ministers come and go. We have chosen to write this story within the framework of the Ministers' periods of service to Trinity. In the main, each chapter is headed by a minister's name and covers the period during which he was stationed at Trinity.

In the early years of the Twentieth Century when ministers stayed for three years, the congregation was almost permanent, except for the seafarers, and even their wives and dependants remained in Penarth whilst they were at sea.

From the forties, the situation altered radically. Percy Watkinson reckoned that two-thirds of the congregation changed during the nine years he was in Penarth. 'Trinity was a giving Church', he said. Thankfully, it is also a receiving Church. Throughout the years, families have joined Trinity to work alongside those who have grown up in the Church.

So, with the precedent of the Acts of the Apostles and the Epistles before us, we do not draw back from mentioning people – some just by name, some with biographical detail – for they are all the living stones of the Church, the worshipping company within its walls.

# CHAPTER 1

## Penarth

Penarth has been called variously 'Clifton-by-the-Sea', 'The New Watering Place for the West of England' and 'The Hampstead of South Wales'. It has chosen to designate itself as 'The Garden by the Sea'.

Its history is comparatively short. Census reveal that in 1851 Penarth consisted of some 21 farms, two licensed houses, and on the Headland the old Church of St. Augustine's with its prominent saddleback tower, a recognised sea-mark in the treacherous waters of the Bristol Channel.

Along with much of the coastal land in Glamorgan, Penarth was owned by the Plymouth, Windsor-Clive Family.[1] They came to appreciate the potential for its development, both as a site for a dock and as a residential town and Baroness Windsor especially took a lively interest in the affairs of the growing town. Present-day Penarth is virtually their creation. The building of the Docks began in 1859, and of the town, which at first consisted of housing for those working there, at approximately the same time. They built substantial dwellings by the standards of the time. The stone houses in Cogan and those lining the streets below the Headland seem modest enough today, but they were held in high esteem by the families attracted to Penarth by the work in the Docks.

For example, Thomas Dewar with his family came to Penarth in 1879 to work as a shipwright. After a year or two he hankered after Glasgow and announced to his wife 'we'll be going back to Scotland next month.' But so pleased was she with her terraced house and the semi-rural situation of Penarth that she was determined to stay, 'If you go you'll have to go alone, the children and I will stay here.' The family were leading members of the Free Methodist Chapel in Cogan.

For the residential town the Plymouth Family had ambitious plans. In a monograph on the Windsor Family of 1879 there can be found the following passage: 'It was planned to make Penarth not only a place of great commercial activity, but to transform it into a beautiful and commodious watering place, a successful competitor with other places of summer resort and one that will be largely patronised by seaside visitors and summer excursionists.'

14

First, however, communications to and from the town had to be developed. Penarth was virtually cut off from the rest of Glamorgan; a winding road over Leckwith and Llandough being the only access, until, in 1867, a bridge and a toll road across the Leckwith Moors were built, but, at first, the road did not go up Cogan Hill. Penarth residents travelled into Cardiff either on foot or by cart or carriage. Later, Solomon Andrews, a Methodist, established a service with horse-drawn buses. The docksmen, who were moving to Penarth by the 1860s, were able to take a ferry from the Beach at Penarth Head direct to Cardiff Docks and this, sailing both at high and low tide, continued into the 20th Century. Later a subway under the Ely River was dug in 1900 for foot and cycle passengers.

With the extension of the Taff Vale Railway from Cogan to Penarth in 1878 the Plymouth Family's plan became possible. Penarth residents could travel easily into the very centre of Cardiff and on to Cardiff Docks and the town became accessible to people living in the Glamorgan Valleys – and beyond.

Penarth: Windsor Road, the main street in 1903.

The population grew fast; in 1881 there were 4,963 residents, in 1891, 9,632 and by 1921, 17,104. As the ground landlords, the Plymouth Family were able to control the development of the town by granting leases of only 99 years and by laying down firm guidelines as to materials; stone only was to be used for building. This is evident in the houses in the older part of the town; the terraces and streets lining the Headland, the first shopping centre in Glebe Street and Windsor Road known as 'The Village' to very old Penarth residents, and in the substantial houses built overlooking or some little way back from the sea. It is reported that when the Earl of Plymouth discovered that some of the houses in Marine Parade and Bridgeman Road were being built of brick he was greatly displeased.

These houses built in 'Elizabethan and other styles' have always attracted comment. A 'Guide to Penarth' as early as 1885 was moved to verse:

> So, might the weary merchant raise
> His mansion where to end his days,
> And here regain that long lost health
> Spent midst the toils of heaping wealth.

This building in stone was not to continue, because the local blue lias became too expensive to quarry and dress. At first, red and yellow brick houses alternated with stone ones but, as the town developed to the west, red brick prevailed, with some stucco in between. At an even later date, most houses were faced with pebble dash or cement rendering.

Penarth did not escape its share of 'brutalist' architecture when the Local Authority built, in the late 1960's, a range of flats on the remaining land in the north part of the town. This it is now attempting to humanise and bring into line with the other housing provision, largely in the west of the town, which is in modest, two-storied buildings and flats.

Easy rail access to Penarth enabled the town to develop as a watering place with boarding houses catering for the weekly visitors, and with facilities for day excursionists who descended on Penarth in great numbers, either to spend the day on the beach or pier or, possibly, to take a Campbell Steamer across the Bristol Channel. There were donkey rides, bathing machines and refreshment tents on the beach and buckets and spades could be bought on the sea-front. A special stretch of the beach was reserved for 'ladies only'. The sight of bathing costumes, voluminous garments at the time, hung out on lines on the beach to dry, offended the eyes of many local people – but nothing was quite as shocking as a glimpse of those who had the temerity to bathe in the nude. The officials of the Windsor Estate were informed of these unfortunate trends, concern was expressed and ways found to discourage such behaviour from the visiting 'rabble from the hills.'

A major disadvantage was that the sand varied in quantity. Riding on the sands was possible in the 1890s along the whole length of the Beach, whereas later it became mainly mud and pebbles, the result of tidal movements in the Bristol Channel and the widening of the Promenade. The water was and is somewhat muddy, and sea bathing has become less and less popular.

Another factor is the orientation of the Front; it faces East, and, although the morning sun can be pleasant, by the afternoon the Beach and the promenade are in shadow. In the evening a walk along the Cliffs is by far the best way to enjoy the view and the sunlight. Indeed, the Penarth residents themselves were often dismissive of the attractions of the Beach, and, when the motor car became a common possession after the Second World War, the day visitors largely deserted it also, for the sandier bays further down the Coast.

The proliferation of motor cars altered the townscape of Penarth as well. Gone were the early days of the 20th Century when the only danger to be faced walking in Plymouth Road was the occasional horse-drawn coal cart or delivery van. When not walking, people were either on bicycles or riding in Mr. Matthews' Taxi, garaged in Station Approach, or, a very few, in their own chauffeur-driven cars on their way to Cardiff Docks. The introduction of the first buses in 1920 presaged the coming of traffic which today makes driving in many of the roads hazardous and parking in the Town Centre almost impossible.

Many of the early houses in the town were built without stables or garages and without room to construct them, other than at the bottom of their gardens. These give on to the remarkable network of lanes which intersect the main roads in Penarth. It is possible to traverse the town almost entirely by these lanes or by traffic-free paths.

Penarth was provided by the Plymouth Family with a system of parks which have been little altered since their creation. Alexandra Park leads from the Town Centre to the Dingle and the Promenade; the Windsor

Gardens look down over the Beach. The parks are still laid out with bedding plants in true Victorian fashion – long since abandoned by private gardeners. The Windsor Gardens maintained its select quality until 1932 by an entrance charge of 1d.

Penarth: Alexandra Park and the Pier in 1903.

The Plymouth Family also gave recreation grounds to the town, The Penarth Rugby Club, with its unusual social mix, shipowners' sons playing alongside coal trimmers, achieved considerable renown, not least because of its annual Good Friday fixture – now abandoned – against the Barbarians. The Family also made available facilities for indoor swimming – the Public Baths, now superseded by the Leisure Centre in Cogan, were opened in 1885, and for golf, bowls, and tennis. The Yacht Club established in 1880 still flourishes as does the Motor Boat Club, though now based in Grangetown. The Rectory Road Tennis Club, with its splendid position in the very centre of Penarth, was the fashionable venue on summer evenings, but the courts were deserted between 7 and 8.p.m. as the members went home for their formal dinners.

A strange incident from the 1960s shows the whirligig of time. The dowager Lady Plymouth, who lived latterly in Penarth, was visited by her two grandsons and she thought it would be a nice idea if they were to play tennis on the courts her family had given to the town. When, however, they started to play in their grey clothes, which were all they had with them, they were told that they were not permitted to play unless they were wearing white flannels.

Victorian developers did not neglect the spiritual needs of the town. William Butterfield's splendid rebuilding of St. Augustine's in 1866, which was paid for almost entirely by Baroness Windsor, set the fashion for the building of churches and chapels by all the major denominations. By the turn of the century, in both the East and the West, spires and towers rose above the roofs of the houses to complete a typical Victorian urban skyline.[2]

The Plymouth Estate gave land for education and for indoor entertainment. The Paget Rooms, which was said to have the best floor for dancing in South Wales, provided a venue for Cinderella dances, with programmes, and later for productions by local amateur dramatic societies, of which the Penarth Operatic and Dramatic Society is the best known and longest established.

Alongside this steady development of the residential part of Penarth the story of the Docks, discreetly hidden under the Headland, is very different.

Penarth Dock was opened in 1865 as the Docks in Cardiff could not cope with the rapidly expanding coal export trade, which was to make Cardiff in the 19th and 20th Centuries 'the Coal Metropolis of the World'. The Penarth Docks, despite their fine Customs House, always played second fiddle to Cardiff and, when trade slackened off and exports slumped, Penarth was the first to suffer. When Barry Dock was developed in 1889 Penarth Dock was immediately relegated to third place, closing in 1936. During the Second World War it sprang into activity again as the Country needed to use all the comparatively safe west coast ports for imports from Canada and America. It was also used to ship men and materials for the North Africa Campaign and for the Normandy Landing. Because of the presence of the Docks and of the proximity to Cardiff, there were a number of air raids on Penarth in 1940 and 1941. These resulted in casualties, and children and expectant mothers were evacuated from the town.

Penarth: the Dock in 1903.

The Docks slumbered on, a place of faded glory, sometimes providing berths for mothballed warships, until they suffered what looked like a final indignity; to be filled in with hardcore and, unfortunately, more active material.

In addition to the problem of the viability of its Docks in relation to the larger docks of its dominating neighbour, the town's relationships with Cardiff have not been happy as it has sought to protect its separate identity. On five occasions Cardiff has attempted to take over Penarth and include it within its boundaries, maintaining that, in reality, it is nothing but a suburb of Cardiff. Penarth has put forward some of the very few residents whose place of business was in Penarth, either at the Docks or at the old established firm of Price Brothers, to refute the claim. The town has resisted the blandishments of Cardiff only to fall into the embrace of the Vale of Glamorgan. The former Chairmen of the Penarth District Council, especially such men as Sam Thomas, and the Urban District Council itself, were forces to be reckoned with. Now, although the Community Council has a Mayor – which sounds more important than a Chairman – it has been forced by Local

20

Government reorganisation to yield most of its powers to the Vale of Glamorgan Borough Council with offices in Barry.

Penarth's relationship with Glamorgan is ambivalent, – so many of its first inhabitants came from outside South Wales and it still attracts many newcomers from England, Scotland, Ireland and other parts of Wales. The Valleys have not forgiven Cardiff, and, by extension, Penarth, for taking a cut on every ton of coal exported through the ports. Nevertheless, it is the ambition of many who do not live in Penarth to retire – perhaps later to die – there. Some Penarth residents are concerned at the large number of retirement and nursing homes, some purpose built, in the town, although many are in the converted larger houses which are no longer suited to the needs of individual families. They fear that the town will become one giant geriatric complex. So far these fears are exaggerated; many young families choose to live in Penarth, although it is somewhat more expensive than other places nearby. The homes create a considerable amount of local employment and enable the frail and the invalid to enjoy living in a pleasant, sedate and caring community. They are staffed now, not by an army of maids – as in the days before the World Wars when they were private houses – but mostly by part-timers. However, Penarth before and between the Wars was an attractive place for domestic service; not so far away from the Valleys as London and not so lonely as the big houses in the country. In the early 1900s Miss Tregellis, a Baptist, was moved to provide a clubhouse where maids could spend their day off in Christian company. Other caring provision was the Penarth Infant Welfare Club, the first to be established outside of London, in 1915 to raise the standard of child care. Penarth was a concerned community.

Penarth continues to be a particularly agreeable place in which to live. There was a time in the 1930s when many of the larger properties became vacant and, if they sold at all, went for a song. For instance, Penarth House in a prime site with its four acres of land sold for £4,000 in 1938. The creation of Cardiff as the Capital and administrative centre of Wales reversed the trend and there seems no limit to Penarth's growth – already 24,000 in 1971 – except for a shortage of building sites. On the East is the sea, on the North, the River Ely. The East Vale Local Plan in 1985 accepted the principle that there should be a 'green wedge' between Penarth and Dinas Powis and that these two 'settlements' should not coalesce. Only to the South was growth possible. Development here however was inhibited by the activity of the Penarth Cement Works, with its extensive quarries, pouring out a daily powdering of cement dust over the neighbouring countryside. In

21

1969, the Penarth Cement Works closed, the chimney was demolished and the adjacent office block became a restaurant. The green character of the neighbourhood was re-established and houses have been, and continue to be, built there.

The quarries remain, now filled in with water from underground springs, and Penarth has discovered that, on its southern boundary it has a remarkable new asset; Cosmeston Country Park. Beyond the Park, to even greater surprise, Cosmeston Medieval Village has been revealed. Excavation and reconstruction are taking place demonstrating patterns of 14th Century living in what was to become the Penarth area.

At the north end of the town a new housing development, the Penarth Marina, an attractive mix of houses of different heights, is taking shape. The former Docks, filled in by the British Transport Docks Board, have been excavated and now provide mooring facilities for crafts of all sorts and sizes. In 1990, the Cardiff Bay Development Company unveiled its plans for the new Penarth Haven. It is clear that this development in the North will more than balance the development in the South.

The town has spawned its fair share of legends. It is true that in 1897 Marconi transmitted the first radio message across water from Flat Holm to Lavernock Point, and that, in the same year the French Impressionist artist, Alfred Sisley, painted six pictures of the Channel from the Cliff Walk. True, also, that the *S.S. Great Britain* sailed on its fateful voyage for Panama from Penarth Dock.

Two celebrated Welshmen, Dr. Joseph Parry, the composer, in the 1920s and the Rev. Elvet Lewis, Arch Druid, in the 1950s, were involved in the life of the, now demolished, Christchurch Congregational Church, and Lord Callaghan, Prime Minister, was the Member for Cardiff South, which included Penarth, from 1945 to 1974 and again from 1983 to 1987. It is however doubtful whether Penarth Head was what Coleridge had in mind, when, in *The Ancient Mariner* he wrote the lines, 'Below the kirk, below the hill . . .' Certainly false is the description, beloved of journalists, that Marine Parade could ever be described as 'Millionaires' Row'; wealthy as some of the residents were; the real Cardiff millionaires were mostly to be found further off in the Vale of Glamorgan.

In the Lias period, Penarth and the surrounding area had been under the sea as the rippled slabs of stone on the beach bear witness. Many of the gardens of the older houses have white or pink alabaster or fossilled ammonite bordering their paths – evidence that the Victorian residents were fascinated by their environment.

Penarth is still a fascinating environment, much of it a Conservation Area, with the Pier a Grade One Listed Building. With the changing of the townscape the seascape, too, has changed. The tides still rise and fall by almost as much as the 70 feet of the Bay of Fundy in Newfoundland, but the shipping has presented a very different appearance over the last 150 years. The Penarth Roads were first filled with large sailing ships and their accompanying tugs – still with us – then with steamers, and now there are the occasional dredger or container vessel, sailing boats and an extraordinary range of water sport crafts.

The Coastguard from their row of cottages and Tower in Marine Parade were much in demand in the earlier days of sail, now the new lifeboat may be called out to rescue water skiers or yachts or motor boats in difficulty.

Seawards there is always activity; Penarth's situation on the Bristol Channel has been its greatest attraction and the changing traffic in The Roads, mirrors the changes that have taken place in the Town above.

Such was the pleasant and prosperous environment in which Trinity Wesleyan Chapel was built on the outskirts of the town just before the dawning of the Edwardian Era.[3]

Mates' *Illustrated Guide to Penarth* published in 1903, three years after Trinity was opened, commented:

> The Methodists have put up a fine building in the southwest part of the town where six ways meet in Stanwell Road. The interior is exceptionally handsome, and has all the newest arrangements for heating and ventilation. It should be seen by visitors.

In the second half of the 19th Century, Penarth was virtually a new town. Within a space of twenty-five years all the major denominations had built places of worship. The Baroness Windsor had provided funds to rebuild St Augustine's and to build All Saints Church, but she was no resident Lady of the manor. Although interested and involved in the town, she did not represent a squirearchy with which the residents could identify or against which they could react. Nor was there a large employer of labour who had built a great mill in which the townspeople worked and a prestigious chapel in which they worshipped.

All the Churches had their leading families, their members who were more or less 'comfortable' and their members who were poor. For some Christians, with a strong denominational loyalty, there was no question where they would worship, but many would attend a particular church or chapel because they were attracted to the personality of the minister or incumbent or by the form of worship offered there.

The relationship between the churches was, in this sense, a competitive one, within a competitive society.

# CHAPTER 2

## Methodist Beginnings in Penarth from 1860 to 1898

## The Rev'd Russell Maltby 1895-1898

The *Cardiff Times* from 1857 onwards never failed in its weekly issues to contain reports of excessive drinking and riotous behaviour in Penarth. There were 13 public houses for an adult population of 1,266 and no other recreational provision of any kind. The plight of the 'Navigators' who were building the docks was recognised by a Miss Morgan who determined to do what she could for their spiritual welfare. To explain her interest, the story needs to go back earlier in the century.

John Wesley preached in South Wales on a number of occasions and one of the results of his preaching was the setting up of a chapel, Bethel, in Cadoxton in 1811. The Chapel was in the Cowbridge Circuit of Welsh Chapels, the services being conducted in Welsh until, as the number of non-Welsh speakers increased, English became the medium normally used. A number of people walked to Cadoxton for the Sunday Services and prayer meetings and amongst them was Jane Dickens, a housemaid at East Barry House. In 1860, a new Chapel was built in Cadoxton and Jane Dickens took her young mistress, Miss Morgan, to worship there. The experience proved decisive, and in 1889, the latter recalled how, some thirty years previously, 'In Barry, I first found Jesus Christ.'

Miss Morgan was the elder daughter of Edward Morgan of Merthyr Tydfil; a man of substance who had moved to East Barry House. She had 'means' of her own and bought a house in Glebe Street, Penarth for Peter Bethell, 'Town Missioner', as he is described in the Census of 1861. 'Bethell, from Halkyn, Flintshire, was cast in the mould of John Wesley and is known to have preached in a roofless stable in the centre of the town to congregations of mixed persuasion. He was at this time thirty-seven years of age. He died aged forty-two and was buried in St. Augustine's churchyard.'[1]

Miss Morgan made him an allowance of £200 a year. The work prospered and there were attendances of upwards of two hundred people at the prayer meetings and services on Sundays. In 1863, an application was made to the Plymouth Estate for a site on which to build a chapel. Designs were submitted to Lady Windsor and a 'sightly building' was

25

stipulated and 'a design applicable to the locality.' The Methodist Church was able to meet these requirements. The Rev. F. J. Jobson had published in 1850 an authoritative book on *Chapel Architecture particularly appropriate to the Wesleyan Methodists* in which a model Gothic Chapel was described.[2] The building which was to be erected in Arcot Street bears a striking resemblance to this. The seating in the Chapel was for 450, with accommodation in the adjoining schoolroom for 500 children.

The foundation stone of the Chapel was laid by Miss Morgan on the 7th October 1863. The Rev. W. Russell Maltby wrote in the Cardiff Conference Handbook of 1911; 'Wild and windy weather prevailed and as the Superintendent Minister began the Service by saying 'We are now going . . .' the temporary platform gave way and the Superintendent and others vanished. Arcot Street began in rain and ended in fire.' Russell Maltby was referring to the fire which later partially destroyed the Arcot Street building in 1898.

The Methodists were not the first of the Free Churches to be established in Penarth. The Welsh Congregationalists had held services in a farmhouse in 1845, and the Baptist Chapel at Llandough, on the main approach to Penarth, was built in 1859. The Calvinistic Methodists opened Sadis in 1861, and from 1860 two Roman Catholic priests visited Penarth regularly to celebrate Mass.

By the 1880s, Arcot Street Chapel was thriving within the Cardiff Loudoun Square Circuit, but the shift of population in the town was to the west of the Taff Vale Railway line; indeed, that part of Penarth was already known as 'The West End.' A number of Arcot Street members 'after much thought and prayer' decided to found another Society and a plot of land on Farmer Morgan's 'Woodland Farm', was purchased, which already had on it a Tin Church known as Playter's Church. This had been erected in 1887 to provide a pulpit for a Mr. Playter, a former curate of St. Augustine's who had been asked to leave for preaching a sermon 'not acceptable to the authorities.' He took a considerable number of the congregation with him to the Tin Church; in time the congregation fell away and he moved to London.

An article in *The Methodist Recorder* of 16 October 1903, reports what happened next: 'The occasion arose for the sale of an iron church and it is doubtful whether any site and building have been bought for Methodism in so short a time. The whole transaction was begun and finished in half an hour and to secure the agreement Sir Thomas Morel

The Rev'd W. Russell Maltby, Minister at Trinity, 1895-1898.

wrote out a cheque on the spot and there was secured for Methodism one of the best sites.' It is said that the decision to purchase the site, if not the signing of the cheque, took place in a railway carriage between Penarth and Cardiff. Sharing the carriage with Thomas Morel were Messrs. Henry Frazer, G. H. Tregaskis and W. B. Gibbs.

The very first Methodist Service in the Tin Church took place on 3 August 1890 and this date marks the beginning of the Trinity Society. However, the building was soon found to be less than ideal as a place of worship: it was hot in summer and cold in winter, and during heavy rain nothing the preacher said could be heard.

The Tin Church, 1887-1898.

The foreword to the first Circuit Minute Book records that at the Wesleyan Conference, held in Cardiff during July 1893, the following Societies were separated from the Cardiff, Loudoun Square, Circuit, and formed into the 'Cardiff, Penarth, Circuit': Arcot Street, Trinity,

Cadoxton, Barry, Porthkerry Road, Barry Dock, Dinas Powis and Eastbrook.

The young probationer minister, Russell Maltby, stationed in the Circuit in 1895 with special responsibility for Trinity, had qualified as a lawyer before offering for the ministry in 1892, and was to become both 'prophet and shepherd of souls for multitudes in Methodism and beyond.' He was the son of a Methodist Minister, educated at Woodhouse Grove and Kingswood Schools, who became known in a wider sphere than Methodism through the conferences at Swanwick, his Fourpenny Manuals which were read throughout the world, and his work with the Student Christian Movement. Archbishop William Temple, when asked who had appealed most during the Thirties to the student classes, replied 'unquestionably Maltby.'

He did not have a good voice nor a commanding presence, nor a degree – until awarded an honorary one by Glasgow University. Mercurial, he was often unable to appreciate that there was anything at all in favour of the other side of the question. It was said of him that he could 'never see any good in anyone in the Bible or out of it who differed from Paul.'

However, most of this lay in the future for the young man, who was ordained in 1896: he was then thirty-one and in the second year of his three years at Trinity. During his third year, the plans for the new Church were drawn up, but it was his spiritual legacy that was outstanding. J. A. Findlay records that 'Groups of thoughtful people were left behind him in circuit after circuit to carry on his work.' The people of the new church in Penarth, such as the Edes, Evanses, Scourfields, Morels and Gibbses, were of that number.

Edward Hornby Ede's grandfather was a Cornishman from Liskeard who became a businessman in Turkey and there married a Hungarian Roman Catholic, possibly a refugee. They had nine children, and one of the sons married into an English banking family, resident in Constantinople. This son became an advocate in the Turkish and other courts but, as an indication of fidelity to his Cornish Methodist roots, sent his son, Edward Hornby Ede, to a school which had been recently opened in Launceston by a Methodist minister, the Rev'd Luke Wiseman, which was 'mainly patronised by dissenters.'

From Launceston, E. H. Ede went to St. John's College, Cambridge, where he obtained a double degree, B.A. and Ll.B. He then returned to

Cornwall to marry Mildred Blanch, daughter of the Rev. Joseph Benson Blanch, who had been one of his schoolmasters.

In 1893, when E. H. Ede entered into partnership with Merrils, the Cardiff Solicitors, they moved to 17, Victoria Square, Penarth. With their three children and, until 1915, with Mildred's widowed mother, Mary Blanch, they remained in the town, and formed part of the Trinity community. Edward was one of the few professional men in the congregation during the early decades of the century.

John Evans moved to Cardiff from Carmarthen and, although an Anglican, attended Cathays Wesleyan Methodist Church after his marriage to Mary Jones, the daughter of a printer who became the editor of *The Western Mail*. On moving to Penarth, John and Mary Evans became deeply involved in the life of the Tin Tabernacle from its earliest beginnings.

They had nine children, all of whom grew up in the church. Of those about whom information is available, one of their sons, Hugh Price Evans, was lost at sea during the First World War, and a daughter, Winifred, became headmistress of Albert Road Infants School.

A second daughter married Cyril Scourfield. Like the Evanses, the Scourfields illustrate the kind of family which were moving to the area around Trinity. Cyril Scourfield's father, David, was an Anglican, a boiler-maker from Pembrokeshire employed by the Taff Vale Railway. Cyril became a member of the choir at the Tin Church. He was a marine engineer as were several Trinity members.

In 1899, Thomas Morel who had purchased the site for Trinity, was knighted. This honour was largely a tribute to the growing importance of Cardiff, of which he was Mayor in that year and which was soon to become a City. In order to distinguish him from his son, also christened Thomas, he will be referred to as 'Thomas Morel' and his son as 'Tom.'

Thomas Morel was the fourth son of a Jersey farmer, Edouard Thomas Morel. The family's ten-acre farm in St. Mary Parish could only support one of the sons, Edouard, the eldest. The second son, Jean, travelled to Cardiff in 1856 to assist his uncle, Philip Le Moignan, in selling the early Jersey potato crop. As soon as he arrived in Cardiff, Jean saw the possibilities offered by the growing port, and sent for his brothers, Philip, aged twenty, and Thomas, aged fourteen. At first they all lived together in Stuart Street and entered the chartering business in which their knowledge of French was a very great advantage. Philip and Thomas moved rapidly into ship-owning, at first sail and then steam, and, by 1888, their fleet numbered some twenty vessels. They were primarily engaged in carrying coal to the French ports and to Bilboa in Northern Spain, and the ships returned to Cardiff and other Welsh ports carrying iron ore for the great iron works at Dowlais and Merthyr.

Philip married Martha Gibbs in 1866 and Thomas married her sister, Susanna, in 1873.

The Morel family had been Methodists on Jersey, perhaps converted by Robert Carr Brackenbury, perhaps by John Wesley himself who, in August 1789, visited St. Mary's Parish. The Morels first took their Methodism to Cardiff, where they became members of the Loudoun Square Chapel. When they moved to Penarth, they worshipped at Arcot Street and, later, were prime movers in the development of Trinity.

The Philip Morels built the imposing Penarth House at the entrance to Cliff Walk and, although active Methodists, were not as committed as their brother and sister. Thomas and his wife, Susanna, spent the winter months at The Lindens in Penarth and the summer at St. Andrews House in Dinas Powis. They had four sons, Tom, Ralph, Clem and John, and one daughter, Gladys; the first and last of whom were to follow their parents as leaders of Trinity.

Susanna was never happier than when at her beloved chapel or at the women's meetings. Thomas had been the Sunday School Superintendent at Loudoun Square and a Society Steward at Arcot Street. He was a widely respected figure in Cardiff and went, on one occasion, to the Wesleyan Methodist Conference. When he died in 1903, *The Methodist Recorder* headed his obituary notice: 'The late Sir Thomas Morel: a Methodist Merchant Prince,' and observed that the name of Sir Thomas Morel will ever be associated with Trinity.' He must have influenced the elaborate style in which the Church was built and he would have contributed largely to its construction and maintenance.

From 1881 to 1884 the Minister of Cathays Wesleyan Methodist Chapel in Cardiff was the Rev'd John Scott Lidgett, M.A., and John Angel Gibbs was the Sunday School Superintendent. His father, William, had arrived in Cardiff via Waterford from Portland, where the family had been quarrymen and deeply committed Methodists. During the 1880s the family had been converted by John Wesley's 'Gentleman Preacher' – Robert Carr Brackenbury.

William Gibbs, whose first home in Cardiff was in Stuart Street and who worshipped at Loudoun Square, was a ship chandler. His second son, John, joined the firm of Morel Freres et Cie in 1869, at the age of twenty. Eight years later, by which time Philip and Thomas had married his sisters, Martha and Susanna, and he had married a young Portland girl, Elizabeth Pearce Scriven, he became a partner.

The firm, now called Morel Brothers and Company, prospered exceedingly, and John and Elizabeth were able to move from their first home in Windsor Esplanade to St. Andrew's Crescent. The family attended Cathays Chapel and John Angel made a considerable contribution to Methodism in Cardiff. On 11 April 1884, John Angel, then aged thirty-five caught a chill; he died a week later, on Good Friday, of pneumonia and pleurisy. The whole Methodist community mourned and on the next Sunday the pulpits in the Cardiff chapels were draped with black.

The funeral address was given by John Scott Lidgett, who remained an honoured name in the family. Twenty-eight years later, he inscribed the Bible given to John Morel Gibbs, the grandson of John Angel, with the following words: 'From his friend John Scott Lidgett on his christening.'

It was decided that the widow, Elizabeth, and her children should move to Number 5 Marine Parade. Elizabeth was not a forceful character and the guiding hand of her husband was not compensated for by the presence of her brother-in-law, William, even though he lived next door – in Number 4 Marine Parade. The children were sent to Methodist boarding schools: William, John and Reggie to Queen's College, Taunton, and Lidgett, who was actually born after his father's death, to Rydal. Later their membership was with Trinity, which they supported to a greater or lesser degree. Elizabeth, the eldest daughter, played the fullest role and became one of the first women trustees.

The unmarried children, William, Elizabeth and Susan, lived on at Number 5 after their mother's death and the household was not broken up until the last of them, Susan, died in 1968.

An incident not immediately relevant to the history of Trinity but illustrating the social background of the 1890s in Penarth in which church had to take its place alongside other institutions is included here.

It concerns two of the young members of the Gibbs and Morel families, when they were 25 and 22 respectively, both lacking a father's influence – William's father had died and Ralph's was busy at the Docks, and involves Penarth Rugby Club.

Some of the most important institutions in Wales were – and are – Rugby Union Football Clubs, and both William and Ralph played for the Penarth Club, then a strong side, in 1899. Then, as now, Rugby League teams from the north of England attempted to persuade talented players in the amateur code to move to the professional code with the inducement of payment for each game and of secure employment. When an agent from Wigan was recognised on the Front while on a recruiting trip to Penarth, William and Ralph pulled him from his cab, dragged him down one of the landing-stages, rolled him in the sand and threw him into the Bristol Channel. Not unnaturally he complained to the Cardiff police, as, in addition to suffering from the assault, he had lost a sovereign in the affray. The police, whose loyalties may have been divided, advised him to return to Penarth to find the coin or the culprits. He decided against taking either course of action.

The incident was reported in *The South Wales Daily News* of 25 January 1899, but the names of those responsible were suppressed. In later years, Gladys Morel would, somewhat shamefacedly, tell the story of her brother's and cousin's involvement.

Incomers from across the Channel or from West Wales or further afield settled in the town, and seafarers putting in to Cardiff or Penarth who thought it would be convenient to have their families near at hand arranged for them to move. Trinity was known at one time as 'The Seafarers Church.' Some brought their Methodism with them; others found their Methodism in Penarth. The Wesleyan Chapels were making their mark on Penarth.

Wesleyan Bazaar at Penarth.

'On Wednesday afternoon, April 3rd 1895, a Bazaar and Sale of Work on an extensive scale was opened in Andrews' Large Hall in connection with the United Wesleyan Churches of the Penarth Circuit. The Hall was tastefully and elaborately decorated under the care of Mr Jones representing Mr Howell of Cardiff. The front of the platform was ornamented with pampas grass, which was so arranged as to hang in arch form with a palm in the centre of each. The platform itself was used as a kind of afternoon tea room, when, for the small charge of 6d, could be obtained bread and butter and cake and a pot of tea specially made all to one's self. The stalls were arranged on either side of the room and contained an immense quantity and varied assortment of goods – some of a very costly character. The stalls were fitted by Mr R Hancock as a contribution to the funds of the bazaar. Mr Andrews gave the free use of the hall and Mr Howell also contributed the decoration free.

The stalls were as follows: Trinity Stall: Mrs Humphrey Wallis, Mrs Thomas Morel, Mrs Arthur Hibbert, Mrs Hicks, Mrs John Gibbs and Miss Davies. Refreshment Stall: Mrs Walls, Mrs Cullis, Mrs W. B. Gibbs, Mrs Hayden and Mrs Pauley. Flower Stall: Mrs G. Frazer, Miss Gladys Morel, Mrs A. M. Stevens and Miss Hilda Chivers.

Each evening, amusements were provided in the form of Tableaux Vivants, the various characters being splendidly represented by, amongst others, the Misses Frazer, the Misses Chivers, Mr G. Frazer, Mr Tom Morel and the young ladies from Miss Sumner's St Maeburne School and under the superintendence of Mr and Mrs Cullis and Miss Ramsdale.

Professor Mayo of Cardiff gave phrenological lectures and examined the heads of many who wished to know themselves. A number of electrical experiments by Mr Butland proved a source of attraction.

The proceedings were opened on Wednesday by Mr Henry Frazer after a short religious service.

We understand that the amount raised was £228 10s 8d or about £50 more than the amount actually required.'

From *The Penarth Chronicle and Cogan Echo* April 1895.

Two Wesleyan Methodist schoolmistresses established a girls boarding and day school at St Maeburne at the bottom of Marine Parade. The pupils included some of the daughters of Mrs Lewis Williams, the 'Miss Morgan' already referred to, Hilda Chivers and Gladys Morel.

The pupils attended services in the Tin Tabernacle. On one occasion, the girls pigtails proved too great a temptation to the Morel boys sitting immediately behind them. During the sermon, the boys tied them to the bar at the back of the pew. The girls were moved one pew forward on the following Sunday.

'St Maeburne' refers to no known saint, but is an anagram formed from the surnames of the two schoolmistresses. Miss Sumner, a formidable woman, was in 1897 one of the first women to be a member of the Circuit Meeting.

St Maeburne was to become the home of Gladys Gibbs in 1919 and, on her death, provided five flats for retired Methodist Ministers.

The Tin Tabernacle which housed the young Trinity Society from 1890 had no building in which children could be instructed. However, within seven years the Sunday School was built, the site being commodious enough to accommodate it and to allow the building to be set back some way from Stanwell Road to enable a fine tree to be preserved.

The original aims of the Sunday School Movement had been to provide the rudiments of education for poor children for whom there was no other provision. Most of these were established in connection with Churches and Chapels.

In 1837, the Wesleyan Education Committee had presented its first report to Conference urging the universal provision of such schools for religious education in the following terms:

> We cannot begin to deal with that portion of the human mind to which we have access at too early a period of life. There can be no wisdom in leaving children and youth to themselves until they are confirmed in habits of unreligion and vice, and then seeking by the use of extraordinary means to instruct and convert them. If it is our duty to evangelise the masses of our countrymen, the sooner we begin with each individual the better. What we wish for is, not merely schools, but Church Schools, which, being systematically visited by the Preachers, may prove doors of entrance into the Church of God: not merely education, but an education which may begin in an Infant School, and end in

heaven; and which will then subserve the high ends of Methodism, which are to fill the world with saints, and paradise with glorified spirits.

By the end of the 19th Century, the Methodist Church was no longer building Day Schools, but the Education Committee in 1889 was urging the desirability – indeed duty – of every Methodist Society to provide its own Sunday School building, so that 'the children of our own people, at least, may be duly instructed in religion and brought to a place of worship on the Lord's Day.'

The Minutes of the Circuit Quarterly Meeting held at Trinity on 28th March 1896 state: 'Rev. W. Russell Maltby referring to the Society at Trinity said that they were desirous of building a schoolroom and vestries at a probable cost of £2,000 and asked permission of the Meeting to proceed.' After some discussion the meeting voted without opposition in favour of the scheme.

The schoolroom was opened in 1897 and was used both as the Church and Sunday school until 1901. It was a lofty building with a large hall, small classrooms leading off, a balcony and fine roof supported by wrought iron pillars. There was a library, a primary room and Church Parlour above. As in so many chapels of the time the Ten Commandments were painted on the wall above the pulpit. The whole cost of £2,600 was raised without connexional grant.

In the main hall and on the balcony, the children sat on benches, boys to the left, girls to the right and the Superintendent, from a raised and railed platform, presided over the gathering. He gave a general address and notices were read out. At an appropriate time boys and girls would 'go into their classes', either in corners of the Hall or in the side classrooms which each seated some ten children, or into the curtained 'rooms' on the balcony. There the teachers would seek to expound and apply the address in the way best suited to the ages of their children. They would then reassemble in the hall for the closing of the proceedings, good order would be maintained and a handbell rung to call the Scholars to order.

Sunday School Treats were a feature of this period. At first, the open country was so near to Trinity that it was merely the matter of going out to a neighbouring field. Later, as land was built over and 'Woodland Place' became but the name of another road, waggonets were engaged. Portable swings which languished in the storeroom well into the second half of the century, were erected for the day. In a field behind Victoria School, the boys played hockey and football; two rugby players, Tom Garrett and Reggie Gibbs, were eventually capped for Wales.

Twenty-two years after leaving Trinity, Russell Maltby was to become the Warden of the Deaconess Order in Ilkley and in 1926 was President of the Wesleyan Conference. A strong advocate of Church Union and of the Ordination of Women, he was reckoned 'amongst the most respected even revered teachers of the faith and of devotional life in the whole of Methodism.'3

Included here is the published text of a sermon by Russell Maltby. He adapted it slightly so that it addresses readers rather than listeners, but the changes are to the surface, the preacher's voice can be heard in the phrasing and so the document provides an indication of the quality of the sermons delivered in Trinity during his Ministry.

'And the Lord turned and looked upon Peter.' Luke xxii, v.61.

Jesus turned and looked upon Peter. Just a look – no more! But a look can break your heart. Someone's look can turn bleak November into radiant May. A look can kill, and a look can make alive. Just a look – no more! But, as you know, a look can say more than a book.

This story of Peter's 'denial' is, of course, one of the classic stories of the world. It is in every civilised literature, but it has not always been very adequately understood. Thomas Hardy wrote a poem about it – mostly wrong. But he stopped at the cock-crowing. The look was beyond him. Perhaps he never had a glimpse of it.

Look again at the situation as it is given to us in the Gospels. Remember that St. Peter, not many hours before, had said passionately, 'Though all men forsake thee, yet will not I.' Yet here he is, a bewildered man in a situation which he has no skill to handle. He stays, partly in desperate resolve to make good his promise, partly out of a pathetic longing to see the end – if it is to be the end – unable to tear himself away from what his eyes can hardly bear to look on. He is challenged and denies. But remember that, having once been challenged and denied, he could have gone out as he came in. If all he had been concerned about was to save his own skin he could have gone, but he stayed, hanging on to the remnants of his boast and to something more than the remnants of his loyalty and love, pitifully helpless and unable to tear himself away from this incredible happening.

It is hard to be courageous when you are utterly confounded. He finds himself a spectator of something unbelievably horrible, something that ought not to be. 'Is there God in Heaven to allow this?' You and I, after all these centuries can see something at any rate of the significance of that cross. We may talk about the victory of the Cross and become rhetorical and even sentimental about it, but all this was impossible to Peter. In the moral earthquake when all the pillars were falling and the solid earth opening at his feet, then bewildered and desperate he is challenged again, and falls back into old forsaken ways such as a Galilean fisherman would use, and fortifies his dreadful denial with oaths.

And 'Jesus turned and looked upon Peter' and Peter looked on Jesus. That look saved him. You may say, if you wish, it broke him. Very well then, it broke him and saved him. Jesus looked upon Peter, and Peter looked upon Jesus, and went out and wept bitterly.

That look! It is beyond us, I know, but let us know as much as we can for it is not all mystery. To begin with, there were some things not in that look. Was it a look of contempt? You know it was not. Was it the look that says 'I told you so.' You know it was not. Was it rebuke? I don't think so; it was not our Lord's way to break a bruised reed. Was it even reproach? I dare not say so. If we were speaking of anyone else but Jesus we should know what was the answer to be expected after Peter's frantic denial. It would be, 'You disown me; so be it. You have made your choice.' But there are some things which I am sure were flashed in an instant in that one look from our Lord to the man who was needing it. Grief, of course, but no surprise. There was understanding. There was forgiveness. You say, 'But he had not repented yet! and we must repent in order to be forgiven.' Don't be too sure. It was the look of Jesus carrying forgiveness with it that made him repent and tumbled him out into the street weeping like a child.

Yes, Peter has denied his Lord, with his lips at any rate; and our Lord turned and looked on Peter, and the look was a message. It did not say, 'Since you disown me I disown you.' Oh no, the very opposite of that. Plainer than words could make it, it said 'You disown me, but I claim you. Ah! Peter, with your wild words you deny me, but it was not you who chose me, but I chose you and you are mine.' Peter caught that glance of grief and love and beheld suddenly the love that would not let him go. That made an end of all his denials and all his boasting too.

Someone may ask whether it is fitting, when we are thinking of His passion, to linger on a mere episode in a chain of events so much more tremendous. To which there is a double answer. Some of us will not see deepest into the meanings of Good Friday by following the cruel stages of a crucifixion or contemplating what tradition calls the stations of the Cross – Jesus carrying His Cross, Jesus falling under His Cross, falling a second and then a third time under His Cross. If such contemplation carries us on to the real suffering of our Lord and reveals again the cost of our redemption so let it be. But were those physical cruelties after all the heart of the matter? Can we not see something so much greater than even these are but incidents? If we would see what is being done during that night and a day, what was meant there – and meant for ever – we may see it as we watch Jesus over against the man he is saving – Jesus and Peter – these two. The soldiers did their part. They scourged Him – till the blood ran, but they did not hurt Him as Peter could hurt Him – or any other man whom Jesus was mightily striving to save. They laid the burden of a heavy cross upon Him, but not so heavy a burden as the burden of turning a man called Simon into the man that was worthy to be called Peter. They drove nails into his hands, but they could not pierce him to the quick as Peter could in one disloyal moment – as any one of us has done or might do.

And there is more. Jesus and Peter – they are both with us. Do not treat it as a commonplace, that He is in the midst of us; so easy it is to say, so hard at times to believe, so hard to behave as though we believed it. Yes, he is with us the same yesterday, today and for ever. But Peter also is here; and if he is not in the person of the reader, he is in the writer, so I know what I am talking about. Peter, with his contradictory motives, his good and evil, his professions and denials, his betrayals and his returns – would you need to look very far to find him? Your face, it may be, is now turned gladly towards Jesus Christ, but have you not denied and could you not do it again? Nobody needs to be told that there are a thousand ways in which we may deny him. It need not be in the clamour of hostile company; we can deny Him by word or deed, by speech or silence, by averting our face or stopping our ears, or sometimes by headlong flight from his presence. We have many ways of denying Him, and I don't know that there are any better than Peter's.

Peter disowned Christ, but our Lord did not take him at his word. His fear, his bewilderment, his resentment were in those wild and wicked words, but his heart was not in them, nor his love and loyalty; for God had planted that love and loyalty too deep to be swept away in a blast of panic. And this is good to know.

It is only Christ who knows how to deal with us at our worst because he knows that our worst is not all there is. He does not accept us because of our confident vows; He does not reject us because we unsay them. We mortals can hardly ever speak aright about sin, for either we condone or we denounce it. But Christ understands all the Peters. He understands what Paul meant when he said that dangerous but pathetic word 'It is no more I that do it, but sin that dwelleth in me.' It was not an excuse, but a cry from the edge of despair. When we are at our best we wonder how we could ever have said or done what we did. When we are at our worst, the best seems so far away than we can almost wonder if it was ever real. But He understands both. And if when they murdered Him, He said the only thing that could be said for them, 'they know not what they do,' I hope that he says it for me also when I am far from my best. He alone knows us well enough to know how to say Neither do I condemn thee, without in the least condoning sin, but only as forgiving it.

So speaking to any Peters that may be among my readers, perhaps someone who has been refusing to look, I say today, Look! for there is One who will meet your trembling look and will claim you with the love that will not let you go. Just to see that is to find salvation and to stand at last in peace.

# CHAPTER 3

## The Building of Trinity 1899-1901

The Society at Trinity was not long to remain content with their dual-purpose building and in March 1899 applied for permission to the Circuit Quarterly Meeting to build a chapel. This was given on condition that they complied with the requirements of the Connexional Chapel Committee. Action was quickly taken and the Annual Report of the Wesleyan Chapel Committee of 1899 carried a drawing and description of the Church to be erected.

The Trinity Minister during the building of the new church was the Rev'd S. Yelland Richards, a Cornishman who had begun to preach when he was fifteen. He was a preacher of exceptional gifts and regarded as a 'judicious, farseeing and wise' administrator; he must have needed all these qualities during this critical time at Trinity.

Yelland Richards was twenty-nine when he came to Penarth. The task of completing Trinity Church building and its dedication was a great responsibility for so young a man.

The leaders of Trinity who had purchased the Tin Tabernacle must have given considerable thought to the type of building which was to replace it. They might have decided that their Church should resemble an eighteenth century chapel, Wesley's Chapel in City Road, or the classical Methodist chapels in Monmouth and Abergavenny, but that would have seemed to them to be looking back to the past when Methodists were a people apart, out of the main stream of British church life. They might have been attracted to a Central Hall type of building, a product of Hugh Price Hughes' 'Forward Movement' which in many places met the needs of the people who were moving in numbers to the new towns, a 'virile middle-class Methodism with its special mission to the poor, the sick, the young.'[1] But if they were to open such a mission as the London Wesleyans had done in St. George's Wesleyan Chapel, they might well see, as in that case, their carriage-folk move to other chapels and their cause divided. They were aware of the Settlement that John Scott Lidgett, having moved from Cardiff, was creating in Bermondsey, but what was suitable for the East End of London was not appropriate for the increasingly fashionable seaside town in which they were to build. The obvious course for them was to build a chapel in accordance with acceptable contemporary taste. This gave them a choice which could be simplified as being between 'the Goths and the Greeks.' When Arcot Street Chapel had been built, F. J. Jobson's precepts in his book of 1850 on Chapel and School Architecture[2] had been closely followed. The Church which was to rise reflected the taste and the aspirations of those responsible for it, and their taste was overwhelmingly for the Gothic. For their houses they might build in scaled down French Renaissance, but for churches, the Gothic style was pre-eminent. It was 'the Christian style', and proclaimed the Christian worship that went on inside.

The Church was not to be a simple rectangle as Jobson had recommended: it was to be a full-blown Decorated Gothic building, with chancel, transepts and a spire to claim its place in the mainstream of British church life. Ignoring the fact that the Gothic style was developed in Britain and on the Continent to express a Medieval Christianity with a Catholic focus on processions, the altar and the liturgy, they adapted it to Methodist worship with its emphasis on the sermon, hymn singing and communion at the Lord's Table. The Trinity Trustees, doubtless influenced by Henry Budgen, the architect and himself an Anglican, placed the Table at the East End of the chancel beyond inward facing choir stalls, and set the organ at one side. The pulpit stood at the left-hand side of the chancel, and the lectern, when acquired, on the right. The main body of the Church was slightly raked – perhaps a nod in the direction of an auditorium; the chancel was raised by two steps and the Table by another. The lofty spire was a conspicuous feature. J. B. Hilling comments: 'The later nineteenth century Gothic chapels are virtually indistinguishable in elaboration from the established church. They illustrate the absolute divorce from Welsh chapel tradition which had by then taken place amongst the Anglicised Nonconformists.'[3] The Welsh chapel tradition was classical and Greek. The 'pagan' associations with this style were not to the taste of the Wesleyans building at the turn of the century.

Trinity wanted to establish its own identity, neither Anglican nor Nonconformist. The Wesleyan Methodist Church had abandoned the use of the Anglican Prayer Book in 1883, before Trinity came into existence and Trinity used the new Methodist Book of Public Prayer and Services. It omitted the Collect, Epistle and Gospel readings for Saints' Days and contained wording for the Services of Holy Communion and Baptism which expressed a Methodist theology for a Methodist Church. However it was still deeply indebted to Church of England Order, of which Wesley had spoken so highly.

The founders of Trinity would never have been troubled by the charge that they were adding just one more church to a town which was already adequately provided with places of worship. Penarth was growing and the Methodists coming into the town wanted to worship in their own way, with an Order of Service with which they felt comfortable, and they wanted to give others the opportunity to join them. At the turn of the century, the Methodists, along with other members of the Free Churches, thought that the future for Christianity in Britain belonged to them and they could see their churches growing in size and influence. Especially was this so in Wales where numerical assessments of worshippers showed a large majority of Free Church members – a consideration which was to lead to the Disestablishment of the Church of England in Wales in 1922.

All Churches were aware of 'leakages' to other Denominations: Trinity hoped that by the dignity and warmth of its Services and by the quality of its preaching, it would attract new members and hold its old ones. This did not always happen, especially when one partner to a marriage came from another religious tradition. As an example from one of the families linked to the founding of Trinity:

> The first two babies born to William and Edith Morel were baptised at Trinity in 1907 and 1909, but when the time came for their third child to be baptised this took place at All Saints Anglican Church, surely at Edith's instigation. This must have caused hurt to most of the senior members of the family, but Edith could not accept her husband's denominational background. She was happy to describe her father-in-law, Philip, as 'a fine Huguenot gentleman.'[4]

She could not accept that he was a Wesleyan of Liberal persuasions.

The move to other Free Churches was usually to the other Wesleyan Church in the town, and so did not involve a denominational break. From 1908 onwards, the Services at Albert Road, the successor to the burnt out Arcot Street, were less formal than those held at Trinity, although the architectural setting was remarkably similar.

In more recent times some ministers and worshippers have found the architecture of Trinity imposes too structured a form of worship and inhibits flexibility – although the front of the Church and the chancel, if built up, can be used for drama, movement and music.

One can speculate that if the Church had been built at a later date there would have been even more uncertainty as to what style should be adopted. It may have been true that 'by the 1890s Gothic had largely run its course.'5 However, it was never specified exactly what form should take its place. Certainly this was true for Methodism until the Methodist Property Division initiated a new building style after the Second World War.

The exterior and the interior of the new Chapel – as the congregation of Trinity would have called it, were safeguarded by the legal requirement that no alteration could be made without the consent of the Trustees, but it was difficult to contain the enthusiasms of members, especially if they were influential. At one period some members with time on their hands, and in an attempt to imitate Anglican practice, covered the Communion Table with a heavily embroidered red velvet Altar Cloth. This eventually perished, and when removed, revealed the simple Table that had been present from the beginning.

*The South Wales Echo* of 27 September 1899 carried the following account of the stone-laying:

> This afternoon the Mayor of Cardiff, Sir Thomas Morel, will lay the foundation stone of a Wesleyan Chapel to be erected in Stanwell Road, Penarth. After the ceremony, addresses will be delivered by the Rev. Frederic W. Macdonald, M.A., President of the Conference, the Rev. Hugh Price Hughes, M.A., and Mr. W. R. Perks, M.P. The structure is estimated to cost £7,500 and when completed it will be an important architectural feature in the neighbourhood.

The platform party assembled for the stone-laying was most impressive when it is remembered that in addition to the well known Hugh Price Hughes, who was the immediate past President, W. R. Perks was later to become Sir Robert Perks, the first Vice-President of the Uniting Conference of 1932. The Rev'd Frederic W. Macdonald was the uncle of Stanley Baldwin and Rudyard Kipling.6

The following 'Description of Trinity Wesleyan Church – Penarth' is taken from the forty-fifth Annual Report of the Wesleyan Chapel Committee 1899.

The Stone Laying of Trinity Wesleyan Church, 27 September 1899. From left to right: the Rev'd W. Maltby, Chairman of the District; the Rev'd F. Macdonald, President of the Conference; unidentified; Mr Robert Perks M.P.; unidentified; unidentified; The Rev'd Hugh Price Hughes; Lady Morel; unidentified; Mrs Humphrey Wallis; Sir Thomas Morel.'

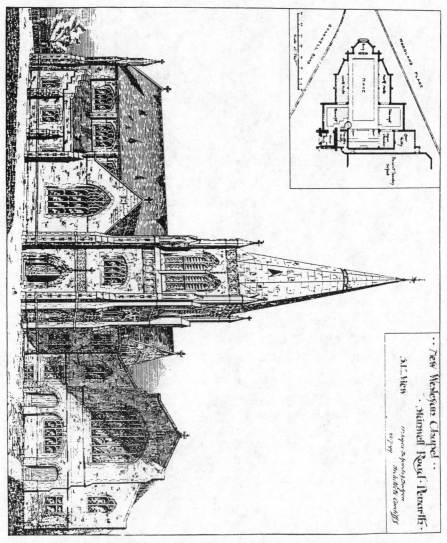

The new Wesleyan Chapel, Penarth, 1899.

*Hayman Christy & Lilly, Ltd.*

*Photo Elchtes, London*

46

As will be seen by the ground plan the site is triangular in shape, thus necessitating a somewhat unique plan to keep within the building line, the ends of Aisles having to be built at an angle.

The arrangement of the plan is Nave, Transepts, Aisles, Organ Chamber, and Minister's Vestry, with a large Choir Vestry having access to the Schools as well as to the Chapel. Further Class rooms are obtained over the Tower Porch and Minister's Vestry, reached from the staircase in the School.

The general style of the building is Decorated Gothic, the facings being of Newbridge stone with Bath stone dressings.

The building is heated and ventilated by Langfield's system of warm filtered air, extract flues being carried to the ventilators half way up the Spire.

Lighting is by the electric light, generated on the site. Gas also is laid on in case of emergency.

The interior will be somewhat ornate, the Nave arcading having Bath stone panelling filling up the spandrels between the arches, the columns being of Saint Bees' red sandstone. The whole of the floor area will be covered with wood block flooring, except behind the Communion rail, which will be of tiles. The Pulpit and seating are of oak, and the windows will be filled in with leaded lights.

The Architects are Messrs. J. P. Jones, Richards & Budgen, 18, St. Mary Street, Cardiff, and the Contractors, Messrs. Jones Bros., of the same town. The cost of the building (including £400. for capitalised ground rent) will be about £7,000. and the seating accommodation is for 650, including the choir.

The Chapel is expected to be ready for opening in November, 1900.

The building to the right of the Tower in the illustration, and joined to same by a semi-circular wall, is the Sunday School, which is now used as a School and Chapel.

Referring to the opening, the Circuit Quarterly Meeting Minutes of 19th December 1900 concluded with the following, 'The opening Services of

Trinity were commended to the sympathy and support of the Circuit generally.'

On the 2 January 1901, Trinity Church was opened by Mrs. Katie Budgen, wife of Henry Budgen, the architect, and daughter of Rabjohn Moxey, a leading Cardiff layman, and sister-in-law to Tom Morel. The preacher was Rev. Dr. Thomas Allen, President of the Conference. The Baptist and Congregational Churches were represented. Lord Windsor sent a contribution of £20, but there were no Anglican clergy present.

In his address, reported in *The Penarth Observer* of 5 January 1901, the President said: 'We must maintain the inward life – be true to our doctrines and see to the culture of spiritual gifts, preaching, prayer and testimony. We cultivate the preaching gift as no other Church does.' But he feared we did not pray as much as our forefathers did, and he also feared that the hearty response was somewhat dying out. He hoped it would not be so where it was the genuine expression of the heart. *The South Wales Echo* had described the Church as 'very much more elaborate than most non-conformist churches.' The President commented, 'Why should we not have beautiful churches? People now have beautiful houses, beautiful shops, should God's House be any less beautiful?'

Trinity was to take its place in a town already well provided with Churches and Chapels, although most of these were grouped in the older part of the town.

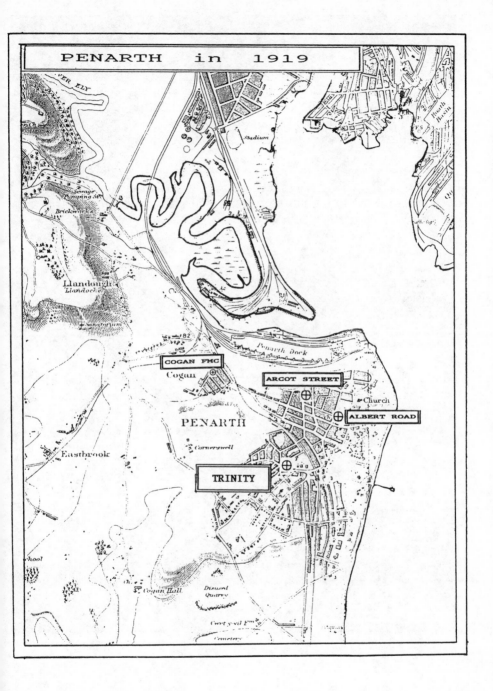

PENARTH in 1919

COGAN FMC

ARCOT STREET

ALBERT ROAD

TRINITY

49

The Rev'd Robert Bond, Minister at Trinity, 1902-1905 and 1908-1911.

# CHAPTER 4

## 1902 – 1915

### The Rev'd Robert Bond 1902-1905, 1908-1911

In 1902, a young minister, Robert Bond, was invited to serve in the Penarth Circuit with particular responsibility for the new Church.

In the Trinity Leaders Meeting Minutes, it was recorded that Robert Bond thanked the Circuit Steward, Edward Ede, for welcoming him and his family when they arrived at Penarth Station at the beginning of the Methodist year in September and for helping them to carry their luggage to the new Manse. This dry minute is fleshed out by a story often told in Robert Bond's family. Robert and Charlotte Bond had, at that time, a two year old daughter, Kathleen, Edward Ede carried her in his arms to the new Manse. The families remained friends and twenty years later when Kathleen Bond and Fiona Ede were undergraduates at Cambridge, Kathleen became engaged to Fiona's brother, Max.

The house, 1, Victoria Avenue, to which the young family went, must have been bought and furnished hurriedly, as the Circuit had the responsibility for housing and furnishing completely the homes of its Ministers. A minute as late as the July Quarterly Meeting reads: 'The matter of purchasing a new and commodious house for the Trinity Minister was carefully gone into and fully discussed and left in the hands of the Trinity friends to arrange.'

In fact, 'Trinity friends' were often inclined to take the initiative and to go ahead with schemes without reference to the Circuit. For instance, in 1904 Tom Morel, who was cast in the same mould as his father, Sir Thomas, bought the Woodland Institute, a hall and ancillary buildings opposite Trinity in Woodland Place, and gave it to the Trinity Trustees, but this was not brought to the Circuit's notice until 1911. Tom Morel first became a member of the Quarterly Meeting in 1895 when he was twenty-three. Later, so considerable was his influence in Trinity, that on one occasion a Leaders Meeting was abandoned because he was not able to be present.

The superintendent of the Sunday School was second only in importance to the minister of a Church; sometimes, indeed, there would be a clash of personalities, but in Tom Morel, a leading Cardiff shipowner like his father, Thomas, there was a man who was first and foremost a loyal member of his Church. He was undoubtedly a forceful individual and Kathleen Ede remembers him as 'someone not to cross'. His shadow lay over Trinity long after his death. Frank Jenkins, who became the Superintendent of the Sunday School in 1920 and who had been one of his young teachers, would say of any innovation: 'Mr. Tom wouldn't like that.'

During Tom Morel's term as Superintendent, Trinity Sunday School stood in very high esteem in the town and its influence was very considerable. The regimented rule which it followed in those days seemed to fit the period well.

For many of the children, attendance at Sunday School was a significant and pleasurable experience on a day which offered few other activities, with the annual highlights: the Sunday School Anniversary, the Treat and Children's Day. Year by year, at the behest of Conference, there was a special Children's Sunday. It was noted that at the Service held in September 1910, which began with a prayer meeting for the staff early in the morning, there was 'a great ingathering of souls and, as a result, three junior class meetings were formed.' The Circuit Sunday School Council meeting in October 1913 recorded:

> regarding the results of Children's Day a very helpful and encouraging conversation took place and it was felt that the Spirit of God was touching the hearts of our young people, some of whom had already come to a decision to love and serve the Lord Jesus Christ.

The early years of the century were generally a time of great increase in numbers in the Circuit and at Trinity, with, for example, the addition to the Circuit membership of fifty-eight in one quarter during 1905.

Robert Bond was greatly loved. In August 1905, as he was leaving the Circuit, 284 members of the congregation, old and young, put their names to a Tribute to him and his wife.

> Your preaching has been an inspiration to us all – so simple that the children loved to hear, so human that we felt we were listening to a brother, so practical that every aspect of daily life was touched and illumined, so stimulating that none could help longing to be more like the Master of whom you spoke.

Thomas Morel   Tom Morel   Teddy Morel
1847  - 1903    1873-1935    1900-1976

In our homes you have been the welcome playmate of the children, the guide and confidant of the young people, the trusted friend and companion of the parents.

You were ever the comfort of the distressed. The bereaved felt your hand clasp theirs in the darkness, you pointed the sick to the Great Physician and the tempted to Him who is able to keep us from falling.

In conclusion, they expressed the hope that they might soon have the privilege of welcoming their dear Pastor and friend back for another term of service. The testimonial is bound in leather covers and in a note to this chapter the names, and as many of the addresses as it has been possible to discover, are listed.[1]

Robert J. Hancock was Senior Society Steward when Robert Bond left Trinity and had an important part in organising the testimonial. He was almost certainly born and raised in Penarth as his father, who died at the age of 101, is buried in St. Augustine's Churchyard. He was a builder and responsible for several roads of houses in Grangetown and for the Penarth Isolation Hospital, and in 1904 he had been Chairman of the Penarth Urban District Council. One of his three daughters was married in the Tin Tabernacle to Ernest Chivers, the son of a well established Wesleyan family who attended Arcot Street and later Trinity.

The Second Steward who arranged the signing of the testimonial was Ivor Hatton Evans, who with his family was to play an important part in the development of Trinity. He led the Brotherhood for many years, and his daughter, Olive, was a formative influence in the Sunday School in the twenties.

Llewellyn Davies was a Welsh-speaking schoolmaster from Abercrave in the Neath valley, whose wife, Lily, like so many Trinity members, came from Bristol. Llewellyn Davies became a quarry owner in Sully, and was Circuit Steward during the Second World War. They had two daughters, one of whom remembered being carried on her father's shoulders at the opening of the new Trinity Church.

A number of the signatories came from Portland. Drawn by the opportunities afforded by Cardiff and encouraged by their Gibbs' relations, the Scrivens, the Hindes and the Pearces formed a distinctive group.

Two of the signatories, Alice and Charles Venn, were recently married members. Alice Smith had come to Penarth as a children's nurse, and as a Wesleyan she attended Trinity where she met her future husband. They were typical of the young people who were to be married in Trinity during the next ten years and to form a network of relationships which stretched into the future. Their family of two boys and two girls were brought up within the Church.

John Cox, a gardener, and his wife moved to Penarth from Somerset and attended Trinity from its beginnings. His sons followed him as gardeners: A. J. 'Bert' the elder, became head green-keeper with the Glamorganshire Golf Club, and, after the War, Fred, the younger, worked at the J. A. Gibbs Home, where boys returning to the Home wanted to see him especially. Bert and Fred grew up in the early days of the Tin Tabernacle, which they attended with their parents. Bert played for the Trinity cricket and hockey teams, and later served as Secretary of the Brotherhood for many years.

In 1906, Bert Cox was married in Trinity, by the Rev. Russell Watson, to Bertha Collins. He later became a trustee and when he died in 1932, Dr. Robert Bond returned to the Church to conduct the funeral service.

Bert's father-in-law had moved to Penarth in order to work in the cement works and initially his children, Bertha, her brother, William, and her sisters attended All Saints Sunday School. However, the evening congregation complained about the state in which the scholars left the premises, and Mrs. Collins removed her children to Trinity. All four were life-long members of the Society. Bertha Cox became a Sunday School teacher, one of the first women members of the Leaders' Meeting, and a class leader.

William Collins, whose wife was also a faithful member, became a Trustee and member of the Leaders' Meeting.

Andrew McArthur, born in 1855 in Old Kilpatrick, Dunbartonshire, was a joiner and ship's carpenter who found work as a foreman in Mount Stuart Dry Docks. He married Emma Goddard, a widow with three children, at Llandough Parish Church, and they had eleven more children. One of his sons, Gordon, used to help him blow the organ at Trinity in the days before 1907, when the present organ was installed. In 1920 he was a venerable figure who sat in the front row of the north transept and was pointed out as one who had had a spectacular conversion. Be that as it may, he was by that time, a devout Methodist who had attended the Tin Tabernacle with his large family. His son, Gordon, married Doris Blackmore from Somerset, a kinswoman of the author of *Lorna Doone.*

Another signatory of the tribute was Alexander Stevenson. His father had come from Scotland to work on the docks at an early stage and he was born at Cogan Pill. With his wife, Alice, from Llysworney, near Cowbridge, he raised a family in Trinity.

Church members are not always sensitive to a new Minister's feelings and when he arrived in September 1905 to follow Robert Bond, the Rev'd Russell Watson must have needed 'the strength of character' and 'natural charm' which his obituary says were his characteristics. Especially must this have been so when the Circuit, on the prompting of 'friends at Trinity', invited Robert Bond to follow him for a second term of Ministry. So anxious were they that they offered to increase their share of the Circuit assessment by £5 a quarter. It was unusual for men to minister twice in the same Circuit. Again, Robert Bond's ministry was appreciated, not only by Methodists but by others, for example, by two young Anglicans who chose to attend Trinity with their nurse rather than worship at St. Augustines where their father was Churchwarden.

During Robert Bond's second ministry, George Chambers came to Cardiff with a firm of Newcastle pit-prop importers. He and his young wife, Jennifer, joined Trinity. They had special links with their new minister as her family, the Kelletts, came from the same Durham village as Robert Bond.

When he left Penarth for the second time the Sunday School gathered at the railway station to wave goodbye.

The Circuit would have extended an invitation for a third term had this been permitted by the Connexion. Robert Bond was an exceptional minister. He was to become Secretary of the Wesleyan Methodist Conference in 1927 and of the Methodist Conference in 1932 and, as Dr. Robert Bond DD, President of the Conference in 1937. 'Quiet in manner, his pulpit ministry was thorough and the fruit of deep personal conviction, an alert mind and wide reading. It was, however, as a pastor that he revealed his great qualities of heart and mind. He had a gift of discerning sympathy, and young and old counted him as friend.' So ran his obituary in 1953. When thanking the Quarterly Meeting on leaving the Circuit, he said '. . . it was no light matter to turn away from Penarth which contained more of his friends than anywhere else.' These friends were both young and old; the Morels remembered how Robert Bond was a frequent visitor at 'The Lindens' where he would play billiards with the younger members of the family.

He never lost contact with Trinity as, during the next thirty years, he returned often to take Services and in 1948 he and his wife moved to Penarth for the third time to live in Coleridge Avenue for the latter part of his retirement.

During the early years of the century the interior of Trinity was being embellished. Most of the stained glass windows were installed during this period and three of them show the continuing involvement of the Morel and Gibbs families. All are by H. J. Salisbury, the brother of the Methodist artist, Frank Salisbury, whose firm was also later responsible for the painting, in memory of Philip Morel and his wife, Martha, of the 'Last Supper', positioned above the Communion Table. A member of the firm went to Italy and spent several months in Milan copying the painting by Leonardo da Vinci.

Robert Bond's 'pulpit ministry' was offered from a gothic-style oak pulpit. However, in 1911 Arthur Hibbert, 'a quiet member of the Society' died at the early age of 51. His widow, Maud, one of the daughters of Philip and Martha Morel, was desolate and commissioned a tall memorial Cross for his grave at the top of Penarth Cemetery which she could see from her bedroom window at 'Penarth House'. She also commissioned an elaborate marble pulpit for her chapel, Trinity. However, within a short time of its dedication, she married the architect of both memorials and moved away to Torquay in Devon.

The Trustees have the right, and indeed the duty, to control alterations and embellishments made to the interior of a chapel, but they were unable, or chose not, to prevent the erection of the Renaissance style marble pulpit which is totally out of keeping with the Gothic character of the Church. Nevertheless, this pulpit, probably unique in Methodism, is now an established feature of the building. Some ministers, notably Arnold Morris, have, however, refused to preach from it, as being an expression of triumphalism for which they had little sympathy.

In June 1912, Trinity and the Circuit were faced with a ministerial emergency. The Rev'd A. R. Edgeley gave notice that, after one year's ministry, he would be emigrating to Australia in the hope that the warmer climate there would improve his daughter's health. At very short notice, the Stationing Committee of Conference sent the Rev'd Alfred Woodward to Penarth. Trinity was fortunate at having such a distinguished minister. He had spent eleven years in Burma where he had been one of the founders of the first home for lepers in Mandalay. His youngest son, Max, later a minister, has only slight memories of Penarth except for going to school at Westbourne House. For his part, Mr. Woodward expressed his appreciation of Trinity and the December quarterly meeting in 1912 when he said, 'It was a joy to meet the classes for the renewal of tickets.'

From John Wesley's time, the weekly class meeting had been an integral part of Methodism where the members met in single-sex groups, witnessed to their spiritual growth and experience, and paid their weekly class moneys for the support of the Society. The membership at Trinity, as was normal, was divided into senior classes, and junior classes for those seeking membership. In 1906, there were one hundred people in senior classes. There is no record of what was said in these classes when they met, if indeed they did meet, as during the twentieth century it would be true to say that within Methodism as a whole their influence has steadily declined. The tendencies of some members to tell *ad nauseam* of their conversion experiences, their harking back to conflicts of long ago and vain repetitions made week after week did not encourage younger people to involve themselves in such meetings. Nevertheless, the division of the Society into classes ensured that most members were pastorally cared for and the work of the Minister was shared with the laity.

In addition to these classes, there were organisations for young people. The Girls League promoted interest and involvement with missionary activity and the Juvenile Missionary Association, J.M.A., dates from this time. The Band of Hope was a temperance organisation, not particular to Methodism, encouraging young people to abjure drink by 'Signing the Pledge', but also introducing them to enjoyable activities; games, concerts, and dramatic presentations, such as *tableaux vivantes*. The Wesley Guild, started in 1896, was another young peoples' society, which held weekly meetings, with devotional, literary and social programmes. Many young people learnt to speak in public, to organise groups and meetings and to 'improve' themselves; not for nothing was it originally known as the Mutual Improvement Society. Guild Rallies brought the young people of the Circuit together in a wider fellowship.

There were afternoon meetings for older women. The Women's Hour, established soon after Trinity was opened, met on Mondays – as it still does. On Monday mornings the family washing would have been done and in the afternoon would be drying, so the housewives were free to attend the friendly and heart-warming meeting with the inevitable cup of tea, before undertaking the ironing later in the evening or during the week. Susanna, Lady Morel, was more comfortable as President of this meeting than when accompanying her husband on his civic engagements as Mayor of Cardiff, and, for her, the Monday afternoon meeting was at the heart of Trinity.

The Sewing Meeting was well established on Tuesday afternoons. Attendance was largely by the leisured women of the congregation, although class lines were not rigidly observed and women with dressmaking and cutting-out skills were welcomed. Articles were produced to be sold at the regular sales of work at which money was raised for Society Funds and other interests, especially Foreign Missions.

Indeed, within the Society, the raising of money ranked second only in importance to worship. Under the Methodist Connexional system, Trinity paid an assessment to the Circuit, for the stipends of the Ministers, the provision and upkeep of Manses and also for 'Connexional Funds'; Ministerial Training, the Sustentation Fund for less well-off Circuits, and the crudely-named 'Worn-Out Ministers Fund'.

Trinity did not forget its surrounding community or the wider world in its giving. There was a Hospital Sunday with a collection for Cardiff Royal Infirmary and special appeals such as that in 1896 for the Distressed Armenian People and the Indian Famine Fund in 1900.

To sustain the Lay Ministry, the Local Preachers Mutual Aid Society received half the collection on Local Preachers' Sunday.

A special Twentieth Century Fund was inaugurated connexionally, to raise not less than One Million Guineas, a truly tremendous sum in those days, for a diverse number of causes which reflected Methodist priorities at the turn of the Century. These were:

To build chapels, schools and mission halls.

For education and training.

For Foreign Missions and Home Missions including Temperance.

The Children's Home; to save all children of Methodists and other nonconformist parentage from Workhouse Schools.

For the children of Methodist soldiers and sailors,·

and

To purchase a site and build Westminster Central Hall.

Contributions were made to all the causes named and the Central Hall was built in the heart of London to take its place alongside Westminster Abbey, and Westminster Cathedral, as the focal point for one of the three largest Churches in Britain.

Year in and year out Trinity and the Circuit, in addition to these commitments, supported Foreign and Home Missions with sacrificial giving. Particularly was this the case where married women were concerned. They seldom had money of their own so they cooked and sewed to raise funds for the Women's Auxiliary of the Mission House. During Robert Bond's time, as Circuit Ministerial Foreign Missions Secretary, the collection rose steadily, but this was not typical. At the 1906 Conference the Connexion faced a deficit of £15,000 on its missionary funds, with the challenge either to retreat or advance. The Penarth Quarterly Meeting in September passed the resolution that 'all our Churches and Sunday Schools should observe October 7th as a Day of Thanksgiving and Intercession for Foreign Missions.'

The great importance of the Edinburgh Conference Declaration of 1910, which committed the missionary societies of the main denominations to avoid rivalry and to work together on the mission field, was referred to at the Penarth Quarterly Meeting, but with no appreciation of what this decision would mean, not only overseas but in Britain, in terms of inter-church co-operation.

At Trinity, the climax of this first period of the Twentieth Century came with the visit of Gypsy Smith in January 1915. The romance of his birth in Epping Forest, his early life in a caravan, his use of an accordion and a violin, and his reputation as a great evangelist broke through any resistance that the architecture of the Church might have offered, and the visit was a 'wonderful occasion.' Alfred Woodward spoke of: 'the spiritual fervour manifested at all the meetings and the great quickening the churches had received. He thanked God for the wonderful results obtained. Those who had been privileged to work in close touch with the mission had had such a spiritual uplift that he hoped would live with them for many days to come.'

The *Circuit Magazine* recorded that: 'following on the Mission in the Circuit there were 230 enquiries and that one third of these were from Trinity.'

# CHAPTER 5

## The First World War

Trinity entered the war years with a strong membership. There is an illuminated Roll of Honour bearing the names of those who served in the War on the south aisle of the Church. This comprehensive list compensates for the sparseness of the other records from this period. The list, compiled in the early 1920's, shows that fifteen women and one hundred and seventy-seven men, connected in greater or lesser degree with the Society, were involved in war service, sixteen of whom were killed in action.[1]

The *Circuit Record* of August 1915 has a moving reference to the death of W. H. Coney who 'was a worthy representative of the Sunday School and who had sung in a church choir while on service in India.' He must stand in for others of whom there is no record.

A name to emerge from this period is John Pearson Griffiths, born in 1878. His grandfather was a grocer in Penarth and the whole family were associated with Trinity from its Tin Tabernacle days. As a young man, he was a member of the Trinity hockey team and in the War was awarded the Military Cross. His wife, Gwladys was a member of the Brethren Meeting in Plassey Street and, unusually, they worshipped separately even after their marriage. An accountant, he served the Church using his financial skills and was both a Trustee and member of the Quarterly Meeting from 1904. However, it was as a very long standing choir member that he was most visible as he sat immediately below the pulpit and was able to prompt or guide the minister if there was a hiatus in the Services at any point.

No minutes of the Leaders Meetings survive from this period and the *Circuit Records* report little as the activities of the Society were restricted because of the War.

From these Records it is possible to see that an increasing number of women were in leadership positions in the Society. In 1894 there were no women; by 1913 there were eighteen. A deaconess, Sister Agnes Gibb who was appointed to Trinity, was sent as a Representative to the District Synod in 1914.

Conference recommended that, because of the War, Ministers should be invited for more than three years and this was to lead in subsequent years to a gradual lengthening of ministries.

In addition to the normal collections, there was now a War Emergency Fund. The *Circuit Magazine* records that the women of the Church were working hard, knitting and sewing for the troops and that books and magazines were being collected for men at the forts in Penarth and Lavernock.

Trinity supported financially two Belgian refugee families. In March 1915 they joined with the Society at Trinity at a lantern lecture on the theme 'Beautiful and Battle-swept Belgium.'

There are indications that the Women's Hour, the Girls' Club and the Guild managed to survive, but records are scanty indeed. There is reference to an Old Folks Party to which people were brought 'in a motor'. Prayer meetings were held and the dependants of those who had enlisted were supported both financially and in other ways. The National Children's Home and Orphanage made an urgent appeal for the orphaned children of Servicemen.

At the Quarterly Meeting in June 1916, there was the first intimation of an approaching storm in the Trinity Society. A Resolution was passed, without recording the mover and seconder, expressing 'the disapproval of the Pacifist Manifesto, issued by a number of Ministers and laymen of the Wesleyan Methodist Church.' How the voting went is not recorded but the Trinity Minister, the Rev. F. J. Pope, almost certainly voted against the Resolution. In his obituary in the Minutes of Conference of 1953, it states; 'His avowed pacifism made his position during the First World War extremely difficult, but those who were opposed to him were in no doubt of his sincerity.'

At the Quarterly Meeting of 14 March, 1917, Mr Pope and two of the other Circuit Ministers were invited, 'with great heartiness to serve for another year.' They all accepted, but Mr Pope at a Trinity Leaders Meeting held on the evening before this meeting had asked permission 'to give three days a week to National Service.' It is not clear what this entailed but permission was given. The Leaders must have been aware of the strain he was under and of the feeling in the Trinity congregation that was building up against him.

Three months later, at the June Quarterly Meeting, a communication was read from Mr Pope, although he was present at the meeting, 'that circumstances had arisen which made it incumbent upon him to leave the Circuit this year', which would mean within three months. The Minutes record great distress 'at such lamentable news. Many friends urged Mr Pope to reconsider his decision and bore abundant testimony to his high Christian character and the magnetic charm of his personality.' Mr Pope was much moved by such a spontaneous tribute, but felt that 'under present circumstances he could not alter his decision.' The Quarterly Meeting accepted it with regret and with appreciation of Mr Pope as a Minister.

A quotation from his obituary of 1953 provides further insight: 'He held advanced social views, set them in a Christian context and defended them with grace and courtesy.' So must he have done at these meetings.

Mr Pope left the Circuit and went on to fulfil a distinguished Ministry in London, Lythan St. Anne's and Southport and to play a leading role in the Christian pacifist organisation; the Fellowship of Reconciliation.

The acceptance at the June Quarterly Meeting in 1917 of Mr Pope's resignation was accompanied by another act at the same Meeting: the congratulating of Major J. A. Gibbs on winning the Distinguished Service Order.'

John Angel Gibbs was the second son of Elizabeth Gibbs and the late John Angel Gibbs. It was in 1909 that John Angel Gibbs and Gladys Morel were married by Robert Bond. John Angel Gibbs, with only the prospects of a junior clerk, had not been considered a suitable husband for his cousin, Gladys Morel, with whom he had been in love for a number of years. Her brothers teased her by saying that in their father's eyes 'only a religious earl would have been good enough for her.' The death of her father in 1903, and even more John Angel Gibbs's success in business, altered the situation. He, of all his brothers, had inherited his late father's flair and ability, and in 1906 he had founded a shipowning company in his own right which prospered to such an extent that by 1909 Gladys's brothers could no longer maintain their opposition to her marriage.

The editor of the *Circuit Record* gave an account of visiting Major John A. Gibbs in April 1917, at 'Eastcliffe', Park Road where he was convalescing after an operation. He reported: 'We talked a little about the operation, more about the skill of surgeons and nurses . . . at

John Angel Gibbs 1880-1917; Susan Gladys Gibbs (née Morel) 1880-1952;
John Morel Gibbs b. 1912.

home and at the front; something about church work; much more about the course, development and ultimate issue of the War, and most of all about the fine calibre of the men and the splendid loyalty and efficiency of the young officers. It was easy to see he was in imagination back in the lines, and again facing the grim realities of war.'

The editor wrote appreciatively of Major Gibbs: 'having enlisted as a trooper in the early days of the war, when a hundred valid reasons might have kept him at home.'

In the same September of 1917 when Mr Pope left the Circuit, John Angel Gibbs was killed at Passchendaele.

After the traumatic experience of Mr Pope's resignation which the Church and Circuit had gone through, it must have been a relief for Trinity to welcome the Rev'd Edwin Owen in September 1917, for he was 'a quietly spoken countryman who loved books and people – but especially people – and whose favourite recreation was angling.'

The casualty list read out at the December Quarterly Meeting was particularly long; it was a difficult time for the Rev'd Edwin Owen to begin his Ministry at Trinity. The Guild and the Band of Hope, which had managed to survive so far, gave up in 1917 but, although nine members were away on war service, the choir still had an average attendance of twenty-one. In 1919, when the organ was re-opened and enlarged, the choir was to present Spohr's oratorio *Last Judgment*, with special soloists.

At the December Meeting, which was held at Trinity, the Superintendent Minister, the Rev'd John T. Watts, sought to bring the members of the Circuit together by the careful wording of a Resolution which was passed unanimously.

> That this Quarterly Meeting of Penarth and Barry Wesleyan Circuit affirmed its belief in the righteousness of the cause for which our Country and our allies are fighting and pledges its loyal support to our Government in their resolve to continue until the triumph of the great cause of right and liberty shall be achieved.

In this the Superintendent was asserting what most Wesleyan Methodists believed, and echoing the sentiment of the President of the Conference of 1915, when he said 'deeply as we deplore the appalling spectacle of bloodshed and widespread misery, we are driven to confess that a righteous war is better than an immoral peace.'

When Major John Angel Gibbs was killed leading his battalion in an attack on the Menin Road, his widow Gladys Gibbs implemented a plan which would not only provide a fitting memorial to her husband but which would also help children and families in need. She and her family bought and furnished the old Penarth Hotel and gave it to the National Children's Home to be a Nautical Branch especially for children orphaned in the War. The decision to make the branch a nautical one was logical. The South Wales' ports were thriving commercial centres due to the continuing demand for Welsh coal, and the Morel, Cory and Gibbs families were able to provide openings for the boys who had passed through the Home as apprentices on their ships. The Royal Navy was also a popular, if testing, choice for boys and there were beginning to be opportunities for promotion from the lower deck to the officers' mess.

The J. A. Gibbs Home was officially opened by the Duke of York in 1921, who commended it as enabling boys to respond to the 'essential calling of the sea.' However, not all the boys were to go to sea: two in particular, Edwin Tabraham and Harold Woodhouse, remained to grow up in Penarth and at Trinity. Edwin Tabraham was the great grandson of a Methodist minister, and both his grandfather and father were Methodists. When the latter failed in his business enterprises and could not support his family, he turned, naturally enough, to the National Children's Home to provide a home for his children. When it had been founded in 1868 one of its objects was to provide for Methodist children an alternative to the harsh provision offered by the State. Edwin was first placed with foster parents, but when the J. A. Gibbs Home opened in 1918, he was moved – then aged seven – to Penarth.

Harold Woodhouse's mother died in 1914 and when his father was called up for military service, Harold and his brother, Leslie, were fostered under the same scheme. The boys moved to the Penarth Home when it opened in order to take advantage of the career opportunities it provided. Harold, like Edwin, was seven at the time.

One of the objects of the Twentieth Century Fund had been the provision of Homes for War Orphans, and even before 1917, John and Gladys Gibbs had decided to provide a building to meet this need. Had he returned it would have been a Thanksgiving: as he was killed, it became a Memorial.

Trinity erected a Celtic Cross outside the main doors of the Church as a War Memorial to her Dead, and every effort was made to ensure that the list of those who died was complete. The War Memorial was dedicated on 4 September 1921 and unveiled by John Evans, the father of one of the Fallen. The Boys of the J. A. Gibbs Home, some of whom had been orphaned during the War, sounded the Last Post.

There is another memorial inside the Church: the Brass Eagle Lectern was given by those men and women who returned from the War in memory of those who had died. The Lessons are read from this Lectern; at first only by ex-servicemen, now by the appointed reader, man or woman, adult or child.

# CHAPTER 6

## The Rev'd John James Johnston 1920-1925

For a year or two after the end of the War there were those who thought it would be possible to return to life – and to life in the Church – as it had been in 1914. However, it soon became apparent that not all those who returned from the War were returning to their churches. Almost a whole generation was lost. The younger brother of Tom Morel, John Morel, who was not actively involved in the War, could ask his cousin Clem Scriven when entering Trinity for a funeral service; 'Can you believe in all this now?' and Clem Scriven was unable to give a simple answer. Men had undergone experiences on the Western Front which were difficult to reconcile with the 'comfortable words' of the Church Services. It was a different world from 1914. The very language had altered: it was as if people could no longer be explicit about 'bringing souls to Christ.' Previously, it had been possible to ask another 'Are you saved?' Now this might be regarded an impertinence. Not everyone realised that a change had occurred and some ministers and local preachers went on striking the old notes, using the old expressions, unable to accept that they evoked no response. A local preacher in the Penarth circuit, hoping to shift the responsibility for the lack of any response from himself to his hearers, said despondently 'I've given them everything I've got.'

As if to point up the difference, the visit of a skilled evangelist, such as that in April 1920 by Mark Guy Pearce, might still make a lasting impression. Although his text was a standard one, 'Bless the Lord, O my Soul and forget not his Benefits,' his method of sermon illustration was vivid. Having slid down the bannisters of the marble pulpit to show how easy it was to go to Hell, he then tried to clamber up them to illustrate how hard it was to get into Heaven. An illustration remembered vividly by Sheila Newton who was eight years old at the time.

In 1920, John James Johnston, then aged forty-four, succeeded Edwin Owen as the Minister at Trinity. He had been born in Cumberland, and, after leaving Richmond College in 1900 with a B.D., had served in five circuits. During the War he went as a Chaplain with the forces in France, and Trinity was his first Church on demobilisation. He and his wife had no children; they kept two chow dogs.

The family pew was still a feature of Trinity and it was difficult to get 'sittings.' In 1917 the Newton family of four could not have their own pew as none was available and for some years had 'sittings' in the Ministers' pew. Mrs Johnston, who was fond of children, would ply Malcolm Newton with sweets during the sermon, much to the disapproval of his older sister, Sheila. Herbert and Jessie Newton transferred from the Wesleyan Methodist Church in Whitchurch. His grandfather had been a Primitive Methodist Minister, and when on holiday Herbert first saw Jessie Goldsworthy at a Sunday School Treat in Newport where her father was a local preacher of long standing. The Goldsworthy family had moved to South Wales from Cornwall, and forebears had been converted by John Wesley at Gwennap Pit.

At this time Cardiff was becoming an administrative centre and large firms were stationing regional representatives in the city. Herbert Newton was at the time a Lloyds Bank Inspector.

Arthur Hosegood, who joined Trinity after the War, was South Wales Manager for the Wilts United Dairies. He had been brought up in a Wesleyan Methodist home, and as a child had attended Church and Sunday School three times each Sunday at Ilminster, two miles from his home. In 1919 he married Catherine Cowell from the Isle of Man, where she had played the organ in the Methodist Church in Douglas. They both became deeply involved in the life of Trinity.

In a similar way, George Knighton was moved to Cardiff as a representative of the London Guaranteed Assurance, which merged with the Phoenix Assurance, and he and his young wife, Evelyn, settled in Penarth. As he was a Wesleyan Methodist from Yorkshire, and she was a dyed-in-the-wool Wesleyan Methodist from Owster Ferry in the Epworth Circuit, they joined the Society at Trinity.

At the December Quarterly Meeting in 1918, A. R. Dawson, M.B.E., was warmly welcomed as a local preacher and one who had served Methodism for a lifetime, retiring to Penarth after serving as an Inspector of H.M. Customs and Excise. He was a Dorsetshire man, with a fund of graphic illustrations from the history of smuggling in the Bristol Channel, and a formidable addition to the laymen of the Circuit.

Another family, the Marsh family, who had been involved with both Albert Road and Trinity Churches, became closely connected with the latter when Jim Marsh and his wife, Olive, became Chapel Keepers in 1922. Jim's father, George, came from Bideford and started a haulage business, working from 46 Salop Place, where his horses were stabled. His wife, Emma Bennet, came from Swansea and they had six sons and three daughters. George was a member of the Brotherhood, and the family attended Trinity, occupying the front pew and so sitting just below the pulpit. When he died, after a fall from a horse, George's funeral service was held at Trinity, conducted by the Rev. J. J. Johnston. Most of the boys grew up to work in the family business, although one, Reuben, was later in charge of the horses belonging to Penarth Urban District Council. Reuben and his wife, Carmen, were members of Trinity, and their son, Glyn, who worked in the Accounts Office of the Penarth Council, was to be the Treasurer of the Trinity Trust for many years.

In 1922, the Minister persuaded the Society to institute the Envelope System, by which members were issued with a set of fifty two envelopes; the members undertook to give a fixed amount each week, and if absent they carried the amount forward. The system operated was a confidential one.

This weekly amount took the place both of the long-established class money to maintain the Society and the pew rent to maintain the building. Thereafter, seats were free and worshippers could sit anywhere, but in practice people felt comfortable in their own seats and Frank Jenkins, even in the 1950's, attempted to defend the pews which he had allotted many years earlier, against newcomers.

The pattern of Worship at Trinity was 'high', though without using the full order of Morning Prayer that had been adapted for Wesleyan congregations by John Wesley. The Lord's Prayer, the Commandments and the Commandments of the Lord Jesus were sung and there was always a sung canticle and psalm.

Although the members of the Society were diffident in expressing their faith in conversation, there was still a confident assertion of faith in the singing of Charles Wesley's Hymns. The anthems by the Choir and their use of music from *The Messiah* gave Grace Prebble the opportunity of voicing the belief of many, when she sang, with the personal assurance sometimes lacking in a professional performance, 'I know that my Redeemer liveth.'

The Senior Departments of the Sunday School slipped into a rut from which they were not to be rescued until much later, but the Primary Department under Olive Hatton Evans reflected the new thinking in

71

children's education.  During the War, she took two courses in Sunday School teaching at Westhill College in Birmingham and her influence on the Primary Department was a lasting one.  She shared her knowledge with the other teachers in the Circuit and the Primary Departments grew; for example in 1923 when, throughout the Circuit, they recorded a quarterly growth of 102.  A somewhat sourer note, however, in February 1931 recorded decreases; partly, it seems, because of the Anglican and Roman Catholic priests who were reclaiming some of the older children who had started in Methodist Primary Sunday Schools.

Olive Hatton Evans appealed in the *Circuit Magazine* for a rug on which the children could sit out-of-doors on occasions, and Joyce Cox, who herself later became the leader of the Primary Department, remembers sitting on this rug on the floor of the Primary room in front of a coal fire while the 'story' was told.  This homely atmosphere was in considerable contrast to the formal regime of the Superintendent's department which was dominated by a bell.  It is not surprising that young men and women volunteered eagerly to teach in Olive Hatton Evans's department.  Arthur Chambers, later to lead the Primary Department and even later to enter the Ministry, records that there were two other men teachers with him in the Department, and he remembers that the weekly training class for the teachers was a 'means of grace.' The teachers had the advantage of feeling prepared to meet the needs of the younger children when many amateurs felt incompetent to face an older group.  Olive Hatton Evans did not neglect the social needs of her teaching group; there is mention of teachers' parties and concerts and warm fellowship permeated all that was done for these younger children.  Two of her favourite precepts were; 'Religion is caught not taught' and 'There is no impression without expression'.  These two sentiments lay behind the growing attempts to provide the young people of the Church, and the neighbourhood, with more and wider youth activities; an evangelism that was implicit rather  than a direct challenge to follow Christ.

Harold Champion offered for the ministry  in March, 1920.  His work at Eastbrook was especially commended and in June of the same year his candidature received a unanimous vote at the Synod.  After Richmond College, he served  in a number of circuits but in 1932, as a result of the acceptance of Methodist Union, he resigned from the Ministry and became the Secretary of the National Brotherhood Movement.

J. J. Johnston revived many week night activities, amongst them the Band of Hope which had closed during the War but which in 1896 had had eighty-two members. He issued the somewhat oblique challenge: 'Are there any parents who wish to get rid of their boys or girls for an hour or so on Wednesday evenings? Please send them along!' The response was good; soon there were eighty members and then 150. The Band of Hope continued to meet at Trinity until the Second World War.

On Wednesday evening there was also a boys' club, led by a gym instructor and with an average attendance of thirty.

The Scout Movement at Trinity began uncertainly. There is mention in the *Circuit Record* in 1917 of the '6th Penarth' but this did not survive the War. In 1924 Sea Scouts were formed, and by the 1930's this became a Scout Troop, the '6th Penarth'.

J. J. Johnston announced that he wished to conduct monthly services for young people, and the *Circuit Record* mentions that Gladys Gibbs presided over a young people's Service in Trinity in 1927. This was attended by the Sea Scouts and the Girl Guide Company – newly formed that year.

Eileen Roberts, nee Chivers, was the first Guide Captain. Her parents, Ernest Chivers and Ethel Hancock, were married in the Tin Church in 1900, and spent their early married life in Llandaff. It was not until 1919 that they moved into Hazelhurst, a large house between Penarth and Llandough, which had been built by her grandfather, the founder of S. Chivers and Co. Ltd., jam and vinegar makers in Cardiff. The Chivers family was active in the Circuit and the Hancock family at Trinity. Eileen settled into Trinity and the Guild, and taught in the Primary Department. Cubs at Trinity also date from this period.

Every Sunday morning, the boys of the J. A. Gibbs Home in naval uniform to show their allegiance to 'the essential calling of the sea' to which the Duke of York had summoned them, marched through the town led by their band, and occupied the front pews in Trinity. Parade Services in the armed forces on Sundays and compulsory attendance at school services were accepted as a matter of course at this period and, indeed, until the 1940's, but, apart from the children's address at Trinity, no special attempt was made to involve them in worship. The boys joined in the Trinity Sunday School sports and contributed musical items on special occasions. Some, who attended the Penarth County School, remained in Penarth after the normal school leaving age and

Church Parade 1930: The return from Trinity of the Boys of the J. A. Gibbs Home to the N.C.H.O. Branch.

were later to join in with Trinity activities, the Guild, and the sole remaining young men's class which was led by Allen Pratt.

Allen Pratt, who had been a young solicitor living in lodgings in Penarth when he had signed the testimonial to Robert Bond, was now a well known Cardiff docksman, soon to move to Marine Parade and was a leading member of the Trinity Society. Arthur Chambers and later Edwin Tabraham and Harold Woodhouse were regular and appreciative members of his class which met for many years.

After the War, two meetings which had been casualties of that War were also revived. The Guild by 1921 was 'going famously' according to the *Circuit Record* with lantern lectures still a feature. So many attended that they met in the Woodland Hall. This, however, was so cold – it was heated only by a pair of 'tortoise stoves' – that a move was made into the Church Parlour.

The other meeting was the Brotherhood which met every Sunday afternoon in the Woodland Hall. By 1921 it was meeting regularly for 'a diligent study of the Bible.' Ivor Hatton Evans was the leader and it was renowned for the large number of gardeners who attended it. There was some rivalry with the Sunday School, also meeting at the same time, when the School could have done with some of the men as teachers for the boys. On rare occasions the Brotherhood and Sunday School met jointly. The Brotherhood's success, perhaps, explained the comparatively poor attendance at Trinity evening worship.

It was J. J. Johnston, himself a keen player, who introduced indoor bowls in the Woodland Hall and a Young Men's Institute also met there. A Church news notes dates from this time but did not survive long.

During the time of J. J. Johnston's ministry at Trinity, the proposed union of the three Methodist Churches: Wesleyan, Primitive and United, occupied the thinking and attention of the Circuit to a considerable degree. J. J. Johnston was involved in the negotiations as an implacable opponent of Union, and this brushed off on the Trinity leadership – but of that in a later chapter.

In his farewell speech of 1925, J. J. Johnston said that the Society he was leaving 'was very different from that he came to in 1921.' This was true, and one of the changes was the shadow of the depression which was to hang over the next years.

# CHAPTER 7

## The Rev'd Percy C. Pegler 1925-1930

During the War the normal period of ministry in the Wesleyan Methodist Church was extended from three years to five. The Rev'd J. J. Johnston had ministered for five years and the circuit hoped that their new Minister would also serve for this period. Percy Pegler was forty-six years of age with a glowing reputation going back to his student days. His fellow students at Handsworth College in 1901 'recognised his pulpit ability and predicted a future of growing influence,' which, was eventually fulfilled in his ministry. 'He had a winsome personality, was a charming companion and enjoyed the confidence of a large circle of friends.' As will emerge, this was to be movingly seen in the closing year of his ministry in Penarth.

J. J. Johnston's ministry and that of those before him was chiefly to the Trinity congregation. Percy Pegler's was to be the first of those ministries which reached out towards the town. He was a graphic preacher and already had a volume of his sermons published under the title *Wheat and Some Chaff* before arriving at Trinity. He advertised the subjects of his sermons to the town at large and did not pull his punches. One, under the title 'The Prevalence of Privet,' castigated households for being isolated behind the privet hedges so characteristic of Penarth. In his series 'Talks for Intelligent People,' he made much play with current advertising slogans, such as 'Prevent that Sinking Feeling.'

The Harvest Festival Service still held pride of place amongst the well attended services. Harvest Services were augmented by visitors from other churches who abandoned denominational loyalties and came to swell the regular congregation – and to appraise the decorations and the display of vegetables. At the Harvest Festival of 1926 the Church was so full that the concealed seats at the end of pews had to be pulled out to accommodate this congregation. The size of the congregation would often be referred to in later years when numbers attending, especially the Evening Services, were declining.

There were other special services. There had, for some time, been a Sunday afternoon Gift Service in the Sunday School before Christmas. Percy Pegler promoted the service to the morning and from 1925 it thus became part of Trinity's Christmas celebrations.

It was in 1928 that the Church was first decorated for the Easter Services.

The Armistice Service of the following year involved the boys and girls of the Penarth Intermediate School, later known as the County School, and the boys of the J. A. Gibbs Home attended. The lessons were read by the Headmistress, Katherine Hughes, and the Headmaster, Basil Judd.

In the months after his arrival, Percy Pegler brought out the first copy of *Notes and News*, a monthly newsletter, less sentimentally named than it's predecessor, *The Friendly Link*. Fifteen hundred copies were printed and the *Circuit Record* reported that 'the congregation had increased as a result.'

*Notes and News* for March 1928 indicated the kind of information contained and provided a summary of activities at Trinity: it listed the events for the month

| Sunday | 11.00 & 6.30 | DIVINE SERVICE |
| | | HOLY COMMUNION |
| | | 1st Sunday in month |
| | 10.00 a.m. | FELLOWSHIP CLASS |
| | 3.00 p.m. | BROTHERHOOD |
| | 2.45 p.m. | SUNDAY SCHOOL |
| Monday | 3.00 p.m. | WOMEN'S HOUR |
| | 6.30 p.m. | GIRL GUIDES |
| | 8.00 p.m. | WESLEY GUILD |
| Tuesday | 3.00 & 3.30 p.m. | FELLOWSHIP CLASSES |
| | 4.00 p.m. | LADIES' SEWING MEETING |
| | 7.00 to 7.45 p.m. | SICK BENEFIT CLUB |
| | | (fortnightly) |
| Wednesday | 6.45 p.m. | BAND OF HOPE |
| | | (fortnightly) |
| | 8.30 p.m. | FELLOWSHIP CLASS |
| Thursday | 7.00 p.m. | SEA SCOUTS |
| | 7.30 p.m. | TEACHERS PREP. CLASS |
| Friday | 8.00 p.m. | CHOIR PRACTICE |

BOWLING AND TABLE TENNIS CLUBS in the Woodland Hall, Tuesday, Wednesday and Saturday Evenings

The news items included congratulations 'to our friends at All Saints on the re-opening of their Church and appointment of a new Vicar. Many of our Trinity people attended the Service in connection with the Induction and Re-opening. . . . We wish our neighbour 'Good Luck in the name of the Lord' and trust that friendly relationship between the two Churches may continue and increase. There is plenty of room for both of us.'

*Notes and News* went on to announce the formation of a Brownie company which would meet on Monday evenings at 6.00 p.m., and asked for a good attendance at the Band of Hope Concert to be given on March 28th and 29th in the Schoolroom. On this occasion the Band of Hope was assisted by the Sea Scouts and the Guides in presenting 'A Round of Song and Dance.' Admission was 6d for adults and 3d for children. On successive evenings two of Trinity's leading laymen, A. R. Dawson and A. W. Hosegood, would take the chair. The proceedings were to be opened by the Troop singing the 'Trinity Troop Song' and would be brought to a close by 'The King.'

In spite of some good things, and more will emerge later, there was a malaise within the life of the Church which perhaps was a reflection of a wider malaise within the Connexion as a whole.

Apart from the Sunday Services, the life of the Church was expressed in a number of organisations, successful in themselves but not integrated into an organic whole.

Discipleship and response to Christ were seen as private matters: maybe diffidence prevented the Minister or members of the congregation from approaching young people. It was felt that they must make up their minds for themselves, although it seemed at times that there was a falling-over-backwards to avoid anything that might seem to be a challenge. No one at Trinity suggested to John Gibbs that he should become a member of the Church and it was not until he was at Cambridge in 1932 that he was received into membership. Before she went away to school, Sheila Newton, at the prompting of her parents, was prepared for membership by the Minister in one session and on her own. She took her first Communion at the monthly Service with the few members of the congregation who remained behind after the main

Sunday morning Service. The Communion Service was announced as an additional service at 12.15 p.m.

An expectation of individual response and of taking up membership of the Church was lacking. It was a time for optimistic humanism, even of hope for the perfectibility of mankind, with only a passing nod in the direction of the Church.

> These things shall be; a loftier race
> Than e'er the world hath known shall rise,
> With flame of freedom in their souls
> And light of knowledge in their eyes.
>
> *MHB* 910

seemed to express the general hope, and Blake's 'Jerusalem' was almost invariably the final hymn for Parade Services.

The Women's Meeting provided opportunities for fellowship, and the Sewing Meeting continued to flourish. While items were still made for sale, essentials had given place to leisure aids; beachbags and bridge-cloths being the most popular lines. The Women's Hour President was usually the Minister's wife, but in 1929 Mrs Pegler was unable to continue. Mrs Wesley Owen, who had been a Wesley Deaconess before her marriage, took over and under her dynamic leadership the meeting flourished as never before. '1930 was the best year yet,' as the *Church Record* reported, in spite of – or perhaps because of, the Depression.

For the members of the Women's Hour their Monday afternoon meeting was perhaps the 'brightest' time of the week. They found encouragement for the coming week by singing:

> Have we trials and temptations
> Is there trouble anywhere?
> We should never be discouraged:
> Take it to the Lord in prayer.
> In his arms He'll take and shield thee
> Thou wilt find a solace there.
>
> *MHB* 538

The Depression, exacerbated in South Wales by the dramatic decline in the exporting of coal, was to have a deadening effect on much of the life of the churches. Whilst Trinity was not to lose large numbers of its young men, as happened in the valley chapels, the numbers of people coming to Penarth declined considerably with the consequent fall in house prices and in general prosperity. There was an overall feeling of depression.

The Trinity Sunday School numbers kept up, however. In 1929 the Circuit Sunday School minutes say 'In view of the general state of affairs, business difficulties, people leaving the district for other fields . . . and the unusually fine summer the increase of 47 in the number of scholars attending may be considered good.'

The Methodist emphasis on thrift, sobriety and education helped the Society in large measure to weather the Depression. There had been a number of marriages between Trinity families in the previous thirty years and these networks were supportive. For instance, when Clem Scriven lost his position with Morel Ltd. his father-in-law, Llewelyn Davies, took him into the quarrying business he was developing in Lavernock. There was still room for local initiative.

The education of their children has always been of special concern to Methodists. For families living near Trinity education was available at the Victoria Board Schools opened in 1897, which, by 1918, were providing education for children up to the age of fourteen.

The Penarth Intermediate and Technical Schools in Stanwell Road, also opened in 1897, were the forerunners of secondary education. As in all such schools, entrance was competitive and fees had to be paid. The fee-paying element at the Stanwell Road schools prevented some of those who had won places, such as Jim Marsh, from taking them up.

In addition, there were private schools which came and went. These included St Maeburne which has featured in an earlier chapter, and Miss Ferris' School, later Westbourne House, which achieved a very high standard of education under its Quaker headmistress. One of those who went to the school, Kathleen Ede, described Miss Ferris as 'outstanding.'

A significant number of children from Trinity families went away to the Methodist boarding schools which had been established during the 19th Century, primarily for Methodist children. Some of these have survived to form the nucleus of the present day Methodist Boarding Schools; however, these never met the needs of more than a small number of Methodist parents.  In 1875 the Leys School had been founded in Cambridge to provide a means of entry to the older universities for the sons of Methodists whose parents wanted them to be educated within the Methodist framework.  As early as the 1880's Philip Morel's two sons had been there.  Some of the Gibbs and Morel boys went to Queen's College, Taunton, others to Rydal in North Wales.  But it was not until the late 1920's and 30's that six Trinity boys went to the Leys, and seven girls to its sister school, Farringtons.

This pattern was to continue in the 1950's and 1960's, especially to Queens and also, since it had restarted taking the sons of the laity, to Kingswood School.  They followed some of Trinity's ministers and their sons to the School which John Wesley had founded to meet the needs of an itinerant ministry.

Those Trinity children who went away to school were by no means always from very wealthy families and many parents made considerable financial sacrifices to send their children to such schools.  It is difficult to assess the effect of an education at a Methodist boarding school: some of the pupils at such schools had their loyalty to and involvement with Methodism strengthened; others were distanced from Trinity and from their peer group in the Church without finding any wider connexional commitment.  They certainly could not be regular members of their own home congregation.

An early attempt at involving the young people in the life of the Church was made when a branch of the Young Leaguers Union was formed with junior as well as senior officers and for some years this raised money through garden parties, plays and a 'Gypsy Fair,' to support a boy at the J. A. Gibbs Home.  However, its membership was largely from middle class families.  The division into social class might be felt inappropriate within a church, but at this time the attitude in the Church reflected that of the world around it.  The upward mobility of Methodist families was fixing the Trinity congregation firmly within a middle class mould.[1]

There were some institutions, such as 'tied' pews and pew rents, and 'free' seats in the side aisles which militated against this. In spite of the introduction of the envelope system, the names remained on the pews. At its best this was a way of affirming loyalty to the Church.  In addition to the tied pews there had always been free seats in the side aisles. A devoted member of the society, Rosina Broughton, a widow with five children, was accommodated in one of these side pews, much to her children's distress. Before her marriage, Rosina Broughton had lived with the Bond family and went away with them when they left Trinity in 1904. Members of her family were to make a great contribution to the life of the Church. Her daughter Gladys, beside being Guide Captain and a member of the choir, was leader of the Beginners Department of the Sunday School for 40 years.

A new Trust for the Church was made in 1928, and attempted to secure a wide representation of the membership. The names and addresses of the thirty-one Trustees are listed, and from this information it is possible to reconstruct the leadership of the Trinity Society at this period. Their addresses indicate something of their social status: six addresses are prestigious, for example, Marine Parade and Park Road; twenty-one are 'middle class', and four are in what could be regarded as, at that time, working class areas – mainly in the streets surrounding Trinity; Rudry Street, Ivy Street, Wood Street and Sully Terrace. The make-up of the Trust probably reflected the membership and this would be in keeping with many suburban Wesleyan Methodist Societies of the period. For the first time two of the Trustees were women. A. J. Cox, the groundsman at the Glamorganshire Golf Course, was aware of some criticism that he should be a Trustee, and his wife, Bertha, a member of the Ladies Sewing Meeting.

The occupations of the brides' fathers, recorded in the Trinity Marriage Registers from 1901 to 1930, indicate a wide cross section of occupations and these are listed in the 'Notes.' In a considerable number of cases, the brides are likely to have been daughters of members.[2]

Trinity Church's relationship with its neighbouring churches was friendly, as was shown when, in April 1926, All Saints Church was burnt down and Trinity was able to offer accommodation to the congregation.

In 1926, Percy Pegler became Superintendent of the Penarth and Barry Circuit. In one of the minutes of the Circuit Quarterly Meeting as early as March 1903, it had been recommended that the superintendency be transferred from Arcot Street to the newly built Trinity. It was twenty-four years before this came about and even at this date it must have caused some distress to the Albert Road congregation – the heirs of the Arcot Street Chapel.

Three young men offered for the ministry during Percy Pegler's ministry. Sidney Ifor Evans offered in 1926, was accepted, and served mainly under the direction of the Home Mission Committee. He died young, in the fortieth year of his life and the thirteenth of his ministry.

Arthur Chambers offered in 1928. He writes:

> . . . during a quiet evening service amid a small congregation it was possible to know something of the 'warmed heart' of which John Wesley spoke, confirming my belief that I was called to offer for the Methodist ministry.

He had a long ministry including a period with Lax of Poplar. At the time of writing, he lives in retirement in Weymouth with his wife, Peggy.

Edwin Tabraham, who offered in 1930, was not accepted. He became a partner in J. G. Progers, Heating and Sanitary Engineers of Cardiff, and for his whole life was a very acceptable local preacher. His son, Barrie, is a Methodist minister.

As the Depression deepened over Britain it was as if it was mirrored in the state of health of Trinity's Minister. In 1928, in the middle of his ministry, Percy Pegler suffered a depressive illness so serious that the Chairman of the District had to act as superintendent of the Circuit for a period. After resting for several months, he took up his active ministry again, but was soon compelled to take early retirement, in Methodist parlance 'to sit down.'

Methodist ministers faced a rigorous medical examination on offering for the ministry and the great majority served a full term, normally forty years. For those forced to relinquish the ministry on medical grounds, there was little connexional provision. It was in this situation that the warm and caring relationship built up between the Minister and his people was displayed. In his sickness, Percy Pegler was supported by his able wife and three daughters, and by the Trinity Society itself.

As it had been arranged that Percy Pegler was to move to another circuit in September 1930 and the manse would be required for the incoming minister, 'Trinity friends' purchased a house in the town for the Pegler family and furnished it throughout. This was an important consideration since at this time Methodist ministers normally owned no furniture of their own. Subsequently the family moved to Budleigh

Salterton, but many of the friendships which the family had made in Penarth were to continue and Percy Pegler returned to take William Gibbs's funeral service in 1943. He recovered sufficiently to preach often in the widespread Devon Mission.

Here is included the full text of the address given by Percy Peglar at the funeral service at Trinity on 8 July 1943 of William Gibbs – previously encountered in these pages as a defender of local rugby talent. It conveys something of the skill of the preacher, the relationship that existed between minister and layman, and illuminates the life of one, who, by any standards, could not be considered an ordinary Methodist.

> William Gibbs was a man of few words and he certainly would not have desired that many should have been spoken about him to-day; but he was so highly esteemed by so many and so greatly beloved by the few who were his intimates, that it would be unfitting for us to separate on an occasion of this kind without paying some brief tribute to his memory.

> Our friend came of Portland stock, and it is not perhaps fanciful to think that something of his native soil found its way into the fibre of his character. He had more than a little of its strength and ruggedness and something too of its reserve; its sense of standing a little apart and living a life of its own. But there are summer days when blue skies are over Portland and when blue seas lap its rugged shores, and flowers deck its rocky sides. William Gibbs could wear this aspect too. For all his strength there was a kindliness and a geniality about him, a friendliness and a warm affection that made him a staunch and loyal friend. He had that broad humanity that loves laughter and sport and the good things of life. But Portland, too, shelters its great Anchorage, offering protection from wind and storm to those who go down to the sea in ships. Our friend of whom we take farewell today, stood between many and the storms by which they were beset. He could never resist the appeal of a distress signal. He was one of those men who are as a hiding place from the wind, a covert from the tempest, and the shadow of a great rock.

> William Gibbs was one of those who bore the yoke in his youth. His father died when he was nine years of age, leaving him the oldest son of his widowed mother, and the elder brother of her young family.

That responsibility fell upon his shoulders and he discharged it with unswerving fidelity. His love and care for his mother through long years, and her love and pride in him were touching and beautiful things, that no one who saw them will ever forget. I knew very little of our friend's business life, but I have no doubt that he was as upright and straight in his dealings as he was in his stature. A man of integrity and good judgement, far-seeing and courageous, and of great native ability; he reaped the rewards of those splendid characteristics. But success and prosperity never spoilt him, and to the end he remained simple and quiet in his tastes and in his pleasures, going his unostentatious and unpretentious way.

He was not one to speak much of his religion. He never lost the imprint of his early training. The pieties and the restraints of his Methodist ancestry never left him, and he loved it with a sincere affection and quiet loyalty. For many years he was a generous supporter of Trinity Church, Penarth, and did all that lay in his power to help its work. No one ever had a kinder heart. When I came to minister here, he put at my disposal a sum of money to be used at my discretion for the help of the needy. he made three conditions. Nothing was to be said about it, no accounts were to be kept, and I was to go to him when I needed more. Every Christmas time he sent me a cheque with instructions to see that no one went short.

William Gibbs was a generous supporter of what are called 'Good causes'; but he was more than that. His kindness to me personally was unceasing, and no one will ever know to how many he extended his unfailing and generous help. He was not the sort of man to 'suffer fools gladly' and life brought him, as it brings us all, into personal conflicts and difficulties. There were those with whom he profoundly disagreed; but in all my intercourse with him I never heard him speak unkindly of a single soul. He knew life's seamy side, as every man with his wide contacts must, but I never heard him say a cynical thing.

May God grant him eternal rest and may Light Perpetual shine upon him.

85

# CHAPTER 8

## The Rev'd George Charnley 1930-1933

## and Methodist Union

Tom Morel was Senior Circuit Steward of the Penarth Circuit. As he was a widower it fell to the lot of the wife of his junior colleague, Herbert Newton, to prepare Pagemont for the new minister, George Charnley and his family. This Jessie undertook with alacrity.

At this time, as we have seen in the last chapter, the Circuit not only provided a house for its minister but also furniture and household equipment, including linen and crockery – a pattern established when ministers often moved circuits every year. With appointments lasting longer, this system came to be seen as more and more intolerable. First, ministers owned their own linen and crockery, and then, in the 1960's, the furniture became the property of the individual minister. In September, the traditional month for moving 'stations', removal vans of the size required by other families now cross and re-cross the country as ministers with their furniture move to their new circuits.

The only good feature of the old system was that the Circuit Stewards's wife and her helpers were able to prepare the house, to make up the beds and lay tea with the manse china to welcome the new family to their new hearth and home. In such a way was the new minister, George Charnley and his wife and son welcomed to Pagemont in September 1930.

George Charnley continued his predecessors' form of ministry. The New Year of 1931 opened with a parade service and there was a large attendance at the Covenant Service. However, he had a stronger commitment to encouraging church membership than his predecessors.

In April 1932, as a result of the Preparation Classes he led, thirty new members, mostly senior scholars or leaders of the Primary Department, were received into membership at a special reception service.

Four young men from Allen Pratt's class, who were already members, made a further commitment.

In 1931, the new Trust undertook the repair and redecoration of the Church. Mistakenly the opinion of the church members as to the colour scheme was not canvassed and many were disappointed when the building was repainted in its former apple green. Arthur Hosegood was so irritated by the repeated criticism that he threatened to resign his secretaryship of the Trust.

Donald James, an electrical engineer with the General Electric Company, and a member of Trinity, introduced, at the Trustees' request, additional lighting in the Chancel. His father had been a marine engineer and a West Countryman who died young leaving seven sons for his wife, a nurse, to bring up. The family attended Broadway Wesleyan Church in Cardiff, but on Donald's marriage to Mebe Evans, they moved to Penarth and Trinity. Donald had met Mebe at the G.E.C. where she was one of the first demonstrators of electric cookers. Donald earned his fellowship of the British Illuminating Society for his flood-lighting of Gloucester Cathedral, and later he was to light all the Trinity Drama Group's productions. He had been involved in Scouting since boyhood and in 1936 became the Scout Master of the Trinity Troop. In addition to the involvement with the Church, he took the 6th Penarth into a leading position in Scouting in South Wales.

George Charnley was celebrated throughout the Connexion for his graphic children's addresses, three volumes of which he had published: *The Skylark's Bargain*, *The Enchanted Highway* and *The Scarecrow's Secret*. Mary Knighton, when she was five years old, remembers services at Trinity:

> Sunday mornings meant going to worship – and best clothes, having to be quiet and sit still, seeing Very Important People who all had their own pews, as did we, though ours was firmly in a side aisle. These Very Important People were all men, though they did have wives and sisters, and they had Hats. From amongst this normally silent band, one read the Lessons each Sunday. The singing, led by the choir, was important. The hymns were usually ones we sang around the piano at home. The pointing of the psalms, canticles and chants needed to be practised and fitted in. There were children there: boys from the J. A. Gibbs Home in their sailor's uniforms, children quietly sitting with their parents. There was always a children's address. Some of them, I suppose 'spoke to me'. I especially remember *The Skylark's Bargain* as we had a copy of the book at home.

George Charnley's addresses were appreciated not only by the children but by the older members of the congregation as well.

Mary Knighton with her brother, Donald, also went to Sunday School. This was somewhat unusual for the children of members who attended Trinity services regularly, since the Sunday School was mostly regarded as a form of outreach. She recalls:

> Lots of us went to Sunday School in the Main Hall and the Woodland Hall. We did the National Sunday School Union Scripture Exams in a little room off this hall. I learnt very well indeed the story of Joseph and the details of St Paul's Missionary Journeys.

Concern was growing that the Sunday School members were not experiencing full Christian worship, and the Superintendent, Frank Jenkins, had been encouraging them to attend the morning Service. In 1933 the order of Morning Star was initiated and, no doubt greatly helped by George Charnley's addresses, proved successful. On 11 March 1934, twenty-five children received the Order's badge, a different colour for each three months of attendance. Many formed the pattern of regular church attendance at this time and maintained it throughout their lives.

In 1933 the new Methodist Hymn Book for the United Church was published. Mary Knighton notes that

> outstanding for me was the year the new *Methodist Hymn Book* came into use. We were to sing 'Soldiers of Christ arise' to the tune 'From Strength to Strength' and in order to ensure that we realised it was a marching tune, Mr Sully, our organist and choirmaster, had us singing it as we marched in solemn procession round the Church.

From these same years comes a memory of Margaret Evans, nee Dewar, and her sister, Aileen:

> We both agreed the one that gave us real happiness and a feeling of awe was the Christmas Tree Service. We must have been quite good children because when we were told to close our eyes to pray we kept them tightly shut, when we opened them the lights were all lit up on what seemed to us a huge tree. As our home

was lit by gas we thought it was a miracle that these little lights could appear.

During George Charnley's Ministry in Penarth Methodist Union was accomplished and an account of its development from 1922, in the ministry of J. J. Johnston, a bitter opponent of the scheme, is included here.

The point has already been made that from 1893, the Penarth Wesleyan Methodist Societies were included with the Churches in Barry, in one Circuit. The Circuit Quarterly Meeting was, Methodistically, the debating forum and decision-making body for the whole of the area. There were clearly weaknesses in this arrangement; for example, difficulties of reaching Barry Dock from Penarth and of catching last trains back, and vice versa, meant that many circuit meetings were poorly attended. But there were advantages too, in that no one Society could take unilateral decisions as to policy and practice, thus avoiding the fragmentation that may result from a congregational system. Methodism is a 'Connexion.'

During the 1920's, the Circuit and the local Churches were being made aware of the discussions which were being held nationally between the three Methodist Churches, Wesleyan, Primitive and United, all of which owed their original impetus to the Methodist revival of the 18th Century and to the preaching of John Wesley. Their union, when the original causes of their division had passed into history, seemed eminently desirable.

For the Penarth Circuit the issue did not present great organisational problems, as, apart from Court Road Church in Barry and the United Methodist Church in Cogan, all the Churches belonged to the Wesleyan tradition.

The possibility of organic union was discussed in the Conferences of the three Churches in 1920, but it was not until the Circuit Meeting in September 1922 that the matter was first mentioned locally.

There are no Trinity Leaders' Meeting Minutes extant for this period so the debate must perforce be followed through the relevant minutes of the Circuit Meeting which are available from 1893 onwards. The impression of this Meeting that emerges is of a gathering of committed Christian men, with a slowly increasing number of women, dealing in love with the affairs of the Circuit. Issues are seemingly decided with

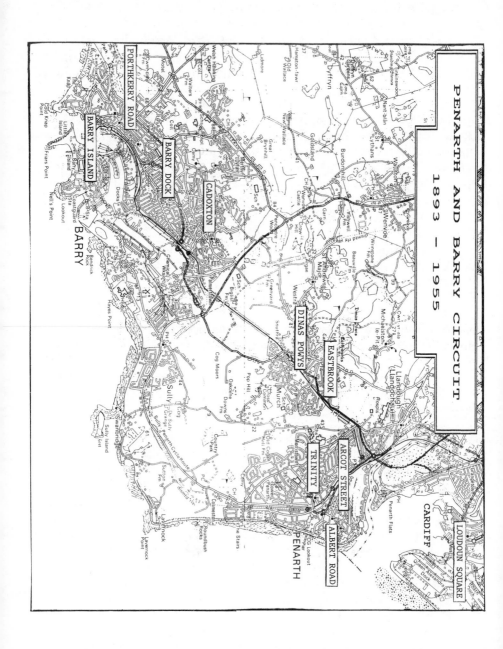

PENARTH AND BARRY CIRCUIT

1893 - 1955

PORTHKERRY ROAD

BARRY ISLAND

BARRY DOCK

CADOXTON

BARRY

DINAS POWYS

EASTBROOK

ARCOT STREET

TRINITY

ALBERT ROAD

PENARTH

LOUDOUN SQUARE

CARDIFF

harmony and unanimity. The wit of Humphrey Wallis of Dinas Powis, a Cardiff Docksman, pervaded the meetings and brought an irenic slant to the proceedings: 'Mr Humphrey Wallis gave another of his racy and statesmanlike speeches.' Tensions may well have been dispersed during the 'Conversation on the work of God' which inevitably concluded the meetings.

At the September 1922 meeting controversy emerged. The Superintendent Minister moved a general resolution, in which the Circuit Meeting 'declared itself in accord with the action of the Conference in reference to Methodist Union and gave its general approval to the Scheme.' There was a proviso that doctrinal requirements from all members, whether ministers or laymen, should be the same and a warning that if differing stipends, as at present existed between the ministers of the uniting Churches, be continued into the United Church this would not make for harmony.

However, the Rev. J. J. Johnston, the Trinity Minister, proposed an amendment. This was not passed, and the general resolution was accepted. 43 voted 'for', 28 'against', and 6 were neutral.[1]

The sides were drawn up, and, on examination, some of the reasons for the division become clear. For example, nationally, the three Churches had in the main a different social class membership, and there were financial imbalances. There were also differing attitudes to the status of the Ministry and there were emotional reactions to the dropping of the name 'Wesleyan'. As A. R. Dawson was to say when Union was achieved, 'They have taken away my Founder.' In the Penarth Circuit, however, the main reason for such a high negative vote was the implacable opposition to the scheme of the Trinity Minster, the Rev. J. J. Johnston and the influence he exercised over his members – who must have formed the bulk of the opposition. Donald Knighton, on discussing with his father years later his father's attitude to Union, was surprised to find that, contrary to his reasonable attitude generally, he had voted consistently against Union 'because of his minister's opposition to the Scheme.' Here is an indication of the influence a minister could have over his members and the value of the circuit system in keeping in check the strong views of one minister.

Herbert Newton was also rather surprisingly against the Union: he was concerned about the difficulty of up-grading the stipends of the ministers of the other denominations to the level of the Wesleyans.

At the 1923 September Circuit Meeting, the Conference recommendation that there should be an interchange of pulpits, that is to say that Methodist ministers should be able to preach in Methodist churches other than 'their own,' was received, but A. R. Dawson proposed that the matter be left to each Church through its Leaders Meeting to decide. There is no record as to whether Trinity took advantage of such an arrangement.

The vexatious question of Union was not discussed at the December Circuit Meeting and the members combined happily to vote unanimously on an issue, uncontroversial in Methodist circles, that: 'The Sunday Opening of the British Empire Exhibition at Wembley would be an offence to the Christian feeling of the country.'

The 1924 Conference persisted and sent down to the Circuit Meetings for their consideration the question: 'Are you in favour of Organic Union of the Wesleyan Methodist and the Primitive Methodist and the United Methodist Churches on the basis of the Scheme now submitted?' In an impassioned contribution in favour of the Scheme at Conference, Russell Maltby, one-time Minister of Trinity, 'delivered a speech of great feeling'. In it he said that the defeat of the Union would be: 'The deadliest blow to Christian Reunion all over the world.'

During the next twelve months the Circuit Meetings of all the Churches voted on the Resolution, with 71.2% in favour by the Primitive Methodist meetings, 66.1% by the United Methodist meetings and 67.1% by the Wesleyan Circuit meetings.

When the matter came to be debated in the Penarth Circuit Meeting in the Woodland Hall during December, 1924, there was a record attendance of 84 members. At the outset, it was resolved to allow each speaker five minutes. A large number of the members participated in the discussion and on a vote being taken by ballot the result was; in favour of the Conference resolution, 56, against 28. The opposition in the Penarth Circuit, presumably of the Trinity members, remained constant.

A final Conference vote was taken in 1928 when J. J. Johnston, no longer a minister of the Penarth Circuit, published an opposing circular: 'The Right Way Out'. This the Conference did not follow, and, when a three-year staged programme was approved, he was the only dissident.

As with the other uniting Churches at the Wesleyan Conference of 1928, a seventy-five per-cent majority was required, and this was exactly what was obtained. A missionary home on furlough from India happened to come into the assembly, where every minister had the right to vote, at the right moment. He voted for union, and his vote settled the matter.

In 1928, Robert Bond, now 'Doctor', became Secretary of the Wesleyan Conference, a very important position in the delicate negotiation which were taking place within the three Churches in preparation for Union, and which gave him much opportunity of exercising the 'tact, wisdom and consideration for others' for which he was renowned.

Consummation of the Union required an Enabling Bill to be laid before Parliament and this was duly moved in 1928. J. J. Johnston, true to the last, was one of the four who signed a petition against the Bill.

In 1932, the three Churches were united as 'The Methodist Church' at a great rally in the Albert Hall with the Rev'd Dr. John Scott Lidgett as President, Sir Robert Perks as Vice-President, and Dr. Robert Bond, Trinity's 'much beloved Minister', as Secretary.

In the *Circuit Record* there is a passing reference to the great service in 1932 in the Albert Hall which brought together three Methodist Churches into one Church. But, apart from the incorporation of the Court Road Society and the Society at Cogan into the Penarth Circuit, its effect on the Circuit organisation was minimal. The former Wesleyan Methodist Circuit Minute Book continued to be used. One gain for Trinity from Methodist Union was that, after it was achieved, more members of the Dewar clan from the United Methodist Church of Cogan joined the Trinity Society where some of the family were already in Membership.

In the first chapter it was noted that the grandparents, Thomas and Margaret, had, in 1879, come from Scotland where Thomas had been a shipwright in the John Brown shipyard. They had seven children and the descendants of at least four of them have been connected with Trinity for many years, serving as leaders, teachers, choir members and, in the case of Jean, as a local preacher.

The later stages of the Reunion Debate did not unduly disturb the ministry of George Charnley at Trinity and after his three years in Penarth he went to North Wales and to three other stations before retiring. He continued to be in great demand as a preacher in other denominations as well as within Methodism.

# CHAPTER 9

## The Rev'd F. J. Bomford 1933-1936

## and Social Issues

Frederick Bomford was 58 when he came to Trinity. He had served as a missionary in British Honduras for seven years and, on his return to Britain, in a number of circuits, largely around London. During forty-two years of active ministry, he never missed a Sunday appointment.

Trinity having become the head of the Circuit was beginning to regret the honour. Almost inevitably, the superintendent of the Circuit was a senior man who had 'travelled' – served as a Minister – for at least twenty years. Trinity looked somewhat enviously at the energetic leadership that was given by the succession of younger men in the other Circuit churches, not least at Albert Road.

Frederick J. Bomford was conservative in outlook and not likely to upset the established pattern of Trinity Church life. As his obituary stated: 'he loved the worship of his Church and rejoiced in the administration of the sacraments.' On his arrival in the Circuit in 1933 he made a strong plea for increased attendance at Communion. This was celebrated after the morning or the evening Service and during the whole of this period was seldom attended by more than thirty people.

Frederick Bomford, also, urged a greater attendance at the Annual Covenant Service. Wesley had emphasised the importance of this Service in which the Methodist people renew their Covenant with God and which is held on the first Sunday of the Year. It is now seen as one of the contributions of Methodism to the universal Church, and has, for example, been included in the Book of Offices of the Church of South India.

Distinguished Methodist figures during this time, such as Dr John Scott Lidgett and Dr William Lofthouse, were invited to Trinity for Church Anniversary Services and the Sunday Services continued to be central to the life of Trinity.

At this time Trinity held a traditional Watch-Night Service at the close of the year.

The Woman's Hour continued to flourish. So popular was the meeting that in July 1937 the 'platform' had to grant a request to reopen earlier in September than planned.

The reference to 'the platform' shows that this weekly meeting was so large that it had to be held in the big school-room, unchanged since it was built and dominated by a high, narrow platform. At one meeting every seat downstairs was filled, and in 1938 three hundred members attended the Christmas party. The Moody and Sankey hymn book was used – to the regret of the pianist, Jessie Newton, who had to play choruses from that collection much more frequently than the hymns of Charles Wesley which she loved.

The Conference Agenda for 1933 reflected the new thinking that was permeating the World Church scene and all overseas work was subsumed under the title: the Methodist Missionary Society. The word 'foreign' disappeared at this time: 'There are no foreigners. All men are of one family from God and before God.'

The Penarth Circuit Minutes and the *Circuit Record* refer constantly to the efforts for Mission. Reductions in giving compared with former years were greeted with dismay and 'redoubled efforts' were demanded. When increases were reported the Societies were encouraged to 'share the joy'.

As in the past, the womenfolk of the Churches would work to raise money for the Overseas Missionary Anniversary throughout the year, and, in addition to their own giving, the men, if they were members of an institution such as the Coal and Shipping Exchange, would button-hole their colleagues on the 'Change and solicit contributions irrespective of denominational allegiance.

Methodist missionaries on furlough were expected to devote much of their leave to preaching and to speaking at Missionary meetings, often using coloured lantern slides which brought pictures of the 'Mysterious East' and its nations into church schoolrooms. The differences between Britain and the non Christian world were stressed and the emphasis was on conversion – conversion away from 'barbaric' practices, such as foot-binding in China and 'suttee' in India – to Christianity. The membership of the home churches were challenged to increased giving and to offer for service in the mission field. Sheila Newton was inclined to shut her ears during such appeals for fear that she would hear a 'call'. The Penarth Circuit reinforced the challenge by performing missionary plays: *The Master's Cup* and *The Ships Go On*, illustrating the way in which the Church was rediscovering the use of drama.

However, the emphasis on those things that separated people was changing to those that united them. In 1929, the Rev'd H. J. Jenkin, who was a returned missionary, came to minister in the Circuit. He and his wife introduced a new and effective note, stressing the similarities between people rather than the differences and reinforcing the concept that 'there are no foreigners'. Mrs Jenkin would wear a sari, so underlining the delight in beautiful clothes shared by women.

With the coming together of the three Methodist Churches the negative elements in their social witness gradually receded into the background and they came to be seen as presenting a more positive image.

Methodism in spite of what some thought to be the narrowness of it piety and the rigidity of its morals, was deeply concerned for the welfare of the whole of mankind. By the time of Methodist Union the three uniting churches had almost identical departments dealing with social issues. Whilst it might seem that there had been a preoccupation with Temperance and opposition to Gambling, soon after the Union the issue of Peace and War was thrust to the forefront of matters which engaged the minds of those who believed that there had to be a social, indeed for some, a political dimension to evangelical faith.

The United Church set up a Temperance and Social Welfare Department which was able to produce a succession of reports and resolutions on such varied subjects as Lotteries and Betting, Sunday and the Use of Leisure, Youth and Citizenship, International and Industrial Relations, Unemployment, The Jews, Armaments and Slum Clearance. As the century unfolded new social issues came to the fore and the Department would prepare reports under pressure from Conference – which would, by and large, accept them and send them down to the circuits.

Temperance, by which was meant total abstinence, was urged repeatedly on the Methodist people as the way of counteracting the evils of excessive drinking. However, in 1943 it was noted that: 'The appeal to Methodists at home and abroad to abstain from the use of intoxicating liquors as beverages is not only disregarded but resisted.'

By 1951, the Department, sensing the wind of change, altered its name to the Christian Citizenship Department. Its new declaration, whilst appealing for abstinence 'not as a burdensome duty but as a privilege of Christian service', added the statement; 'the Conference has not at any time imposed total abstinence as a condition of membership, nor does the reiterated appeal imply the imposition of such a condition.'

The Trinity Society was as confused and divided as any over the issue. Many of the men who played rugby were caught up in a tradition in which drinking was part of the sub-culture. Many of the women members, however, including Gladys Gibbs and Jessie Newton, were members of the Blue Ribbon organisation which worked single-mindedly for total abstinence, perhaps because they had relations who were heavy drinkers. It is reliably reported that Elizabeth and Susan Gibbs took the drastic step of watering the whisky in their brother William's decanter. He complained of its weak consistency to the distillers in Scotland which had supplied it. A representative of the firm was sent down to investigate and he had to report that, while the whisky had left Scotland crated at full strength, there was a considerable addition of water when it was served in the decanter.

A proportion of Trinity families accepted the pattern of social drinking and did not heed the Conference appeal. They often absented themselves from Church on Temperance Sunday when they guessed what the burden of the sermon would be.

The Conference of 1898 had stressed 'the importance in future of electing in the Church as officers only those not employed in the drink traffic.' The Penarth Circuit Meeting accepted the resolution on a divided vote, but it was never implemented at Trinity where Herbert Bishop, the leader of the Senior Department, was the local sales manager of Whitbread's, the brewers.

When Jack and Maureen Moody from Ohio 'exchanged' ministries and manses with Percy and Eileen Watkinson in 1954, they were surprised to be offered alcohol in many of the Trinity homes in which they were entertained. This was alien to American Methodist practice at the time.

A good number, however, of the Trinity families followed the Conference teaching and this number included Tom Morel, Gladys Gibbs, and Jessie and Herbert Newton. At Sheila's wedding the Newtons provided a splendid reception with a marquee in their garden.

Alcohol was not served, although some of the guests were observed to have recourse to hip-flasks during the proceedings.

The Band of Hope continued until the Second World War and Temperance Sunday was observed at Trinity from, at least, 1898, until it gave place to Christian Citizenship Sunday. It might have seemed to an observer that at one time all John Wesley's social concern had been channelled into the temperance movement; but, gradually, a more balanced attitude has prevailed. The Conference Declaration of 1977 stated that the rule prohibiting the consumption of intoxicants on Methodist premises did not apply to ministers' houses or private accommodation, and it is not uncommon to be offered wine with meals taken with a minister and his family.

Perhaps now, as Rupert Davies writing in his book on Methodism put it, 'the image of the Methodist as a holier-than-thou sourpuss, implacably hostile to the harmless enjoyment of the people can be buried.' (Rupert Davies, *Methodism*: p.157.)

There is, however, another field to which this stereotype applied, and a Church with such a distinctive response to the alcohol problem was hardly likely to neglect the somewhat similar problem of Gambling.

The 1933 Conference failed 'to discover any good results following from gambling but only economic, social and moral disaster occasioned thereby.' The Conference reaffirmed the prohibition of any form of gambling on Methodist premises or on behalf of Methodist causes and urged Methodists as individuals to avoid all forms of gambling practices 'particularly in their business and social relationships.'

They were especially urged not to participate in lotteries which were being increasingly used to raise money for charitable purposes. The Methodist Church took the high ground on the issue, arguing that the main motive of gambling was economic self-interest, and that the gains to winners were made at the expense of the losers. Gambling was also seen as a misdirection of the spirit of adventure and a debasement of sportsmanship. The more widespread gambling practices became, the more evident the evil results were in the record of crime, commercial disaster and human tragedy. It was even claimed that resort to gambling was a denial of faith in God and an ordered universe, putting in its place an appeal to blind chance.

The Conference of 1964 confirmed the standing order forbidding gambling on Methodist Trust premises, but added that games of chance, including card games played primarily for entertainment, were not covered by the prohibition.

Whilst Methodists, by and large, accepted this teaching there were exceptions, particularly among the 'great', of the Methodist Connexion. As changing patterns of entertainment meant that new uses had to be found for old cinemas, Lord Rank, head of the Rank Organisation and a prominent Methodist, was caught up in the extensive growth of Bingo Clubs. Lord Mackintosh, also a Methodist, was prominent in the promotion of Premium Bonds, in which the interest on a deposited sum is gambled.

Nearer home and within the Trinity family, William Gibbs became a director of Chepstow Racecourse and a box holder in the stand. Ted Morel, son of Tom Morel, towards the end of his life, owned a small string of horses which he raced at national meetings. As a simple dichotomy, the distinction may be made that, of the followers of John Wesley and his horse, a number of the Gibbs Morel family followed in the footsteps of Wesley and the others followed his horse or horses.

By and large, however, the Methodist people followed their Church's teaching on the gambling issue. The effect, when applied to Trinity Church bazaars, involved hair-splitting judgements. Straight raffles clearly fell under the prohibition, but guessing the number of peas in a glass-jar or the name of a doll squeezed by on the grounds that the first involved mathematical calculation and the second was an exercise in human psychology.

The equating of the purchase of a raffle ticket with commercial gambling on a huge scale is one that Methodists are finding it increasingly difficult to make and in the ecumenical climate of the 1990's equally difficult to sustain. This does not negate the long-established tradition of opposition to gambling, nationwide, on those grounds identified by the 1933 Conference: criminal activity, commercial disaster and human tragedy.

The 1933 Declaration of the Methodist Church in respect of its 'Attitude to Peace and War' concluded with the following paragraph:

> It is in regard to individual participation in war that the application of the spirit and teaching of Christ may be most

severely tested. Should War come there would be those sincere lovers of their country who, nevertheless, out of loyalty to Christ would feel compelled not to take up arms. With equal sincerity of conviction there would be others who would feel bound by obligation to the body politic, and the Methodist Church would recognize that, in present circumstances, both decisions may express their loyalty to personal spiritual conviction, and an earnest endeavour to do the will of God and serve the highest interests of mankind.

Sheila Newton was deeply affected by a performance of *Journey's End* which she saw in London in 1929. She was away at the Methodist school Farringtons and seeing this play was a deep spiritual experience for her, which was reinforced by a visit to the school by the Rev. Owen Spencer Watkins who had been a chaplain during the 1914-18 war. At this period she felt very deeply that 'it must not happen again.' By the 1930s it was becoming apparent that it was going to happen again. She began to attend meetings of the Fellowship of Reconciliation, which were held in the Friends' Meeting House in Cardiff.

In 1931 John Gibbs went up to Cambridge University. He had been at the Leys School where he had done badly, but, at this time, entrance to Cambridge was not academically demanding. Apart from those on scholarships and those who had bonded themselves to teach and were on county grants, the minimal entrance qualifications were the passing of Little-Go – and the ability to answer in the affirmative the question 'Can you afford three hundred pounds for three years?'

At this time, the Methodist Church was strongly developing its work among students based on membership of small groups. For John Gibbs membership of a Group which included Charles Coulson, Stanley and Mary Worrall, Harry Haigh and Gar Pask, was a remarkable spiritual experience.

Membership of the Group certainly marked him out as being unsuitable material for recruitment into the Communist Party: he was not approached by Blunt, and did not become involved with Burgess or Maclean. Cambridge also gave him the opportunity to explore Methodist theology and to make a personal commitment, in no small measure as a result of the writing of Russell Maltby, who had been the minister at Trinity in its earliest days.

Social issues were of great concern and the Group held lengthy discussions on what should be the individual Christian's attitude to war. War was envisaged in terms of the 1914-18 War with the practicability of individual protest, rather than of the Holocaust and the carpet-bombing of Dresden that was to come.

In December 1934, the Trinity Guild presented a reading of a Russian play about a conscientious objector who suffered for his belief, and in 1937 held a debate on 'War and Peace'. But the Conference Declaration, with its acceptance of both standpoints, would have prevented any hurtful divisions within the Society.

In one of the Cambridge vacations, Charles Coulson and Stanley Worrall preached at Trinity, and, as a consequence, a group of Trinity young people started to meet to discuss the implications of their Faith.

In 1933, the Guild at Trinity debated the question 'Should cinemas be open on Sundays.' The motion was moved by Harold Woodhouse, the Secretary, and opposed by Edwin Tabraham. At that time they were living in a hostel in Penarth, and they must have carried with them memories of Sundays in the Methodist National Children's Home and Orphanage, which would have been worship oriented with little except an afternoon walk to break the monotony of the day.

Their experience was, broadly, shared by many of their contemporaries in Trinity: Sunday was the occasion for wearing 'Sunday Best' and for a limited range of activities. Mary Knighton recalled that even after the Second World War she was expected to wear gloves to church. In the Newton family there was no sewing, no gardening and no playing of card games on Sunday; it was a special day and there were opportunities for those activities on other days. Gladys Gibbs walked to Trinity, a twenty-minute walk, with the feeling that it was not right to be dependent on her car. She had a driving licence, but this attitude may have harked back to the days when it was felt one should not get the coachman and the horses out on a Sunday unless it was necessary. Cars were not often taken out of garages on Sundays. Most Trinity families avoided playing games in public places on the 'day of rest'. The Gibbs family was one of those which permitted the playing of croquet on Sundays. However, this did not pass without censure and even as recently as 1975 a retired Methodist minister expressed disapproval of the practice.

Sunday was a day for family visits, and modest pleasures. The Conference Declaration of 1933 on 'Sunday in the Church' stated:

> The earliest impression of Sunday made upon children should be that it is a happy and pleasant day, rather than a day when pleasant things are forbidden. Indeed, there was much to be said for associating specific hobbies and activities with Sunday.

Sheila and John, much involved with the production of plays at this time, were not discouraged by their parents from rehearsing on Sunday evenings.

The second part of the Declaration had to do with 'Sunday in the Community.' It was not so much the Sunday opening of cinemas but the massive development of broadcasting and later television on Sunday that had a dramatic effect on patterns of worship in Britain. Attendances at church services were drastically affected – and have never really recovered. Church-going on Sunday evenings at Trinity suffered in line with most other congregations.

Trinity was also affected by two other issues with which Conference was concerned: the impact of unemployment and the increase in juvenile delinquency. In 1934 the Temperance and Social Welfare Department presented to Conference a statement on 'The Church and Unemployment, and the means by which the Churches are attempting to grapple with the problem.' The impact of unemployment on Penarth was all pervasive. Scarcely a family but had one or more members out-of-work, if not in Penarth then in the area around. Young people had to move away in search of work. Although Trinity did not suffer as badly as the Valley churches where the members of a Class might be decimated overnight as young men moved away to the Midlands or Dagenham, yet in one Leaders' Meeting thirteen removals were reported. In some roads in Penarth almost every other house was for sale, sometimes for as little as four hundred pounds.

Reflecting another social concern, the treatment of delinquents, the J. A. Gibbs Home became, in 1936, a Junior Approved School. The Depression had forced many local shipping lines out of business and training boys for a nautical career was no longer practicable. The decision to change was reached after much heartsearching by the committee. The thinking of Gladys Gibbs, influenced by John Wesley's precept 'Go to those who need you most', was crucial, although John Angel Gibbs's brothers and sisters disapproved of the decision. The name was changed to Headlands School.

Susan Gladys Gibbs with some of the boys of the J. A. Gibbs Home at camp, Ogmore by Sea, 1932.

Of the boys who went to sea in the Merchant Navy, Stanley Greenaway rose to the rank of Captain, whilst Leslie Woodhouse became a Lieutenant Commander in the Royal Navy. Harold, his brother, remained in Penarth and a member of Trinity. He was almost a second son to Gladys Gibbs and, after going to Cardiff University, became a Wrangler at Cambridge.

Some of the boys now came to the Home through the courts but their physical and emotional care was still in the hands of members of the National Children's Home Sisterhood, many of them devoted Methodists. The boys no longer wore uniforms, nor did they march through the town to the strains of a band to attend Trinity. In small house groups they went to the church of the sister's choice, very often Albert Road, which was much nearer to the Home.

During Frederick Bomford's Ministry the life at Trinity continued in somewhat muted key. The Sunday school, Band of Hope, Scouts, Badminton Club and Guild all carried on. John Pearson Griffiths led a class of young men. A Men's Fellowship was started in the Manse at 8 p.m. on Thursdays and Mrs Bomford formed a Young Women's Class which was so successful that when the Guild collapsed it took over instead.

The new Methodist Hymn Book made a much wider choice of hymns available. These were not always to the taste of the congregation, especially if new tunes were involved as well.

Sheila Newton and John Gibbs were involved with the presentation of plays through the Mask Society which had evolved out of the Y.L.U. The Trinity Hall, still dominated by the high, narrow platform, was quite unsuitable for their dramatic productions and the All Saint's hall with its larger stage became the centre of their activities. At the manse, there was now a young family, two Kingswood boys and a younger sister, and two of them were included in the Mask Society productions.

At this stage the leadership amongst the Free Churches had passed to Christ Church Congregational Church in the centre of town under the ministry of the Rev'd Idris Evans with an imaginative programme of social outreach and concern.

Within the town, Trinity, as a Church, did not play a leading role, but the service of one of its members, Tom Morel, to the South Wales community was recognised by his being pricked as High Sheriff of Glamorgan in 1933. It was unusual at that time for those who were not members of the Anglican Communion to hold this high office. The duties were largely nominal and consisted of entertaining and supporting the judges as they presided over Assizes. Tom Morel chose as his chaplain the Rev'd Thomas Naylor, the Chairman of the Cardiff and Swansea District: it would never have occurred to him to have invited anyone other than a Methodist minister. Tom's wife, Edith, had died after a mental illness that lasted twenty-two years, and in 1926 he remarried. His second wife, although an Anglican, supported him loyally in all that he did for Trinity. When he died in 1935, the Methodist press and the South Wales papers recorded his passing, and the *Circuit Record* of July 1935 gave a Circuit view.

We think of Mr Tom Morel as a loyal and generous-hearted Methodist, who in Synod and Circuit stood out as a tower of strength in counsel and debate, who lived for Christ and his Church, and set an example of devotion that called out the best in others. His keenest interest was in Trinity, but his great heart took in the whole Circuit. The smallest Society could count on his sympathy and generous help. His presence in the Quarterly Meeting was a great assistance in all our discussions. He brought to its affairs a wisdom and discretion that often lifted the whole tone of the meetings. He had a Connexional outlook. Home and Foreign Missions, and the larger Methodist interests were not forgotten in his concern for the Circuit. To him it was more than a mere business meeting. It was the centre from which the work of God throughout the whole Circuit could be dealt with. We were sure to hear the right way to solve our problems if Mr Morel expressed his views.

# CHAPTER 10

## A Spring Postponed 1936-1939

### The Rev'd Stanley Dixon and the Rev'd James Parkes

For September 1936 the Circuit Stewards of the Penarth Circuit achieved a spectacular coup: Stanley H. Dixon, BA, BD, was invited to serve Trinity – and accepted. A youngish man with a remarkable record, the new Minister had been born at Haroldswick in the Shetlands in 1889. The influence of a manse home and Kingswood School prepared him for the call to work amongst Chinese students. After being trained at Didsbury College and spending two years in the north of Scotland and Truro whilst waiting for a passage in wartime, he reached the Winchang District in 1916. Anio gave him his introduction to Chinese life and thought, and he then exercised a ministry amongst pupils and students in the Winchang Middle School and the Central China Christian University. In the uncertainty and dangers of the nationalist revolution in 1925 he proved himself a tower of strength to all. Home service in Edinburgh followed and then the call to Penarth.

The Trinity Society, stratified and set in its ways, must have distressed him. Within days of his arrival in Penarth he preached at his Recognition Service on 'The togetherness of believers in faith, fellowship and service' and he was to bring inspiration in all these fields to Trinity. He urged that the Church, in addition to being the most beautiful and elaborately embellished, should also be the most friendly. Members were engaged on further elaboration within the Church: a new organ stop was added, Allen Pratt gave an oak door for the South Transept and an oak screen was in process of being erected at the back of the Church in memory of Tom Morel.

To match these embellishments Stanley Dixon urged the congregation to make new ventures in fellowship. He asked members to invite to their homes those from other groups or organisations whom at present they did not know. Some members took kindly to the suggestion, although Jessie Newton, who sometimes annoyed her children by her inability to go shopping without talking to many people, was somewhat taken aback. As a result, the Chivers invited the Youth Club to use the tennis court in the garden of their house in Victoria Road once a week. Gladys Gibbs had recently bought Worcester Cottage, a house by the River Usk in Llangynidr, and she asked the Sunday School Leaders to visit it for their annual outing. This happened again in 1938 and the 6th Penarth Trinity Scouts established a tradition of using one of the fields for their annual camp. Stanley Dixon suggested that the Ladies Sewing Meeting should make garments for the Penarth Social Services instead of the not strictly necessary items on which they were engaged. Members were at first unhappy about this as the money they made by selling their handiwork was their contribution to the upkeep of the Church. Stanley Dixon met this objection by suggesting that the Bazaar should be replaced by a Gift Day thus freeing the Sewing Meeting for other work.

Stanley and Gladys Dixon brought a young family to the Manse: Arthur, who was a pupil at Kingswood School, and Margaret. The Dixons became very friendly with Evelyn and George Knighton, and Margaret with Mary. Mary Knighton writes: 'The advent of the Dixon Family was a milestone for me. Margaret was much the same age as I was and we quickly made friends and spent a lot of time together. 1, Victoria Avenue changed from 'the Manse' to their family home as we played hide-and-seek, had midnight feasts in her bedroom, ate Cornish pasties and splits with clotted cream and golden syrup. I began to see Trinity as part of something bigger: The Methodist Church world-wide – and especially in China.'

In March 1937, there was a Service of Dedication, the first of its kind, for those engaged in Sunday School work and other church activities. Outings for the older children, at Stanley Dixon's inspiration, were by motor coach to Monk Nash Lighthouse, rather than to the traditional field at Lavernock. Somewhat to his surprise, George Knighton was appointed as Superintendent of the Sunday School as Stanley Dixon wished to edge Frank Jenkins, with his limited vision, out of this office. In this he succeeded, although Frank Jenkins, a faithful servant of the Church but one inclined to see it in terms of the fabric rather than the people, came back later. The Sunday School at this time had 40 in the Primary Department, 36 in the Juniors 30 in the 12-14 age group and 7 over 15. They all were presented with New Testaments at the special Service to mark George VI's Coronation which was held on 9 May 1937.

At a service in July, Stanley Dixon broke a long-established pattern that only ex-serviceman should read from the lectern. Two young men read and the collection was taken up by young people. Young mens' and young women's clubs were started and visits made to Loudoun Square Coloured Mission, as the old Church in Cardiff Docks was then known.

In June 1937, Stanley Dixon took the opportunity of a meeting which brought together the Circuit Sunday School Council and 'Young Methodism' to challenge Trinity and the other Churches to rethink their strategy. He asked them to 'put their house in order' in the light of success of the youth work in other parts of the Methodist Church, and he asked the following questions: Do our Wesley Guilds meet our present needs? Do they not appeal chiefly to older members, rather than the youth they were framed to serve? Are the Scouts and Guides able to meet the need of our young people or are they too secular in their interests? Do the Junior Classes serve their purpose or should they be organised, as at Albert Road, into a Children's Church? Are the office bearers in the Churches too staid and should they make way for younger leaders? If our organisations are felt to be satisfactory, should they not be supplemented by other methods for keeping the young people in touch with one another during the week? Did not young people dislike being termed 'scholars'? And, should not these same young people be invited to express their views on the situation?

The meeting took fire and it was proposed that a residential conference such as were being held at Swanwick should take place during the following March. Over the summer a full survey of the youth work in the Circuit was undertaken.[1]

During the summer it was learnt that Stanley Dixon was to be 'lifted out' of the Penarth Circuit for an immediate appointment in September as one of the General Secretaries of the Conference of British Missionary Societies at Edinburgh House in London.

Trinity was deeply unhappy. Mary Knighton, for example, was 'distraught' and it was as if the promise of a spring was withdrawn – although, as future development were to show, it was more a spring postponed.

As we have noted the Overseas Mission workers at Trinity, preoccupied with their money-raising activities, had not been particularly concerned about the effect of the resolution passed at the Edinburgh Conference of 1910 which had allotted spheres of influence on the mission field. This provided an example of co-operation little followed in Britain, except in the coming together of the three Methodist Churches in 1932. But the effect of the expansion of the Christian churches in Africa and Asia now affected the Trinity Society in a direct, and totally unexpected manner – by the withdrawal of their Minister.

At Stanley Dixon's last Service in Trinity just four new members were received – a small harvest, but the impact of his one year-long ministry was to be felt in the years which followed. Mary Knighton voiced the feelings of many when she wrote: 'The influence of the Dixon family left an indelible mark on my life and Christian experience.'

Stanley Dixon was the first of the Trinity ministers to drive a car; earlier they had travelled by train, bicycle and, often, on foot. One evening, as he was driving down Victoria Road, he passed Sheila Newton and John Gibbs walking together. He was to return in September 1937 to assist at their marriage in Trinity.

At Edinburgh House, Stanley Dixon began a service to the Protestant Churches in their work of world mission which carried the stamp of his integrity and Christian joy. He helped to launch the China Relief Fund at the time of the Japanese War and later became chairman of the Sino-British Fellowship Trust which provided overseas scholarships for Chinese students. He served as Secretary of the Overseas Literature Committee and when he became a supernumerary minister he spent much time at the Mission House helping with China records. When he died in March, 1960, he was remembered as a man courageous yet humble of heart, and a gallant Minister who loved the things of Christ and cared for all his neighbours.

One of the initiatives he had taken in the Circuit failed to bear immediate fruit: interest in the Swanwick-type, residential conference was not sustained and, as an alternative, two identical series of meetings for the two centres of the circuit, Penarth and Barry, were planned. In the event these were failures – not because of the quality of the lecturers provided by the Sunday School Department in London but because, as was reported to the Circuit Meeting: 'the teachers showed a disquieting lack of interest and . . . there was great disappointment at the attendance.'

Because of Stanley Dixon's unexpected removal, the Stationing Committee of Conference would have had to review the list of ministers who had no circuit appointment. These appointments were often arranged two years before the September in which ministers were due to move – and to find a minister for Trinity at such short notice was not easy.

In the event, Stanley Dixon was followed by James Parkes, who was heir to a fine Methodist family heritage since both his father and grandfather had been Wesleyan Methodist ministers and had served overseas. Following the normal pattern, he had been educated at Kingswood School. When he arrived at Trinity, he was sixty-two years old and had served in ten circuits.

The itinerant system which Methodism had devised and continued with, although the periods of service in any one circuit were lengthened considerably, told hardly on the older men. In most occupations it is tacitly understood that when nearing retirement one will be able to exert less energy than was possible in one's prime. Not so with the Methodist Ministry. When a minister took up a new appointment in a circuit, the society expected a vigorous and innovative lead whatever his age, and it was inevitable that Trinity was disappointed to receive a man who was so near to retirement. James Parkes, too, must have felt the challenge of leading the newly awakened Society at Trinity a daunting prospect. His obituary described how he brought a keen mind and balanced judgement to the discharge of his circuit duties and that he 'lived for preaching'. But it is understandable that after two years he became a Supernumerary Minister in 1939.

Many of Stanley Dixon's innovations continued during the two years, but the dynamic was missing. George Knighton continued as Sunday School Superintendent and at the annual Christmas gift service a play, *Inasmuch*, produced by Enid Stokes and lit by Donald James, was presented by the scholars. This 'gave promise of further efforts in the future'. Enid Stokes was also the leader of a much appreciated girls' class: 'It was superb,' Marion Scourfield recalled many years later.

The Children's Sunday on 16 October became a Children's Weekend. There was a teachers' conference and a parents' evening at which George Knighton, characteristically, 'spoke briefly'.

In 1939 Donald James with the leaders of the Guides, persuaded the Leaders' Meeting to institute a Third-Sunday-in-the-month Parade Service, at which colours were carried into the Church and the whole Service was adapted to the younger Congregation.

After their marriage in September 1937, John and Sheila Gibbs moved to London where John was doing an MA at University College under Cyril Burt, and training as an Educational Psychologist at Guy's Hospital. It was, however, his work at Clubland in South East London, in which Sheila joined him, that was later to have a considerable impact on Trinity.

A summary of the contribution of Jimmy Butterworth and Clubland to youth work within Methodism is provided by George Thompson Brake in his *Policy and Politics in British Methodism, 1932-1982*, and is an illustration of the youth work in other parts of the Methodist Church to which Stanley Dixon had referred when he challenged the Circuit Sunday School Council to 'put their own house in order.'

There have been ministers and others who have pioneered youth clubs in Methodist churches, often in the face of opposition from established youth organizations and unimaginative trustees, and no account of Methodist work among young people can be given without reference to the quite exceptional enterprise of Clubland, created by James (Jimmy) Butterworth at Walworth in South London. Butterworth left Didsbury College, Manchester, in 1922 and was appointed to the Mostyn Road Wesleyan circuit. It was in this appointment that he had a vision of a Temple of Youth for the under-privileged youngsters in the neighbourhood of his church, which was built in 1812, 'about the time Napoleon was retreating from Moscow.' Butterworth saw this old church pleading to serve a new purpose. A few stalwarts had saved it from becoming a warehouse or a cinema, and when it was eventually pulled down and a new building erected both the 1812 and the 1929 foundation stones were laid together as a symbol of the continuing church. Butterworth believed that the new era would not have dawned but for an elderly woman who opened her home to lads before the clubs were built. When her parlour proved too small the club moved to a 'dug-out' at the church, taking the parlour furniture with them.

After six years' adventures, failures, successes and many struggles, new premises became a necessity. Without a penny in sight a notice was chalked on the grime-washed walls of the Dug-out that by the help of God we would build the first Clubland Church to cost £28,000. Why that figure no one knows. Two years later the builder's tender was about that amount.

The scheme met with opposition, resignations and diminishing congregations, but Butterworth found he could not run away from the call, or adapt himself to tasks which he knew were futile. At the point of desperation a generous friend gave Clubland its chance, and so began a work which by any standards was unique. The spacious premises which were built brought a new dimension of church enterprise in a run-down area of South London, and the

111

youngsters who came into Clubland found that they had become members of a community which changed their personal habits and mode of dress. At the heart of it all was the Chapel which had an immeasurable influence on the young people, guaranteeing among its members reverence for God and respect for themselves and each other.

Until September 1939, Sheila and John were mostly concerned with the production of plays at Clubland, amongst them *On the Frontier* by Auden and Isherwood, and *Tobias and the Angel* by James Bridie.

In August, they accompanied the Club on their annual camp to Guernsey, and in September took over the running of the Boys and Girls Clubs for a period which included the first year of the War. It was the high standard of furnishings from Heals and Edwin Maufe's design for the Chapel and premises that gave them an insight into what could be achieved structurally in Methodism, and a challenge in caring for youth that they later attempted to reproduce at Trinity.

# CHAPTER 11

## The Rev'd J. Clark Gibson, 1939-1942

## The Second World War, Part One

John Clark Gibson was fifty-two when he arrived at Trinity in the fateful September of 1939. He, too, was a son of the manse and had been educated at Kingswood. Before arriving in South Wales, he had served in a number of Home Mission stations and, during his term at the West London Mission, had gained experience of open-air preaching: he had had a regular weekly stand at Speakers' Corner in Hyde Park and had drawn large crowds to his question and answer sessions.

At the outbreak of the First World War he became a chaplain to the Forces and served in the Dardenelles Campaign, being twice mentioned in dispatches. Demobilised in 1919, he served in a number of churches before being invited to Trinity at what was to prove a difficult time. However, Penarth offered opportunities which he would not have had in many other places.

Mary Knighton remembers that it was during morning Service on Sunday 3 September, 1939, that she heard the expected, dread announcement that 'this Country is now at war with Germany.'

The announcement was made during J. Clark Gibson's first Service at Trinity: he thus began his ministry under sad and demanding circumstances. The impact was felt on the very conditions under which worship and church activities took place; the Church had to be blacked-out, and so did the Woodland Hall and Schoolroom. The new Minister started a youth club and the members not only filled sand-bags but also helped elderly members to black-out their homes.

As the *Circuit Record* of October put it: 'War conditions with unlit streets and Churches with darkened windows create a new problem for those responsible for the usefulness of Methodism.' The Royal Army Service Corps had their headquarters at the Drill Hall, at the top of Woodland Place, and so Trinity was already close to such military activities as there were in the town. Clark Gibson organised community singing on Saturday evenings in which soldiers joined with the young people of the Church. The *Circuit Record* noted that during December 1939 there was a male voice choir on one Saturday night, the Penarth

Ladies Choir sang on another night and on a third there was a performance by the Mario Puppets. A canteen for the soldiers was started in Woodland Hall, run by the Church and open every evening.

It took Penarth – and most of the rest of the country, some weeks to realise that the effects of the War were not to be felt immediately. Daytime activities resumed slowly, but it was some time before people gained enough confidence to let their children attend activities in the black-out.

J. Clark Gibson preached a series of special Sunday sermons during January 1940 on 'God and the War.' But it was not so much War as the 'phoney war' and that continued into the early Spring, when Norway was invaded and the Maginot Line breached.

King George VI issued a call to the nation to set aside Sunday, 26 May 1940, as a 'Day of Special Intercession for Peace.' Sheila Gibbs, evacuated from London to Penarth as she was expecting a baby, was at the Service and made the following entry in her diary:

> Trinity was absolutely packed. For a moment it seemed quite laughable to see people rallying to God as a last line of defence, but the service and sermon were so good that this impression soon disappeared. Clark Gibson was excellent. There was nothing vindictive or Old Testament about the sermon. A simple appeal to God to forgive us, help us and give us opportunity and grace to build a better world.

On Saturday 30 June, there was an air-raid in which several houses in Penarth were damaged. When the congregation arrived for Service the next morning they found the Woodland Hall in use as a Reception Centre for victims of the bombing.

But, strangely, at times the effect of the War seemed almost peripheral. It is odd not to find any reference to the conflict in the minutes of the Sunday School Council for 9 March and 6 June – except in comments on the difficulty of providing for the treats in a time of rationing, especially as the later date was when France was falling and troops were being evacuated from Dunkirk.

In contrast to the Sunday School Council minutes, those of the Trust for 19 July are startling in their immediacy:

Minutes of the Emergency Meeting of the Trustees and Leaders held in the Games Room of Woodland Hall.

Present: Rev. J Clark Gibson in the chair; Mrs Gibbs, J.P., Miss Gibbs, Mrs Morel J.P., Messers Llewlyn Davies, J.P., L. H. Allen Pratt, J. T. Dewar, John Williams, Ivor Evans, R. M. Evans, A. E. Barnes, J. C. Francis, C. S. Scriven, W. Collins, F. A. Sully, A. W. Hosegood, sec'y.

Rev. J Clark Gibson stated that owing to enemy bombing on the previous day, 18 July, when the Church and schoolroom were seriously damaged, he considered it necessary that the Reading Room in the Woodland Hall be made safe as an air-raid shelter immediately. He stated that he had been in touch with a Home Office expert on shelters and he had advised that the ceiling be strengthened with iron supports and the windows bricked up.

It was pointed out by R. M. Evans that the ceiling had been specially strengthened some twenty years before when a full-sized billiard table was put in the Games Room.

Arthur Hosegood stated that the damage caused to the roof of the Church was so extensive that he had been advised by Henry Budgen, the architect, that it was not worth repairing.

In the absence of Herbert Newton, the Chapel Steward, he was getting estimates for repairs and re-roofing. He was not dealing with the roof of the schoolroom as this had been requisitioned by the Air Ministry.

F. A. Sully stated that the organ was in danger of damage by rain and he was asked to take necessary steps for its protection.

It was decided to hold services in the Woodland Hall till further notice.

The raid of July 18th occurred at 11.00 a.m., just after about a hundred people had dispersed from a prayer meeting

The *Circuit Record* of July 1940 gives an account of the rapid transformation carried out by a very willing team of workers each Sunday to transform the Woodland Hall from a makeshift canteen to a place of worship. The re-roofing cost £559.2.6 and was completed by 16 October. This bears witness to three things: the seriousness of the situation, the efficiency of the stewards, and the underemployment in the building trade at that stage of the War.

During July 1940, the Air Ministry requisitioned the school buildings, but did not occupy them until December. Penarth had become a reception and fitting out centre for the R.A.F. recruits and so from this time on until the end of the War only the Church itself, the minister's vestry and the choir vestry were available to the Trinity Society. The Reading Room and the Games Room were available in the Woodland Hall. The Hall itself was used as a canteen in the evenings, but could be used in the daytime by the Church.

In December 1940, the No. 1 R.A.F. Recruit Centre moved to Penarth. In addition to the Trinity Schoolroom, a great number of halls and private houses were requisitioned. A permanent member of the Attestation Section, centred on Trinity, was Bert Scriven, who worked as a clerk. He describes how the section Warrant Office occupied the platform in the schoolroom, under 'The Ten Commandments', the clerks were in the main hall and the recruits on the balcony. Recruits were documented and assembled in groups of fifteen or twenty and then conducted to the church parlour to be 'sworn in' if they were conscripts, or 'welcomed' if they were volunteers. One of those young recruits was John Ashplant of whom more later. The recruits only spent one night in Penarth after being kitted out in the Paget Rooms.

Trinity's contact with both the Drill Hall soldiers, the permanent staff of the Attestation Section and the R.A.F. School of Accounting which later moved to Penarth, was through the canteen, and through the chapel keeper, Olive Marsh, now a widow.

Olive Marsh was much appreciated by all the R.A.F. staff, and sometimes they helped her out with the cleaning of the Woodland Hall. She was the natural link between the Church and its 'lodgers', she entertained a number for supper and some of them joined her two daughters in a local tennis club. Bert Scriven, who had been a chorister in London, joined the church choir and at one time there were three airmen in it. He was posted to India in December 1942 and so disappears from the Trinity chronicle for a time.

As Winter 1940 drew on, recruits who had been in camp at Lavernock were moved into billets, and many Trinity members found they were providing homes for young men and women just as their own sons and daughters were being called up and sent away. It was a time of great upheaval for all. The Minister asked the Trustees to authorise a service for the troops before the morning Service and for a film service after evening worship, and permission was given. However, Clark Gibson alienated the Trustees because he did not make it clear to them that he intended making a hole in the schoolroom wall so that his projector could be safely operated from the Library. A small, square hole remained for many years as witness to the enormity of altering church premises without Trustees' permission, an almost unforgivable action, even when undertaken by the Minister, and in wartime.

From 1940 onwards, activities were carried on in the premises remaining to the Church, especially the Games Room and the Reading Room in the Woodland Hall. Cubs met on Saturday afternoons under Audrey Scourfield as leader, and the Scouts, with Donald James as 'Skip', even managed to hold their camp at Llangynidr. The Brownies and Guides continued, although the latter were reduced at one time to four members. The Women's Hour met regularly, now under Bertha Pratt, Allen Pratt's sister. The Primary and Beginners Departments of the Sunday School held classes in the Choir Vestry, which the young Donald Knighton accepted as a perfectly normal arrangement having known no other. The older children met in the Woodland Hall premises. Missionary Meetings continued bravely, but attendance at Circuit Meetings was reduced because of 'air-raids going on at the time'. On occasions meetings began late and 'as soon as the all-clear sounded friends hurried to Dinas Powis.' Nevertheless, in March 1941, it was reported that 'in spite of premises having been commandeered and teachers called up, Sunday schools were carrying on well.' Penarth was neither an Evacuation Area nor was it a Reception Area. Despite the air-raids it was considered one of the safer areas of Britain and there were some private evacuees in the town, so Church and Sunday School attendance increased.

The Society rose to the challenge of welcoming these newcomers and Clark Gibson must have been pleased to learn of the way his people responded. 'I should like,' ran a letter written to him on 14 September 1940, 'to express our gratitude to those who made it their job immediately we had been to our first Service to make us feel at home. For my part, I have never before in my life found so many people in a congregation willing to chat to me without fuss . . . their spirit of friendship and fellowship was something new to me, even in a Methodist Church, and should be a great help to you in your ministry. As a result we were able to bring along another 'evacuee' – a woman of good intellect who had not been to a Church for twelve months, but who enjoyed her visits to Trinity during her last few weeks in Penarth.'

The number of prayer meetings increased, as did attendance at them. There was an intercessory meeting before the Sunday morning Service and a Thursday morning Service regularly attracted as many as a hundred people.

The Church building was repaired and reopened in time for the Golden Jubilee Services in October 1940 which commemorated the move to the present site from Arcot Street. Dr Bond, who had been 'planned' to take the Services, was held up by transport difficulties but arrived in time to take the usual Saturday night canteen service. The next morning he preached in the newly restored Church and received twenty young people into membership. That afternoon he baptised John Newton Gibbs, the first of five brothers to be baptised by him.

John Gibbs, at this time, having registered as a conscientious objector on religious grounds, had to appear at his tribunal at the Law Courts in London. Jimmy Butterworth and Dr Kimber, the leader of Hertfordshire Psychiatric and Child Guidance Service in which he was working at the time, supported his application and he was granted 'unconditional exemption'. He continued throughout the War to work in the Hertfordshire service as an Educational Psychologist.

Trinity thus met at first hand the dilemma faced by young Methodists as described in the Conference Declaration of 1933 on Peace and War. For the most part, members of the Society accepted that there was more than one way for a Christian to respond to war, and enfolded those who held differing opinions.

In October 1941 the YMCA took over the running of the canteen in the Woodland Hall 'for the duration of the War. Rent free, subject to their paying all expenses connected with the premises and a dilapidation clause.' Trinity members continued to staff the canteen, now under the direction of Mr Duckett and with the assistance of volunteers from other churches. The facilities for cooking and washing-up were meagre by present-day standards, but the meals served were quite ambitious under the circumstances. The canteen, which was open from 5.00 to 9.00 each evening, offered a choice of fish and chips, bacon and reconstituted egg, and beans on toast.

The gates and railings around the Church were commandeered and removed to make armaments. It is interesting to note that some fifty years later, in September 1992, the Church responded with horror to the idea of replacing them. Although considered a deprivation at the time, a later Society appreciated worshipping without bars between them and the world.

On the night of 5 March 1941, in the course of a very heavy air-raid, All Saints' Church, Trinity's near neighbour, was destroyed. The Trustees, through the Minister, immediately offered the Church in Wales congregation the use of the Woodland Hall for Services. On 9 March, Gladys Gibbs noted in a letter that 'Trinity is being really well used at last. The All Saints people have it at 8 o'clock and there were a lot there. Then, the troops at 10 and our Service at 11 o'clock. Of course, the Woodland Hall is very useful too.'

During the air-raid of 18 July 1940, the west window of Trinity had been damaged. The broken glass was collected and stored, but the question of the safety of all the windows was clearly an immediate one. After much discussion it was decided at the Trustees' Meeting of 16 October 1941 that the windows should be stored in a cellar belonging to the Transformer Electric Station at Gilfach Goch near Bargoed. They were transported for £1 and stored rent free until they could be reclaimed at the end of the War.

Within the Circuit, some of the established practices survived. Preachers from Barry came to Trinity on a regular basis and the Society Stewards arranged for them to be entertained between the morning and evening Services. Mary Knighton remembers:

> Sunday lunch was always the highlight of the week. Mr Collins, our butcher, did as well as he could for us. Always roast and usually Yorkshire pudding even in rationing times. When there was a visiting preacher, he would often join us, and, somehow, Mother managed to stretch the rations. It was probably early in the War when Father was Society Steward that he would retire to the front room after dinner to re-count the morning collection rather than do the washing-up. My brother Donald's reaction to this was, I remember, 'I'm going to be a Society Steward when I grow up.'

The ministry of John Clark Gibson in the Circuit came to an end in 1942. He had dealt with unprecedented situations with initiative and aplomb. The following is taken from his obituary:

> He was greatly troubled by the materialism of our time, particularly with its effect on young people for whom he had great sympathy.

In Penarth and in wartime he had to deal with these problems in an acute form.

For the last ten years of his ministry from 1946 onwards, he served with distinction as the Secretary of the Church's Council on Gambling, which gained national recognition for its research into and monitoring of the gambling scene in the United Kingdom.

# CHAPTER 12

## The Rev'd Robert Hingley 1942-1947

## The Second World War, Part Two

In 1942, with the War still in its darkest phase, Robert Hingley arrived at Trinity. He had entered the ministry from teaching and whilst at Richmond College had taken an honours degree at London University. After graduating in 1913 he was posted to the Edinburgh Mission and while there followed a post-graduate course in psychology at the University, specializing in the effects of shell-shock. This provided some of the background to the book he later wrote on psychoanalysis. To Trinity, he brought his fine, disciplined mind and his love of people. An intellectual evangelist, a pastor who listened with expert understanding, he 'counselled' with great skill long before the profession of counselling came into being. Eleven young men from 'his' Churches successfully offered themselves as candidates for the ministry: six from Woodford alone. Long before ecumenism became fashionable, he had, and shared with others, a vision of a renewed Methodism leading the ecumenical movement. When the effects of the War were eventually lifted, Trinity was to have a burst of new life under his leadership which was to result in the Church taking on the characteristics of a community centre as he understood the term.

Initially, this was inevitably inhibited by the lack of human resources: both young men and young women were being called up as soon as they reached eighteen. There were also problems of premises and priorities: most of the Church buildings continued to be requisitioned and the nation was primarily concerned with the need to pursue the War with all possible energy and with all available resources.

Those who were not actually called up were so occupied with their billetees and with their work and war work that their Church activities were largely restricted to attendance at Sunday worship. Women were playing increasingly important roles. For instance, Gladys Gibbs became a Circuit Steward, one of the first women in Methodism to serve in this position, and in 1944 she attended the Methodist Conference in Leeds as a Representative of the Cardiff and Swansea District.

Joyce Cox, although only in her early twenties, was in a 'reserved occupation' in an insurance office, and her account of life at this time illustrates the limited extent to which people could engage in Church activities. Her weekday evenings and even nights were occupied in voluntary work as an Air Raid Precautions telephonist. Only Saturday nights, when she prepared her Sunday School lesson, and Sunday nights, when she served in the Woodland Hall canteen, were 'free'. Her contact with Trinity was limited to the Sunday morning Service and to leading the Primary Department's Sunday afternoon sessions. She had become leader of the Department in 1940, when Laurella Dewar moved with the B.B.C. to Bristol, and remained in this position until 1979.

Mary Knighton has provided a memory of Trinity life and the impact made by Robert Hingley at this period:

> Ronald Hingley was the Minister who in my teens enabled the opening up of faith and commitment. There was a special series of Services about 1942 and, uncharacteristically, one evening he invited those who so felt to make a public commitment of faith. June Marsh, Donald and I made that response and embarked on a course of preparation for membership, much of which I can still remember. We were duly received and shared for the first time in Holy Communion. So that was what the reredos of the Last Supper was about! But no one had told me before.

This testimony falls in the middle of a period, 1940 to 1944, for which no copies of the *Circuit Record* are available. However, from the Trustees Minutes it is possible to see that by 1944 the clouds were, indeed, lifting. At that time it was no longer necessary for the R.A.F. to have a fitting-out centre in Penarth and, in August, notice was received that the requisition order on the Church buildings was to be lifted. Robert Hingley moved quickly to ensure that church organisations should have full use of the premises and any attempt by the Trustees to let the rooms profitably was forestalled. All the premises, albeit cold, dark and dilapidated, would be needed by the reviving Society.

The Roll of Honour placed on the south wall of the Church lists the seven members of Trinity who were killed in the Second World War. They have all featured in the pages of this book or belonged to families which have.

D. G. Dewar was a grandson of Thomas and Margaret Dewar and the son of George and Lilian Dewar.

F. A. Evans was the brother of Dick Evans, a Trustee and Circuit Steward.

H. N. G. Evans was the son of Ivor and Elizabeth Evans and the nephew of H. P. Evans who had been lost at sea in the First World War.

Graham Hosegood, the son of Arthur and Kitty Hosegood, was a stalwart young Christian of great promise. He died while a Prisoner of War in Burma.

A. G. and C. A. Venn were the sons of Charles and Alice Venn, who were thus doubly bereaved.

Harold Woodhouse, who had become a bomber pilot, was shot down over Holland in 1943.

Those who had survived began to return, some, such as Norman and Eric Collins from prisoner of war camps, all marked by their experiences. Robert Hingley and his wife gave a dinner party to welcome back as many as possible, but, as after the First War, of those who came home not all returned to the Church.

The end of the War, V. J. Day 1945, was, it was reported, 'celebrated by people flocking to Church,' and with peace, Robert Hingley's Trinity Community Centre began to come into being. He wrote about his ambitions for Trinity at this period:

> The aim is to bring the different sections of the Church into closer contact and co-operation; each closely linked with the whole. Its success depends on the quality of thought and devotion we bring to its services; thought and devotion deeply rooted in true love for our God and Saviour.

The concept of a 'Community Centre' was quite new in those days, it suggested a warm welcoming organisation within the Church which could enfold those returning and those who had remained behind.

Robert Hingley's ability to involve people had full play as men and women were demobilised and returned to Penarth, and as those who had not left were less tied than previously.

The Guild was the channel through which the Community Centre first found expression, thus fulfilling the original aims of the movement. Its secretary was Norah Morgan, who, with her family had come to Trinity in 1929 when her father, a railwayman was promoted to the signal-box at Penarth Dock Station.  She writes:

> I attended Membership Classes led by the Rev'd George Charnley and became a member during his Ministry.  He made his own version of *Pilgrim's Progress* and we especially looked forward to the next instalment.  I became a member of the Choir and started to teach in the Sunday School.  The meeting on Friday evenings for the preparation of the lessons was a very necessary and valuable time.  Looking back, I think folk of my age and younger were privileged to be part of such a wonderful Church which included people of an unusually wide variety of different social standing.  The Wesley Guild was an important part of the life of Trinity.  It brought us together in the planning of programmes each winter and enabled many of us to preside over meetings.

Norah Morgan became a local preacher, one of 'the band of charming young women' about whom an elderly Supernumerary Minister from Dinas Powis spoke appreciatively.  In a production of J. M. Barrie's *Quality Street,* she was to play Phoebe, the heroine.  All this was to stand Norah in good stead, when, after leaving Trinity and serving as residential secretary at Methodist Guest Houses, she married a Methodist Minister, Graham West.

During the War, there had been a realization that the Sunday School Department and the Wesley Guild Movement were not meeting the needs of the younger members of the church, nor of the young people who were outside the church.  A new Youth Department and a Methodist Association of Youth Clubs were brought into being and they were to revolutionize the approach to young people in all the churches of the Penarth Circuit and throughout the Connexion.[1]

In 1945, a youth club was tentatively started in Trinity by John and Sheila Gibbs.  When they had been evacuated to St. Albans they had attempted to run a club such as they had experienced at Clubland, but they had failed.  The failure was partly because of the blackout, partly because they were attempting to impose their pattern on the boys and girls who attended, but mainly because there was nothing to build on in the life of the small ex-Primitive Methodist Church in St. Albans that was the venue for the club.

These conditions did not apply at Trinity. There were excellent premises, there was a lot of young life in the Sunday School, the Scouts and Guides, and there had been a history of clubs from time to time so that the new club grew out of the activities that were on-going, such as a table-tennis team which played in a Circuit league. Barn and square dancing were all the rage, so there was often a social with dancing on Saturday evenings. On Sunday evenings, the Club met after Church as a discussion group. Tuesday was the main Club night with table-tennis, billiards, chess and an epilogue. On Fridays, the Club was part of the Drama Group. Soon Frank Dewar took over the leadership, and one of his contributions was to start a magazine.

In 1945 the Trustees gave permission for the lowering and extending of the platform in the hall. Wood was in very short supply but the floor was taken up from a redundant decontamination centre and relaid as the new stage. This was to prove the first step in the conversion of the hall over the next few years into what could be, for a week or so, a Little Theatre, with a stage 20 feet by 15 feet and tiered seating for 220. The lighting equipment gave Donald James the opportunity for lighting plays to his professional standards. Many responded to the opportunities provided: apart from those who were involved in acting and singing, there were various supporting groups. With scenery designers and makers, wardrobe staff – a new sphere here for the Ladies Sewing Meeting, stage crew and front-of-house management, a production might well involve and extend as many as seventy-five people; the Community Centre in action.

During the summer of 1945, the Church decided to use the theme 'Home and Family Life' in their 1945/46 winter programmes. The uniformed organisations made a point of inviting parents to their meetings, the Drama Group produced plays with family themes, and the Guild invited speakers on the subject. The Guild also arranged Brains' Trusts – a very popular format at the time, on such topics as 'When you consider the world, do you think it a fit place to bring a child into?' and 'Will the social services have an effect on parents' control of children?'

When the Dixon family returned for a weekend, they were presented with a demonstration of what was happening in the Community Centre. The Women's Hour sang 'O brother man, fold to thy heart thy brother' – there being no concern about gender specific language at that time; the Scouts and Guides performed an enroling ceremony; after the Junior Sunday School made a contribution, the Drama Group acted out a rehearsal. At the Service on the following day, the lessons were read by two young members of the Church.

This was the last Service for which F. A. Sully played the organ. A bank manager in Cardiff, F. A Sully found his real vocation at Trinity where he was organist and choir-master for thirty-three years. The music was regarded as a fine feature of the services and this tradition had been maintained under adverse conditions during the War. F. A. Sully was succeeded by E. Macmillan Ewens, who had previously been the organist at Holton Road Baptist Church in Barry.

On the ecumenical front, Trinity Guild asked members of other churches to discuss with them the role of Christians in the postwar world, and much attention was given to an Anglican report, entitled *Towards the Conversion of England*. Whilst Miss Carey Evans of the Oxford Group was optimistic about this approach, the Rev. Thomas Jones of All Saints' Church was extremely doubtful whether the initiative could succeed.

The Sewing Meeting on Tuesdays had continued throughout the War, knitting comforts for the troops, and Robert Hingley turned them into a Minister's Class. They met at three and, after the class meeting, had tea and a social hour.

Sheila Gibbs, building on experience she had gathered at St Albans, started a Young Wives' Group. The Group's annual garden meetings proved particularly popular and were open to young women from other churches – and none.

Concern for the church overseas continued and considerable sums were raised. Increasingly the emphasis was on similarities rather than differences: for instance, at one Overseas Anniversary the Rev'd Cyril Davey introduced the Trinity children to games played in other parts of the world. In the first years of peace the Monday Women's Meeting held its first Anniversary Service in the Church.

During the War, the Senior Sunday School, which still met on Sunday afternoons, had been in the doldrums. George Knighton had resigned the superintendency to lead a young men's group and the ever-faithful Frank Jenkins had, for a second time, taken over responsibility for the School. Whilst the Beginners, the Primary and Junior Departments were in good shape, the Seniors were offered an uninspiring programme. Apart from the occasions on which Robert Hingley led the class, the boys and girls sat in a circle and read verses aloud one after the other. There were still some thirty who attended the class regularly which suggests that the success or otherwise of an activity at this age depends on just being together. Fellowship, to use a somewhat overused word, is more important than what actually happens or what is taught in the group. It must also be said that there were few alternative attractions in the town on a Sunday afternoon.

The Minister asked John Gibbs, recently returned to Penarth, to sit in and report on a session. He quickly found himself appointed Sunday School Superintendent – a dated title if ever there was one, and he proceeded to institute changes. These were initially based on current British Lessons Council material, and later, in the 1960's, on the *Partners in Learning* scheme introduced by the Youth Department.

Robert Hingley had a way with him: he could persuade people to do what he thought was right for them. The previous paragraph indicates how he approached John Gibbs; Mary Knighton writes about her experience as follows:

> In the summer of 1947, when I was a university student, Robert Hingley came to our house – to my great surprise, to see me, not my parents: 'We don't have a preacher to go to Cogan on September 21st. Will you go?' 'Me?' I remember cycling there but even more I remember climbing up into the pulpit to find, sitting at the back, J. T. Wells, a senior, respected local preacher – *horror*! Why couldn't he have taken the Service? There was none of the normal local preacher's drill, no being 'on note', no going to Local Preachers' Meeting, no being urged to take exams.

In 1946, the Sunday School Anniversary was resurrected in all its former glory, indeed with some additions since theatrical entertainment was offered on the Friday and Saturday evenings. A double-bill was presented consisting of *The Happy Journey* by Thornton Wilder, in which Robert Hingley took part, and *Bread* by Leslie Davidson. On the Sunday, there was a school choir of fifty voices, who introduced the congregation to special hymns from the Sunday School Hymnal which was to be published in 1950. The young Derek Jefferson from St Athans preached and impressed both young and old.

During the spring of the same year, Trinity joined with the rest of the Circuit to hold an Eisteddfod. This particularly Welsh phenomenon brought the people, particularly the young people, of Penarth, Barry and

127

Dinas Powis Churches together. Those who were to enter either the individual or the group competitions went into training. Mary Knighton remembers her parents preparing hard for the Bible Quiz and her brother rehearsing St Paul's speech at Athens. The occasion was primarily directed towards teenagers, but there were sections for adults and for quite young children. The final set-piece for senior choirs was fraught with tension and the hapless adjudicator needed all the tact he could muster as the Holton Road and Porthkerry Road choirs from Barry competed against each other.

Robert Hingley, despite his natural tact, did not have an easy ministry at all levels. This was partly as a result of the increasing tensions between the Penarth and Barry ends of the Circuit. The two communities sprang from very different beginnings: Penarth from the Plymouth Family Estate and the Taff Vale Railway; Barry from the development of Barry Dock and of the Barry Railway by 'Davies, the Ocean'. There were class differences too: Penarth was becoming increasingly middle class, while much of Barry remained sturdily working class.

These tensions were prone to surface during the Quarterly Meetings, or, if not to surface, to lie uncomfortably close to the surface so that many members of the meeting did not anticipate these circuit gatherings with any pleasure. The members were tempted to ask: 'Can any good thing come out of Penarth? – or Barry,' respectively. None of this tension was allowed to intrude into the Circuit Minutes which George Knighton, as Secretary, spent many evenings writing and rewriting so that as much distress as possible was avoided. But the strain of Circuit meetings told on the Chairman, Robert Hingley.

The itinerant system of ministry provided another source of conflict. At this time, a good proportion of laymen were residents of long standing in their communities; the ministers came for some five years and then left. It was the intention, usually achieved, that the ordained men should bring their individual gifts to the ongoing life of a circuit and, if necessary, guide it in new directions. This could, however, be deeply disturbing to the members, who might be tempted to ask: 'What will my position be?' Or 'Why this change. We've never done it that way here?' In general the respect for the Ministry enabled proposed changes to be accepted, but this was not always the case. It was some of the local preachers from Barry – a group that should have been among the first to welcome spiritual development – who met Robert Hingley's innovations with suspicion and sometimes with downright opposition.

A small number of the local preachers were 'ministers manques' who felt that they were as competent as the ministers and that they made up in knowledge of the local situation what they lacked in college training.

John Gibbs, attending Local Preachers' Meetings for the first time, was astonished and disturbed by the acrimonious note that crept not infrequently into the discussions. Some of the local preachers made no attempt to hide their critical attitude to the Ministry and he saw something of the 'seamy side' of Methodism which Tom Morel had warned him against, when he saw his nephew becoming more and more caught up in the organisational side of the Church. It was necessary to accept that no church is a completely redeemed society. Robert Hingley, with a distinguished book on psychoanalysis to his credit, would have been able to understand the causes of these tensions and to come to terms with them. But the hurt remained.

There is, incidentally, no evidence that there was an English Welsh divide: almost all the members of the Methodist churches in Penarth and Barry, not excepting the local preachers, were 'incomers' – as were nearly all of the ministers.

Robert Hingley left Penarth in 1947 for Evesham. Even after he became a supernumerary he continued to serve, and, at the age of seventy, he took pastoral charge of Little Common, Bexhill, where, such was his enthusiasm, he increased the membership from fifty-five to ninety-two.

Almost the last event in his ministry at Trinity was a Conference at Worcester Cottage, Llangynidr. This was at Whitsun, 1947 and Mary Knighton recalls:

> . . . the sense of relaxed fellowship and the beauty and freedom of the place and the excitement of the wild flowers, especially finding for the first time in my life, on an island in the River Usk, a globe flower. Derek Jefferson was there, sharing the leadership for part of the time, but we had no special interest in one another – then. The evening finished with evening prayers. Next morning, Sunday, most of us enjoyed the unique opportunity of not only attending but actually joining in an Anglican Communion Service. Another session of our conference was held later in the day. Our last session was on Monday morning when in the light of all that had happened since Friday we set our house

129

Trinity Away Weekend at Llangynidr, 1952.

in order. We freely discussed if and how any of our Community Centre activities could be improved and the next year's programme was talked over. We ended on the note that the past, even if not finished with, was over, and that it is for the future that we must plan and pray. No one who was present at the week-end will ever forget the experience.

# CHAPTER 13

## The Rev'd Ernest Pickard 1947-1951

Ernest Pickard, born in Cowbridge in the Vale of Glamorgan, was the first Trinity minister to have been born in Wales. He was fifty-nine when he came to Trinity. He had attended the renowned Cowbridge Grammar School and, when his training for the Wesleyan ministry was completed, was called to supply a ministry among the soldiers on Salisbury Plain. By this appointment he was introduced to a sphere of service that he enjoyed very much and in which he was to continue until almost the end of the 1914-1918 War, serving in Gibraltar and then as chaplain to the forces in France. After his health broke down he returned to circuit work, and spent almost the whole of the Second World War in Bristol.

Throughout his ministry his quiet word often brought new light to bear on the problems of his flock and the business of the Circuit Meeting. He was a deep thinker who kept himself abreast of the times and was not afraid of new ideas. However, he was distressed by the lack of response he encountered at Trinity on some issues.

In September 1947, rehearsals began for the Drama Group's first full-length play, *A Midsummer Night's Dream,* which aimed to reproduce the conditions under which the play might have been presented at Shakespeare's Globe. Great scope and considerable challenges were offered to the needlewomen of the Church in the making of costumes, for, although materials were still 'on coupon', surplus war supplies were not rationed. The fairies were dressed in net originally intended to be stuck to windows to prevent splintering during air-raids, and the cloaks for Oberon and Titania were made from green and brown camouflage silk. Anne Evans and Jean Dewar played Puck on alternate nights, and Donald Knighton was Flute, one of the Mechanicals. The production involved some sixty-eight people, established Trinity Drama Group as a theatrical presence in the town and introduced it to the Connexion.

The Winter and Spring of 1947 gave Trinity an opportunity to show the new Minister how it worked as a community centre, through its involvement in town and circuit life, and in an eisteddfod. In 1946 Ronald Ashman had moved to Barry to become Ministerial Youth Secretary with John Gibbs as the Lay Secretary. Writing in 1992, Ronald Ashman said:

131

Both of us were anxious to carry out the policies of the newly created Methodist Youth Department; the chief of which was to help circuits and local churches present 'The Way of Christ and His Church' to the young people of Methodism, especially to those who had grown up during the Second World War.

One of the ways they used was the Eisteddfod, the second of which was held in March 1947 and the third in 1948. The *Circuit Record* of 1947 considered the role of the Eisteddfod and asked: 'Is the Eisteddfod the way to win men and women for Christ, to make Christians?' And provided the following answer: 'Not in itself, but it has great possibilities for good.' This possibility was translated into reality when, later the same year, it was reported that forty-three of the young people in the Circuit's youth clubs had been received into membership of the Church.

The *Circuit Record* reported that, at a Youth Service in Trinity:

> Fifteen were received by the Rev'd E. R. Pickard; we feel that each of the fifteen will long remember Mr Pickard's inspiring talk to them as competitors in Life's arena, taking part in the greatest game of all, and watched by a great crowd of witnesses.

A feature of Ernest Pickard's Ministry was the role played by the Circuit and the extent of the activities which drew the Methodist Churches of Penarth and Barry together. Beside the Eisteddfods, there were the Circuit Weekends and weeks at Llangynidr. Ronald Ashman writes of one:

> It commenced on a Friday afternoon and concluded with a Communion Service after lunch on Sunday. The theme was 'What does it mean to be a Christian in the middle of the 20th Century?' The Saturday afternoon was used to organise a climb up one of the mountains around Llangynidr. This was greatly enjoyed, especially as the climbers had been promised a 'roast' for the evening meal. It is worth noting that food rationing was still in force, and it was only with the help of the Glamorgan County Council Youth Committee that we had been able to obtain special ration coupons to purchase the roast for twenty people. Unfortunately the Aga went out and in spite of tremendous efforts by the two cooks, a minister's wife, Gwen Ashman, and Norah Morgan, a Wesley Guild Secretary, it would not relight. However, all was well by Sunday lunch. But it was not only the

dinner that was enjoyed. All the young people who attended returned to their respective Churches and youth groups talking of their experiences. All had experienced real Christian fellowship, and some had caught a vision of their tasks as Christians in the post-war world. Other circuits in the District wanted to know if they could have a similar conference and soon groups were coming from all over South Wales. Incidentally the charges were: 17/6 per person for each week-end, and 30/- for a week – excluding transport.

At a Trinity Leaders' meeting, Ernest Pickard referred to 'the spiritual enthusiasm' he had observed during recent conferences at Llangynidr – thus underlining the value of residential experiences for church members.

In January 1948, three of the choirs, Albert Road, and Trinity from Penarth, and Porthkerry Road from Barry, joined together to perform Haydn's *Creation* in each other's Churches. The following year a pageant entitled *Militant and Triumphant,* written by John and Sheila Gibbs especially for Circuit production, was mounted throughout the circuit. The different Churches presented their own episodes which featured Christians from different centuries: from Peter and John, through Blandina, St Francis, John Bunyan, Susanna Wesley and Elizabeth Fry to the present day, with Cankerapple, John Gibbs, the Recording Angel, Sheila Gibbs, and an Apprentice Devil, Anne Evans, to provide continuity. The play, published by the Youth Department, was put on by a considerable number of groups throughout the country.

The period covered by Ernest Pickard's Ministry marked the heyday of the circuit system in Penarth and Barry: during it the Methodist Churches worked together closely. The circumstances in which the circuit system had been created in a time of rapid growth, with its emphasis on extension and support, was passing away; new alliances were coming into being, and common ground between Christians in particular places was being recognised. There was to be less and less interaction and mutual support between the Methodist Churches in Penarth and Barry as other groupings emerged, notably the Free Church Council of Penarth and, later, the Penarth Council of Churches.

An illustration of the fragility of circuit togetherness, and, incidentally, of the loose connection which might exist between youth club and church, was provided when the pageant was put on at Barry Dock Church. Even though the host church was responsible for an episode, the youth club showed no interest and continued with its activities, billiards and table tennis, in another part of the building.

The Drama Group contributed to a Penarth production of *Militant and Triumphant* with the other Free Churches and, to look ahead to 1951, presented *Everyman* as part of a Festival of Christian Drama within the larger celebration of the Festival of Britain. In this instance, Trinity collaborated enthusiastically with All Saints, Tabernacle Baptist Church and Christ Church, at a time when the feeling that the country had finally put the War behind it was paramount.

Ernest Pickard was not so impressed by the spiritual enthusiasm in Trinity's regular life. Indeed, he was distressed by the absence of sustained spiritual activity during the weekdays. With the exception of the Tuesday Women's Fellowship, the Men's Fellowship – which was soon to close, and the occasional devotional meetings of the Guild, there was nothing. Only three Class Leaders were in office and although assistant leaders were appointed, there was little or no pastoral oversight of the membership, other than that supplied by friendship and normal, neighbourly concern. Of the new young members received, few became deeply involved in the spiritual life of the Church, and attendance at Sunday evening Services was declining.

The Methodist Conference had heard a rousing call in 1946 when Dr Harold Roberts introduced the report on *The Message and Mission of Methodism*, and commended it for study and action throughout the Connexion. Its scholarly and authoritative analysis of contemporary Britain and of Methodism's historical role led into proposals for a programme for action in every church. There were four main recommendations. 'That every church should examine the nature and reality of its life in fellowship. That, in view of the need for world-wide evangelization, every church in Methodism should plan periodically a campaign to commend Jesus Christ as Saviour and Lord to those outside the churches. That Christian homes should be opened more freely as centres of fellowship, and that house to house visitation should be reinstated. Finally, that young people, before they leave home to embark on careers 'should be adequately equipped to bear their witness.'

Ernest Pickard urged the Leaders to arrange meetings to discuss the Call from Conference, even to have a joint meeting of Trustees, Leaders and the Youth Council, but the Minutes of the Leaders' Meeting record postponement after postponement, and it does not seem that anything was ever done. This illustrates the difficulty of translating the will of Conference into action at the local church level. Conference may propose, but the congregations tend to dispose. A programme which may seem right to the Methodist Church sitting in its highest court, the Conference, may have great difficulty in commending itself to the ordinary members 'in the pew.'

There were, however, encouraging features in the life at Trinity. Worship on Sunday mornings continued at the high level that had been established. The Sunday School was thriving and year after year reported a total membership of some 300 – the numbers in the Senior Department were keeping up particularly well. New teaching methods and aids were introduced at all levels, and in 1948 a film-strip projector, one of the first in Penarth, was introduced. It was used regularly, unlike many which were acquired by churches in a first flush of enthusiasm and thereafter left forgotten at the backs of cupboards.

Parents in Penarth, unconnected with the Church, were willing to send their children to Sunday School at 2.45, and many were prepared to put in an appearance at the Sunday School Anniversary – an occasion on which there was a flowering of new dresses. But few, if any, were interested in becoming involved in the life of the Church despite the special Services and occasions which were planned to attract them.

However, there were others who were attracted to the church premises. Now that the restrictions of war time, with the blackout and the 9.00 pm limit on Church activities, had been brushed aside the Youth Club, Uniformed Organisations, Guild and Drama Group attracted large and enthusiastic followings. The Trinity Youth Club organised a visit to the M.A.Y.C. Weekend in London in 1949.

Esme Bryant provided an account for the *Circuit Record*:

> As our Club had only recently been affiliated to MAYC this was our first experience of such a gathering. With three fellow club members, I arrived at Clapham Underground Station on the Friday evening and we were greeted by young people, easily distinguishable by their little green and yellow badges, who showed us the way to the Underground Shelter where the delegates were to sleep for the week-end. It was really grand to find so many young people with the same interests as ourselves and there was so much to talk about that it was hardly surprising that we had little sleep during our stay.

135

On Saturday morning we were up at 5.30 and after tea in the canteen were all ready to see the sights of London. The Congress took place in the afternoon in the Westminster Central Hall and it was a most impressive sight to see the vast hall packed with young people of all ages and from all walks of life, yet all members of our large family – MAYC. The Rev Douglas A. Griffiths, 'Griff', spoke to the Congress for the last time as Secretary and was thanked by his successor, the Rev. Len Barnett.

At the conclusion of the formal business the real work of the Congress began. The subject for discussion was 'Club, Community and Church.' Under the sub-title of 'Can MAYC make a difference to things?' Mr Sid Hedges in opening the discussion stressed the need of a close link between Club and Church, Club and Sunday School and also between all people outside Methodism engaged in Christian Youth work who were ready to follow the same Master.

After three most impressive speeches by the appointed delegates it was most encouraging to see others ready to speak as soon as the discussion was open. All were anxious to tell the Congress the ways in which they were bringing young people into the fellowship of the church. Before the Doxology, 'Griff' handed a lighted torch to a representative of a London Youth Club, who was to bear it to the Royal Albert Hall for the display.

After tea, the delegates made their way to the Albert Hall where they formed the main body of the packed auditorium. The theme being 'The Pilgrim Flame' the runners, to an opening fanfare, led the procession of torch-bearers around the arena where they remained throughout the display. The varied programme, which showed the high quality of the activities of our youth Groups was brought to a conclusion by the performers who carried lighted torches assembling in the arena. The climax came when the pilgrim flame was handed to Len Barnett while the hall rang with the strains of 'The Church's one foundation is Jesus Christ our Lord.'

On Sunday morning, the closing devotions of the Congress were held in Wesley's Chapel in City Road where delegates filled extra seats in their eagerness to join in this final act of worship. The sermon by the Rev. Peter Morley in which he spoke of our

Christian Pilgrimage was a fitting conclusion to a most inspiring week-end.'

We came home feeling that M.A.Y.C. does make a difference and looking forward to meeting our newly-formed friends again next year.

This lively description of an MAYC Week-end could be repeated with minor variations year after year as the Trinity Club attended, and not infrequently took part in the Albert Hall display.

The younger members of Trinity were enabled to realize that as young Christians they 'lived on a large map,' and the Weekends provided an experience similar to that of going on pilgrimage in other Communions.

The Trustees at this period had to deal with two difficult problems. The first was the offer by Allen Pratt of a carillon of bells. These were to be electronically played and amplified through the belfry at the base of the spire. Considering such pretension to parish status inappropriate, the Trustees were able to cite 'disturbance to the neighbouring households' as their reason for turning down the offer. If only the Trustees of the 1900's had been as strong minded when faced with the gift of the renaissance style pulpit.

The second concerned the traditional and indeed, actual, date of the Church Anniversary. Dr Eric Baker, the Secretary of the Methodist Education Committee and later the Secretary of Conference, had been invited to preach at the Church Anniversary Service in January 1948. The invitation was technically in the hands of the Secretary to the Trustees, as the Trust benefited from the collections on these occasions, but the Trustees did little, it seems, to gather together a worthy congregation and the attendance was very poor, the weather being atrocious. Dr Baker was greatly displeased and communicated his displeasure so widely that Trinity lay under a connexional cloud. The Trustees decided that they had, indeed, been courting disaster with the January date and for the next year moved the celebration forward into the more salubrious month of May. The days, however, of the great Church, Sunday School and Mission Anniversaries with nationally known preachers were beginning to be numbered at Trinity, and the church members, if they were happy with their minister, were happy that he should preach on these occasions.

Trinity, it should be said, guarded its pulpit jealously. The Minister was normally appointed for at least one of the Services each Sunday and the other circuit Ministers would take their turns. Thus laymen, although accredited, and, like A. R. Dawson, well established in civic life, were seldom 'planned'. On the Circuit Plan women local preachers in the Penarth and Barry Circuit were few enough, and they were only rarely 'planned' at Trinity. An exception was made in the case of Norah Morgan, who was considered 'acceptable.'

At this time, so soon after the end of the War, with materials in short supply and a Government committed to giving housing high priority, the Trustees began work on the only development for which they could realistically expect to obtain approval: the creation of a Chapel Keeper's flat in the Woodland Hall. The completion of the flat coincided with Olive Marsh's retirement, and, as the position was advertised with accommodation, many applicants came forward.

In 1948 an article had appeared in the *Circuit Record* on premises, 'begging people not to take Trinity in its dilapidated state for granted, even though at that stage the buildings used by the Sunday School compared favourably with those of many day schools.' It pointed out that three years after the War people had managed 'to sweep and garnish their houses.' And asked 'Are we to be satisfied with a lower standard for our church premises?' In making alterations to the premises when it is possible we should not feel we are being ungrateful for what our forebears built for us. They served their age and we must serve ours.'

Such pleading was at length to bear fruit. In the spring of 1950, modest structural alterations were made to the buildings, three of the small class rooms were turned into lavatories and cloak rooms and the outside of the Church and Trinity Schoolroom and the Woodland Hall were painted. The work was completed in time for the April 1951 Jubilee Celebration, on which occasion Dr Wilbert Howard D.D. was the guest preacher. The celebrations included an 'At Home' at which the older members of Trinity were guests. There was the expected Appeal – in this case for £1000 'so that Trinity may be handed on as a living church where men may seek the means of grace and, above all, worship God.'

The final meeting of the Guild in 1951 took the form of a social evening for the entertainment of students from overseas currently training in the United Kingdom. The *Circuit Record* noted:

Although the number of visitors was small we feel that a repetition of this on some future occasion would very likely bring more guests. In view of the great and terrible danger from zealous Communists which these students from abroad have to face, it is surely up to the Christian Churches of this land to extend hospitality to them, and to welcome them into the family circle at home.

A more positive approach was adopted by those who began to think about the provision of residential accommodation for overseas students. Their concern found concrete expression in South Wales when International House was built in Penarth during the 1960's.

As a result of his efforts and the work of the congregation, Ernest Pickard was able to hand on a church in good heart and in good shape to his successor. He went to Blackwood in the Sirhowy Valley Circuit and spent three years there before moving back to Bristol as a supernumerary and becoming Warden of Charles Wesley's House. This final appointment lasted nine years during which he used his time and gifts without stint in the interests of the thousands of visitors from all parts of the world who followed the John and Charles Wesley Heritage Trail to Bristol.

# CHAPTER 14

## The Rev'd Percy S. Watkinson 1951-1961

Percy Snowdon Watkinson was born in 1895 and came to Trinity towards the end of a very distinguished ministry spent at the Wigan Central Hall and in circuits in the seaside resorts on the Lancashire coast, to which the cotton magnates, who had built their churches near to their cotton mills, moved in the nineteenth century and where the mill workers went for their wakes weeks. He came from Yorkshire farming stock with a great Christian tradition, and was very much the product of his background and training,. He had immense physical vitality, combined with a great love of cricket and rugby, and these gifts, together with his enjoyment of life and his rich personality, enabled him to communicate the content of his message to his hearers. When he preached, others listened. It was, as Winifred Evans said, 'as if Dr Bond were with us again.'

His ministry at Trinity began inauspiciously. His son Peter, drawing partly on his mother's recollections, wrote as follows about his father's first reaction:

> South Wales represented a very big cultural and geographical leap, but I never remember any move being made with relish. As to the Manse, Mother has memories of stone steps leading down to the pantry and Father regarding them as dangerous and, apparently, later, Mother did fall down them. During our first night in Pagemont, Father said 'Let's go home.'

John Gibbs, the Circuit Steward, and Sheila who had attempted to make the Watkinson family welcome, remember Percy saying 'What a dreadful house!' When no suitable alternative property could be found at a price Trinity could afford, they had done what they could, to make the manse as easy to work as possible. A new floor had been laid in the morning room, the scullery had been modernised, an immersion heater had been installed, the hall had been decorated, the second floor shut off from the rest of the house, and the bannisters had been 'boxed in'. This was thought, at that date, to be a labour saving measure. With the help of their young sons, they had cleaned and tidied the house after the decorators had left. Little enough done, perhaps, but building restrictions still applied and improvements, such as fitted kitchens were still rare. A garage, by then a connexional requirement, was by this time necessary.  Percy Watkinson drove a car but preferred to do most of his visiting on foot.

Percy Watkinson protected his wife, Eileen, fiercely.  She was younger but more frail than he, and he resented the tendency in Methodism at that time to take a wife's services for granted and to use her as an unpaid curate.  They arrived with their two children, Peter, who was just about to go up to Oxford, and Mary, who was still at school.  This was to prove a ministry of the whole family.

Methodism's system of itinerancy causes some strains and stresses, and increasingly so when wives have their own careers.  However, the system also brings great advantages: for the minister there is a new challenge and an opportunity for trying out a new approach and new ideas; for the congregation a new voice and a new personality to respond to.  Penarth was a surprising station for Percy Watkinson and he revelled in it.  Trinity received nothing but good from the new Minister with his sermon illustrations which drew on life on his family farm in the Dales, or experiences of life in Lancashire  mill-towns.  He could coin telling phrases: of the Israelites spending forty years in the wilderness, he would say, not infrequently: 'They had to get the Slave out of their souls.'

A stationing usually had a known termination and this, too, could be an advantage: the Minister would know that the itinerant system would provide him with another station if the strains of a particular appointment were mounting, and the people would know that, in the same way, at a point in the future there would be another minister in their pulpit and the manse.

For some of Percy Watkinson's ministry the Circuit Minute Book and the Trinity Trust and Leaders Meeting Minute Books are all in existence, so it is possible to see how the Methodists in Penarth and Barry exercised their responsibilities and how the life at Trinity proceeded.

These three meetings between them enabled the Methodist people to be the Methodist Church in any one locality: the Quarterly Meeting of the Circuit, the boundaries of which had been fixed by Conference, the Trustees' Meeting of the particular Church, and the Leaders Meeting of the Methodist Society in that Church.

In 1951, the Penarth and Barry Circuit had five ministers and ten places of worship: five at the Barry end of the Circuit and five at the Dinas Powis and Penarth end. It was run by a Circuit Meeting which met quarterly.[1]

It was clear from the situation prior to 1951 that the Circuit was under strain and when Percy Watkinson appreciated the situation he set in motion the constitutional steps necessary to divide the Circuit. This required District and Connexional approval. The move had the support of the Penarth and Dinas Powis Societies and, to a lesser extent, of the Barry Societies. They could see that the civic interests of the two towns often diverged, but there was regret for the breaking of contacts between the Churches – of which the disappearance of the *Circuit Record* and the narrowing down of circuit youth activities were the most obvious.

This separation took effect in September 1955. The records of the Circuit Meetings hereafter of the new Penarth Circuit, with its two ministers and four churches, contain no hint of tension or strife. The members must have been thankful that they no longer needed to make the twice yearly visits to Barry – more if they were on other Circuit Meetings, to conduct circuit business.

The new Circuit planned joint activities. At Trinity, the annual Covenant Service in January 1960 was organised as a circuit occasion and was televised by the B.B.C. During March 1960, 150 members of the Circuit, led by the Trinity Drama Group, performed the Biblical episodes in the pageant, *Set My People Free*, which was presented in the Albert Hall on the occasion of the Bicentenary of the Methodist Missionary Society.

In addition to the Circuit Meeting, the Trustees' Meeting of each Church had responsibility for the fabric of the Church and its ancillary premises, and, legally, for what went on inside them.

The Trustees appointed the chapel stewards, the organist and choir master, the door stewards, the sidesmen and the chapel keeper, and they had doctrinal and general oversight of the type of worship offered; they had to rule, for example, whether drama could feature in a Service. They had especial responsibility for the Church Anniversary and the Harvest Festival. They had responsibility for letting the ancillary premises within Conference's directives. The Trustees of Trinity who had been appointed in 1928 were, by the 1950's, either dead, elderly, or had moved away. Those who remained rarely took the initiative, and were reluctant to be persuaded that action should be taken because, for example, the lighting was defective, the lavatories smelly, the kitchens primitive or the Church cold – although their years probably made them aware of this last problem.

Sometimes the Trustees responded to a real need. In 1951, the Glamorgan Education Committee applied for accommodation pointing out that six years after the War had ended, the children born in 1946 were stretching the schools to breaking point. In February 1952, the Trustees let the Woodland Hall and the Primary Room, from Mondays to Fridays from 8.00 am to 5.00 pm at a rent of £135.0.0 per annum. The arrangement led to continual problems about caretaking and it was a relief when, six years later, the tenancy ended. In the meantime, however, the Education Committee had, with the Trustees' approval, installed two extra lavatories in the Woodland Hall. It was only too easy, however, for the Trustees to become out touch with the life of the Church or of the times.

It had been the custom that those who paid pew rents had their names on their pews and the pews were reserved for them until five minutes before the service began. So assiduous were the property stewards in collecting the pew rents that even in October 1940, when the Church had been bombed and was temporarily unusable, they sought guidance from the Trustees as to whether they should continue to collect them. The idea of reserving pews became increasingly unpopular, especially as it was reported that visitors were being asked to move from seats they had chosen. The Leaders Meeting and the Annual Society Meeting repeatedly sent representations to the Trustees asking that the names should be removed and that all seats should be regarded as free.

The Trustees 'felt that the removal would not be carried out without breaking faith with the past – a name in a pew, even though that person was unable to attend – was an indication that a covenant had been made to contribute to the support of Trinity.'

Prime movers in this agitation were Glyn Marsh and Ernest Moss. In 1952, Ernest and Irene Moss came to Penarth from Swansea where they had both been deeply involved in Brunswick Methodist Church in which Irene had grown up. She met Ernest at a Christmas party, given by her Sunday School teacher, who was also Ernest's aunt. His mother was a Methodist and his father a Salvationist, but the whole family attended a Forward Movement Church of the Presbyterian Church of

Wales. He was a coachbuilder and wheelwright by trade and worked on horse-drawn carriages in his youth. Not surprisingly he suffered unemployment in the '20s and he and Irene had a difficult courtship, as she was caring for her widowed father. In 1927 Ernest got a job working on the repair of the bodywork of buses owned by South Wales Transport. He was always very left-wing in his politics and a strong union man: but his marriage to Irene and their strong affiliation with Methodism prevented his becoming a Communist. They felt that Donald Soper often articulated their own feelings.

Ernest had always wanted to teach. In 1930, he attended night school and obtained his City and Guilds Certificate, and when a Training Centre was set up in Swansea by the Department of Labour he was employed as an instructor in coach-body repair. However, after a few years the Centre was closed. This was a blow as Ernest and Irene now had two teenage sons, Geoffrey and Donald, who were doing very well at school. However, a Rehabilitation Centre was opening in Cardiff and Ernest became an instructor there.

During their first month in Penarth, they tried out both Albert Road and Trinity Churches. 'The Chapel Methodism' of Albert Road was more akin to their experience, and they thought the welcome there was the warmer. However, they found Percy Watkinson 'down to earth' and decided on Trinity as it was nearer to their house.

Both Geoffrey and Donald write that their parents really enjoyed their time in Trinity. The family threw themselves into the life of the Church for the seven years they were in the area, particularly into the Sunday School and Drama Group.

Ernest's over-riding ambition, which he shared with Glyn Marsh, was to remove the remaining name cards from the pews, which he felt were unworthy of the Church. To this end he supplied ammunition for sympathetic leaders to fire at their meetings. Both their sons went to University and one of their grandsons is an Anglican Clergyman. It was not until two years after he had moved to Birmingham to a new job that the cards were finally removed.

The Trust was renewed in 1956. Some younger and very able men were appointed, but no women, and selection continued to embody the middle class, almost professional, image that the Church, together with Penarth itself, was coming to reflect.

Despite reluctance to make changes on pew rents, the Trust Minutes do report requests that were acceded to. These included the conversion of the North Transept of the Church into a children's chapel, the upgrading of Trinity Hall, the provision of what were then considered modern 'Pel' steel and canvas chairs and the painting of the Hall – which was undertaken by the Scouts in 1956.

Percy Watkinson, as was Methodist practice, chaired the Trustees' Meetings as he did every other Trinity meeting. He was not a committee man: he disliked long discussions of policy or practice, and after about three-quarters of an hour assured the meeting that 'I know you all want to get home early so we won't be long.' Especially did he dread the item 'Any other business,' and he himself talked up to the time the meeting was expected to close, so that there would be no time for matters to be raised under that heading which he feared might be contentious, or even worse, hurtful.

The last of these meetings, the Leaders Meeting, was closer to the members of the Society, any of whom might find themselves appointed to it if they showed a desire for involvement. The Leaders Meeting consisted of the Society Stewards, the Stewards of the Poor Fund, representatives of the various groups in the Church, and elected members from the Annual Society Meeting. By courtesy, the local preachers whose membership was in Trinity were co-opted. It could thus be a large meeting. Many were women and there was a constant attempt to elect younger people from this period onwards.

This meeting had the responsibility, with the Minister, of running the Society. The Society Stewards had the oversight of Sunday worship, with the fearful responsibility for leading the service if the appointed preacher did not appear. The Poor or Communion Stewards had the responsibility for stewarding the Communion Services and, originally, for distributing the Poor Fund monies to those in need, a task which the Minister had by this time undertaken.

The Leaders' Meeting kept the membership figures of the Society under constant review. The existence of quarterly figures and membership details for the greater part of Percy Watkinson's ministry reveal his practice, which was similar to that followed by virtually all Methodist ministers. He pursued the policy, after removing the names of those who had died, of waiting until a number of new members were received and could be recorded, before removing from the membership roll the names of those who clearly had, for one reason or another, ceased to be members.

Through this system, a membership figure was returned each quarter which was remarkably close to the previous one. The total membership at Trinity, as returned for each quarter over the ten years of Percy Watkinson's Ministry, fluctuated between 243 and 260.

More generally, at Trinity the number of those in membership has moved between 240 and 350 for the years for which figures are available from 1930 to the present day. They show little decline and little advance, some ten or fifteen members up in one year and then down by a similar figure in the next. In British Methodism, three hundred seems to be the optimum number for any one Society.

The stability of the Trinity figure does not follow the pattern of the Methodist Church in Britain as a whole, which shows a loss of some 51,470 members over the fifty years from 1932 to 1982. This will include a loss of membership from churches in areas, such as the Welsh Valleys, which have experienced a dramatic decline in population over that period. Penarth, in contrast, has recorded a steep increase in population, so that the numbers at Trinity should have advanced each year since the 1900's. By 1990 the congregation should have been in the thousands – as perhaps it would be if in America.

A constant anxiety of the Leaders Meeting was whether the Sunday collections would enable the stewards to meet the quarterly assessments and perhaps, in addition, to help with any Trust debt that had accumulated. The Envelope System did not usually provide enough income and it was necessary to arrange 'efforts', which went by different names, to raise additional money.

The Leaders Meeting also made small benefactions, and these led to time-consuming discussions out of all proportion to the importance of the matter. The size, for example, of the contribution to Local Preachers' Mutual Aid was regularly debated at length. There was often little enough time to attend to the real business of the meeting: the needs of the Society and the pastoral oversight of its members.

Once a year, an Annual Society Meeting, which all members were entitled to attend, was held at which reports on the various activities of the Church were given, and elections of representatives to the Leaders Meeting were made. At the Annual Society Meeting in January 1954,

Percy Watkinson 'stressed the necessity of strengthening the family spirit among the members of the Church. In the spiritual and cultural fields there is everything in the life of Trinity to satisfy the spiritual hunger of young and old. We all must seek to offer these gifts to those about us.' He said that he was glad to see the increasing number of young people in the congregation and thanked all who had contributed to making the life and service of Trinity what it was.

Percy Watkinson leads prayers before a production of Henri Gheon's *The Comedian* in 1955.

The reference to 'cultural fields' was partly an allusion to the production of *Pride and Prejudice* adapted from the novel and with which the Watkinsons had been welcomed to Penarth in September 1951. With fifteen women's parts, some of them excellent, it was made to measure for the Trinity Drama Group. The company included many who were involved in Methodist life in the town and who had responsibilities within the Church: two were on the staff at Headlands and some seven were on the Leaders Meeting. Anne Evans, one of the group's best actresses, played Kitty, the fourth of the Bennet daughters.

She had just seven lines to speak, an illustration of the Group's policy of sharing leading roles between members and expecting those had played leading roles in one production to take small parts in others. After the production, Glyn Marsh who played Darcy and Richard Garrett, Bingley, were added to the Lectern Rota, but opportunities for women in this direction were still limited. Daphne Bryant was the first woman appointed to read a Lesson. Afterwards, an elderly Trustee said 'We don't want any more of that!'

*Let's make an Opera* by Benjamin Britten, 1954.

The Circuit Stewards continued to be concerned that the Manse was not altogether suitable. When bearing in mind his initial reaction to the house, they suggested to Percy Watkinson that perhaps they should be looking for a more modern manse, his response was 'Whatever for? What's wrong with this one?' Number One Victoria Avenue, 'Pagemont', had become his home and Trinity his Church. So protective was he of the latter that he found it difficult to allow any money to go elsewhere. In the Autumn of 1952, he suggested to the Leaders Meeting that the collection taken at the Christmas Morning Service should go to the Sunday School, instead of to the National

148

Children's Home as was the custom. Much as the leaders were predisposed to fall in with anything he suggested, in this instance he did not carry the day: the usual pattern was followed.

John and Sheila Gibbs during his Vice Presidential Year, 1958, with their five sons: John, James, William, Andrew and Simon.

In 1953 Sheila Gibbs was appointed as a Representative to Conference from the Cardiff and Swansea District. Percy Watkinson, also a Representative that year, impressed her with his Methodist 'savoir-faire'. She was a little shocked at how lightly he sat to the sessions, and his invitation to have coffee when she was zealously attending to every word. His knowledge of the ways of Methodism was shown when he said, with reference to the voting for President and Vice-President: 'We must get John's name on the Vice-Presidential list, you know.' John Gibbs' name did indeed appear on the list in 1953, and in the years which followed moved up steadily as more and more people voted for him. It looked likely that he would be nominated in 1956 at the age of 45, but just before the ballot Philip Race, an even younger representative from Lincoln, made a brilliant speech on Methodist finances, 'Taking the Collection: Where?' This lifted him to first place, and it was not until the following year that John Gibbs was designated.

He served as Vice-President, the highest office in the Methodist Church open to the laity, in 1958.

At the Leaders Meeting on 1 March 1954, Percy Watkinson announced that he was to exchange his pastoral responsibilities for six weeks with the Rev'd Jack G. Moody of Mount Vernon, Ohio. Such British – American exchanges were becoming possible with the return to normal everyday life in Britain, and offered a revelation of the similarities and differences between two traditions owing their origins to one founder, John Wesley. Following the American War of Independence, American Methodism had gone its own way.

Percy and Eileen Watkinson, Peter and Mary experienced as much as they could of American life at a time when crossing the Atlantic was still a comparatively rare experience. The Manse in Ohio was comfortable and full of labour saving devices. Percy Watkinson's preaching was a revelation to his temporary congregation, one which filled the Church completely and reminded him of his time at Adelaide Street, Blackpool in the late 1940's.

Each minister returned home with new ideas. Percy Watkinson introduced weekly, cyclostyled news-sheets to Trinity which removed the need for announcing the total of the previous week's collection and the reading of notices for the subsequent week.

Jack and Maureen Moody revelled in the warm welcome they received and were delighted by the countryside, the narrow country roads and by the gypsy encampment, with traditional painted caravans, then established beside the Cardiff – Penarth Road.

They were the first American Methodists to make an exchange of their pastorate and their 'parsonage' with a minister in Wales. They found life in Britain 'difficult and drab' and were amazed at the simple fittings in the kitchen and scullery in the Manse. They were momentarily depressed by the small number of cars outside the Church, when they went to Trinity for their first Service. But, inside, there was a splendid congregation, and they were very impressed by what they felt to be the spiritual depth of British Methodism. This they compared favourably with church life in Ohio where Methodism was the largest denomination, with some dilution of commitment which that usually implied.

The 6th Penarth Scouts in Camp at Llangynidr 1954: Brian Lea, Peter Timney, Richard Tarn, Donald James with Maureen and Jack Moody.

As with Percy Watkinson in America, so Jack Moody held the Trinity congregation by the depth and concern of his preaching, helped by his enthralling accent, which sounded very like that of a western movie hero. The Moodies were surprised to find that it was not a popular thing to be a Christian in Britain and amazed when one of the Trinity members was rejoicing because a Christian was coming to his Department at the University, as there were only three other Christians on the faculty. This was in considerable contrast to the position in the States where churchgoers numbered about 40% of the population.

Trinity Drama Group also benefited from the cross-fertilization of ideas brought about by the American exchange. Jack and Maureen Moody suggested a Christmas play in the porch such as they had produced at their Church in Ohio. The Drama Group produced this on the evenings leading up to Christmas in 1955. A tape recording of appropriate readings and carols was made and there was a continuous cycle of a series of tableaux: shepherds, nativity, kings. In Ohio, one of the shepherds had fainted with the cold, but fortunately the weather in Wales was not so bleak. The *Play in the Porch* was repeated for a' number of years in its commanding site and was only brought to an end when more and more of Trinity young men were employed in delivering the Christmas post, and as a result, were unavailable.

The Junior Church Department of Trinity Sunday School with the American Exchange Minister, the Rev'd Jack Moody preaching in 1954.

Among other plays, the Group put on a memorable production of Maurice Maeterlink's *The Blue Bird* in 1955. This had a cast of eighty-three from six years upwards and a percussion orchestra from Headlands School, numbering thirteen. So many children were involved that when they were not acting they were entertained back-stage by Ian James, son of Donald James, who later became a member of the Magic Circle. One memorable night there was a snow storm: all the members of the cast turned up, but on this occasion they outnumbered the audience.

The Youth Club grew and was flourishing when, in 1955, Frank Dewar's work took him from the town and Michael Nance took over the leadership. As a young club member in 1949, Michael Nance and Esme Bryant had attended the MAYC London Week-end.

Michael Nance's grand-father had come to South Wales from Cornwall in the 1850's, bringing his knowledge of tin mining to the booming coal industry. The family had strong links with Methodism – ancestors having been converted by John Wesley[2] and Michael Nance led the Club until 1958, when the time came for him, too, to leave Penarth.

It is the norm for a church which nurtures its young members to see them move away because of their work. However, Trinity also benefited from moves made in the other direction: for example, Bert Scriven had returned to Penarth, and, on 13 June 1946, married Audrey Marsh. They settled in the town, where Bert practised as a commercial artist, and became more and more involved in Trinity, beginning with the Rover Scouts and the Drama Group. He writes:

> I didn't become a member of the Methodist Church until the Ministry of Percy Watkinson, who was a great influence and encouragement to me. He held regular church membership classes on Sunday afternoons. I joined the Sunday school staff also in the early 1950's and taught in the Junior Department under the leadership of Jean Good. I joined the Club as an Assistant Leader. I took over the leadership in 1958 until my retirement in 1969. Those were ten happy and eventful years when we enjoyed a thriving membership of 100 plus with a waiting list of many more.

Bert lists some of the former Club members, who include a nuclear scientist working in the USA, a high ranking member of staff on _The Times_, a producer and lecturer in sound broadcasting with the BBC, and, locally, a mayor of Penarth. There were many others who took their places in the life of the Church and the community. The Trinity Youth Club was regarded as a youth movement in the town where exciting things happened. Bert Scriven again:

> During the ten years we attended the MAYC Weekend every year and performed the final religious mime in the arena of the Albert hall on three occasions. We produced numerous club revues, where our dramatic heritage, nurtured on Friday nights, was fully exploited, entering plays for the Local Authority and MAYC Drama Festivals, and took an active part in sporting and social events sponsored by the District MAYC and Welsh Association of Youth Clubs. We raised many thousands of pounds for the church overseas and for other charitable causes.

Bert's leadership of the Trinity Club was recognised in South Wales and by the whole Connexion. It made Trinity a leading Youth Club in the 1950's and 1960's.

Evelyn and George Knighton's two children, Mary and Donald, have already been mentioned and quoted. Neither reacted against their deeply Methodist home life which was loving and liberal. In the chapter on Robert Hingley's Ministry at Trinity there was an account of how Donald and Mary Knighton and June Marsh had made a commitment to Christ. Donald was then ten years old, and Robert Hingley encouraged him to read widely and lent him books, sometimes, such as Thomas Carlyle's *History of the French Revolution*, well in advance of his years. After a period at Penarth County School, Donald won a scholarship to Kingswood School. He started there in 1945, and his links with Trinity Church and Drama Group were limited to the school holidays. He left school in 1945 and, after doing a shortened period of National Service, took up a scholarship to read history at Oxford. Peter Watkinson, his minister's son, led the Methodist Group of which he became a member.

Anne Evans was born in 1934 into a family which she was always proud to claim was absolutely Welsh. Her father, a miner, had been deprived of work during a lock-out in the 1920's and became a deep-sea trawlerman. He died when she was ten, and Anne and her two older brothers were brought up by their mother, a nurse, greatly in demand in both medical and pastoral roles. She worked very hard to educate her three very able children.

The Evans family first lived in John Street at the top end of Penarth and attended Albert Road Church. When they moved to Grove Place they attended Trinity, largely on account of Anne's involvement with the Drama Group. Anne made a full contribution to the life of her Church: Sunday School teacher, Guide Leader and, later, Youth Club Leader. After leaving the County School, she went, with her close friend Mary Watkinson, to the Cardiff College of Domestic Arts, to take a three year education course in Home Economics.

While at Oxford, Donald had become a local preacher. After graduating, he took a job with the Ministry of Labour in Swansea and worked there for three years, but he was increasingly drawn to the Methodist Ministry. While working in Swansea, he returned to Penarth every week-end, where he taught in the Sunday School and where his friendship with Anne developed. In July 1958, they became engaged, and in the same year he was accepted for the ministry. He began a two-year BA in theology at Wesley House, Cambridge while she remained in Penarth.

During his time as a probationer, he and Anne were, in accordance with Methodist practice at the time, unable to marry. It was not until 23 July 1960 that Percy Watkinson, who had given them great encouragement during his whole ministry and who was then in his last year at Trinity, officiated at their wedding.

The Wedding of Anne Evans and Donald Knighton at Trinity, 23 July 1960.
Donald and Anne Knighton, Henry Rack, Mary Parr, Evelyn and George Knighton, Annie Evans with William Evans.

In September Donald and Anne Knighton moved to Birmingham and Donald's first circuit. From that time their contact with Penarth grew less: they were 'released' into wider Methodism and, eventually, into the World Church.

Percy Watkinson had intended to become a supernumerary minister after his ninth year, but he had his eye on a young minister, Deryck Collingwood, at that time in Handsworth, Birmingham, who he wanted to succeed him. Since Deryck Collingwood would not be free until 1961, Percy Watkinson offered to remain in Penarth for an extra year.

He had brought into membership, while he had been minister, a number of young families, amongst them the Ponsfords and the Harold Williamses, but he left it to his successor to enfold them more deeply in the work of the Church feeling that a younger man would do this more successfully.    Characteristically, although he received fifteen new young members just before he left, he did not put them on the Membership Roll: he let his successor have the satisfaction of doing that.

On leaving Trinity, he moved even further south, to Bournemouth, for retirement in an area somewhat over-populated by Methodists.    Peter Watkinson, who went on to become headmaster of Rydal, wrote later that his father looked back on his ten years at Trinity as the happiest ministry of his life.

# CHAPTER 15

## The Anglican Methodist Conversations:
## An Ecumenical Encounter

The British Council of Churches came into existence in 1942 and local Councils of Churches had sprung up and become active in parts of England at that time. It was not until 1962 that, in Penarth, the Christian Council, later the Council of Churches, was formed as a meeting place for the Churches in the town. Up until then the Church in Wales and the Free Churches had little common ground on which they could meet, and the initiative of Geoffrey Fisher in his Cambridge Sermon of 1946 to the Free Churches to 'take episcopacy into their systems' sounded as a note from a far away place which had little reference to the church life of the Welsh seaside town.

However, the Methodist Conference, after some hesitation and having cleared their response with the other Free Churches, decided to take the matter further. Their organisation and history made them the Church most likely to succeed in the undertaking: they stipulated that liberty of interpretation of Episcopacy was maintained and that their relations with the other Free Churches were not disrupted. Precedents had already been set, notably in India. The Methodist Church was a member of the Church of South India, which had already achieved a union between Anglicans, Methodists and Presbyterians.

In 1955, the Methodist Conference accepted the Anglican invitation and the Conversations began between twelve ministerial and lay members of both Churches. The Commission came fairly soon to the conclusion that intercommunion – the goal set by the Cambridge Sermon – was not satisfactory in itself, but should be regarded only as a first stage on the way to organic union. So it formulated the idea of union in two stages, and the main thrust of the debates was how to bring about Stage One. Not much was said about the second stage of unity, organic union, on the ground that it was too early to be specific, but practical problems which would arise once the first stage was inaugurated were dealt with in a preliminary way.

As the Church in Wales is a separate Church from the Church of England a panel was set up in 1963 of eighteen members of the Church in Wales and eighteen members largely from the Methodist Districts in Wales to consider the Scheme with reference to its application to the

Principality.   On the Methodist side this was led by Dr. Maldwyn Edwards and John Gibbs was one of its lay members.  The Welsh Joint Panel met on three occasions and in 1965 published a set of papers generally favourable to the Scheme.

The main Commission had presented its full report in 1963 and it was endorsed in principle by both Churches with overwhelming majorities. The Methodist Conference sent it down to the Synods and Quarterly Meetings for study and discussion.

The main recommendation included the proposal that Methodism should accept Episcopacy into its system and that there should be a Service of Reconciliation at which the ministers of each Church would be commissioned by representatives of the other.  After that, ministers of each Church would be entitled to conduct services and administer the Sacrament of Holy Communion in both Anglican and Methodist Churches and lay members of each Church would be able to share in the Sacrament of Holy Communion in both Anglican and Methodist Churches.  This would be known as Stage I.  Stage II would be the actual uniting of the two Churches.  This might not take place for some years, but it was to be understood that when either Church accepted Stage I it would be with the determination to find means to proceed to Stage II.

The Service of Reconciliation was to be visually symbolic: the Methodist ministers would kneel before the Archbishop of Canterbury and other clergy and receive a 'laying on of hands with prayer'.  The action was to be accompanied by a prayer that each according to his need 'might receive the Spirit'.  Then the Archbishop and Anglican priests would kneel before the Methodist ministers and receive their laying on of hands, and the Methodists would pray in the same words for them.   After the Service, the bishops would consecrate some Methodists as Bishops and all future Methodist ministers would be ordained by bishops.

In a speech to the Conference of the Canterbury Diocese in October 1968 Archbishop Ramsey movingly set out his thinking on what would 'happen' in the Service of Reconciliation and that, by it, his Ministry would have new significance and authority.[1]

All the Anglican members of the Commission signed the 1963 report but only nine of the Methodist members.  The three who did not sign were led by Dr. Kingsley Barrett, whose opposition was based on a

New Testament interpretation of the Church, on his objection to episcopacy and on an interpretation of the Service of Reconciliation as an 'ordination'. Certainly all agreed that the Service contained an ambiguity, and once the word ambiguity had been thrown into the arena a suspicion of disingenuity was introduced. This was illogical and unfair because not all ambiguity is evil, but only the ambiguity that is intended to deceive. John Gibbs remembers that when this very point came up in the discussions in Wales he drew on his psychological training and pointed out that all understanding is subjective; we all 'see' things in different ways and no single interpretation of what is happening or what something means can have final significance. In the Anglican–Methodist Scheme it was openly stated that the words said at the laying on of hands would be taken by some to mean ordination and by others, emphatically, not to mean that. Members of the two Churches were encouraged to discuss the Scheme, and to get to know each other and each others'standpoint. In most cases, members had only the vaguest idea of the theological stance of the other Church – and most of their ideas were based on folk memories: these included tales of the overweening bishop and of uncouth dissenters.

The Penarth Circuit invited the Rector of St. Augustine's, the Rev. Grosvenor Stephens, and members of his Church Council to be present at the Circuit Quarterly Meeting on the 4th March 1964. A taped address by Dr. Maldwyn Edwards was played at the end of the normal business. The Rector, who had been the first chairman of the Penarth Council of Churches and was consequently used to ecumenical encounters, expressed his confidence that; 'the two Churches would be in full communion by 1967, the fact that the Church in Wales was already disestablished would help the move towards union; the basis of real union is local fellowship and integration', and he was confident that 'the idea can be put through without difficulty'.

His successor, the Rev'd Norman Griffiths, was neither so sanguine nor so well informed. He invited Shëila Gibbs to speak to his women's meeting, but it became clear that he was extremely unclear as to who these Methodists actually were. This was largely the case through Wales, except for those Anglicans who had worked beside Methodists in the larger centres of population. In rural Wales the only Methodists the Anglicans knew were the Calvinistic Methodists – the Presbyterian Church in Wales. At the first meeting of the Welsh Panel, John Gibbs had to explain to one of the Anglican laymen on the Commission, T. I. Ellis, that it was the Methodist Church with whom he was conversing and that his diligent preparation in reading up about Howell

159

Harris, the founder of the Calvinistic Methodists, was not strictly relevant.

In 1965, the Convocations of the Anglican Church in England and the Methodist Conference tested the feelings and opinions of the local Churches. Two Questions were sent down to the Circuit Meetings for debate:

1. Do you desire closer relations with the Church of England?
2. Do you consider that in broad outline the main proposals of the report point the right way forward to full communion between the Church of England and the Methodist Church?

The Penarth Circuit met on the 10th March in Albert Road Church. The first question was considered and unanimously approved by the sixty-seven members present.

To the second, three amendments were proposed. The first came from the Dinas Powis Leaders Meeting and looked to two differences of practice, with which the Scheme, being one of union and not uniformity, would not be concerned. With reference to the Holy Communion, the amendment required that the principle of the Open Table should be safeguarded with respect to regularly communicating adherents and that non-alcoholic wine should be allowed in the celebration. This, although strictly not relevant on this occasion, was passed with sixty-three in favour and four against.

The second amendment, proposed by J. T. Wells, was a direct negation of the motion with the alternative that a permanent negotiating committee be established to examine the various objections and suggestions that had been made, with a view to action when a substantial measure of agreement had been reached. This was defeated, with fourteen in favour, fifty against and three abstentions.

The third amendment, proposed by two other Local Preachers, was that the Conversations should be broadened to include other Nonconformist Churches, and went on to claim that Anglican insistence on the retention of the Thirty-Nine Articles, the closed Communion Table, Episcopacy and the opposition to Disestablishment would hinder larger unity. Here clearly were serious misunderstandings. Since 1865, only general assent to the Thirty-Nine Articles had been required within the Anglican Church. The closed nature of the Table was a matter of Anglican discipline, Methodism generally had never renounced

Episcopacy and the Anglican Church in Wales was itself disestablished. Three voted in favour, sixty-one against and there were, once again, three abstentions. The first and the third amendments revealed the depth of misunderstanding at large at the time.

When the substantive motion was put, the result was fifty-seven in favour, six against and four abstentions. The majority was over 83% – which compared with an average vote throughout Britain of 55% in the Quarterly Meetings. The larger issue of a uniting Christendom took precedence over narrower considerations.

In order to produce an informed vote at Conference in 1969, there were numerous gatherings of Anglicans and Methodists throughout the Principality, parallelling those in England. A Day of Fellowship, held on neutral ground – Windsor Place Presbyterian Church in Cardiff – on 24th March 1966, was addressed by Dr. Maldwyn Edwards and Eric Roberts, the Arch Deacon of Margam, later to be Bishop of St. David's.

A week-end residential conference was held at Coleg-y-Fro towards the end of November 1969, which was attended from Trinity by Joyce Wells, Howard Ponsford, and Sheila and John Gibbs. Once again Dr. Maldwyn Edwards spoke in his inimitable way on John Wesley and the Dean of Brecon spoke on the Church in Wales. The Dean showed clearly the traumatic experience that disestablishment had been in 1922 and how the Church in Wales had turned to its Celtic Christian heritage as a result. Pauline Webb, a formidable Methodist Laywoman and a 'revelation' to the Anglicans, looked to the future: 'A New Church, Coffin or Cradle?'. For the Methodists in Wales, the prospect of becoming part of a Welsh Church, greater certainly than the present Church in Wales, but undoubtedly Welsh presented itself in all its starkness for the first time. We were forced to realise that we might lose our direct connection with the British Conference, the cross-fertilization of our ministries with British Methodism and our links with Methodism world-wide, indeed, our 'connexionalism'.

On the 8th July 1969, the Anglican Convocation at Church House, Westminster, and the Methodist Conference meeting in Birmingham, debated the issue, by arrangement, on the same day. The Conference easily cleared the 75% hurdle, which, in accordance with the Anglican arrangement, it had accepted as necessary. The Convocation, in spite of support from both Archbishops and of a large majority of bishops, reached only 69%. Of the three Houses, the lower House of Clergy produced the smallest vote in favour. An alliance between Anglo-

Catholics and Evangelicals had torpedoed the Scheme – as it did the second attempt in 1972.  But the issue had come to a fairly close vote and if only a comparatively few opponents of the Scheme, or of those in the middle had voted otherwise, the whole course of Church history would have been changed.

Sheila Gibbs was a member of the Methodist Conference.  She wrote of the events of 8th July:

> All day we sought to know God's will.  All day we listened to speeches for and against the Scheme.  One thing was apparent: everyone spoke in favour of Unity, everyone wanted Unity, the question was whether this was the way to achieve it.
>
> The whole day was steeped in prayer, and we spent from 6.30.p.m. to 7.00.p.m. in guided silent prayer.  At 7.00 o'clock the ballot was taken and at the same time Convocation voted at Westminster.
>
> In ten minutes the result of the Methodist vote was announced: 77% in favour of the scheme, 23% against.  There was absolute silence and a deep upsurge of feeling for those who had voted with the minority, a desire to enfold them in love and fellowship.
>
> Then came the announcement of the Anglican vote: 69% in favour.  It had been decided only to proceed to Stage 1 if both Churches achieved a 75% majority.  The Anglicans had diligently sought to know the Will of God too.  How could He answer Yes to one, and No to the other?
>
> The next morning I felt I knew why.  We were not to be torn in two: one taken and the other left.  In caring we must go forward to the Unity we all seek, to real oneness.

The Governing Body of the Church in Wales did not vote until September 1969.  The voting was 293 in favour and 104 against, a majority of just over 72%.  Even if a 75% majority had been achieved it was almost unthinkable that Wales could and would have gone ahead unilaterally; the Provinces of England and Wales being closely bound together doctrinally.

If the Scheme had been approved the effects on the Methodist people in Wales would have been far reaching.  The discussions they had had with the Church in Wales had never touched on the particular problems that Methodists in Wales would have to face. How would it be possible to avoid a virtual cutting off from English Methodism, the severing of the links with Westminster and Manchester – often grumbled about, but nevertheless deeply valued – how to adjust to moving, perhaps withdrawing, into a nation-based Church with defined boundaries? How to be loyal to John Wesley: 'I look on the whole world as my Parish'?

It might be that the uniting of the Anglican and Methodist Churches would have great advantages as each brought their particular gifts to the new Church, but it would be very hard for the small Methodist element in Wales to make a worthy and visible contribution to this.

The relationship between the two Methodist Churches in Penarth and their two neighbouring Anglican Churches would have been thrown into the melting pot. Would it be proper for a United Church to maintain six properties, two Methodist and four Anglican in close proximity? Would Trinity feel that it was proper to spend large sums on repairing its premises if, within three hundred yards, there was another Church with which it was united?

The vote on the 8th July, 1969 postponed for the foreseeable future, the need for the members of Trinity to agonize over this particular issue.

The Rev'd Eric Baker had said that Methodism might have to die denominationally so that it might rise ecumenically, and the Methodist Conference had indicated that the Methodist people were prepared for this to happen: but this was not yet to be required of them.

Archbishop Ramsey was devastated with the result of his Churches' vote. Two days after the debate, the Lord Mayor of London entertained the bishops to dinner at the Mansion House. Ramsey took advantage of the occasion to speak frankly:

> It is not the first time that the Methodists have been the leaders of Christianity in this country. . . . In these latter years we Anglicans have liked to think of ourselves as being the leaders in the matter of Christian Unity. But at the moment we are not; it is the Methodists who are the leaders now.

163

# CHAPTER 16

## The Rev'd. Deryck Collingwood 1961 - 1969

Deryck and Dilys Collingwood, together with their four children, Linda, Nigel, Gillian and Deryck, were delighted with Pagemont, 1 Victoria Avenue, when they arrived in August 1961. It was roomy and the family decided that the 'closed-off' top-storey was ideal for a club room. It soon became an out-station of Trinity as the children decorated it with Beatles posters and, most evenings, filled it with their friends and contemporary music.

Deryck Collingwood had been born in Burma where his father was in business. On his father's side the family were traditional Anglicans, but his mother's family were Huguenot refugees and had later come under the influence of the Wesleys in Lincolnshire. In consequence, with his brother John, Deryck was sent to Wycliffe College in Gloucestershire – then a Methodist School. He was converted during an evening service in the School Chapel and at sixteen became a local preacher. In his final year he was head prefect and then moved from Gloucestershire to Leeds, where he was a student at Headingley from 1936 to 1940.

After serving in Retford, Barnsley, Leicester and Birmingham, he was forty-five when he took up his appointment at Trinity – the perfect age in the estimation of the Circuit Stewards. Because of his wide experience before arriving in Penarth and the distinction of his ministry, it was only too possible that he would be 'lifted out' for a connexional appointment – as Stanley Dixon had been. Trinity was spared this and Deryck Collingwood remained for eight years. Later the almost inevitable happened and he was made the Chairman of a district – the London North East District as it happened, one of the most taxing appointments in Methodism.

A description of his ministry is made easier in one sense because the Trinity Magazine, *Contact*, is available for the whole of the period, but more difficult as there is a plethora of news and views from which to select. Deryck Collingwood contributed an article to almost every issue of the magazine and used it as a platform on which to set out his concept of Trinity as an 'Open' Church. He wrote:

> The 'Open Church', the brilliant Vatican report of the struggle to open the Church to the modern world by Michael Novek (1962),

made a deep impression on me. Also a remarkable S.C.M. paperback *Pro-Existence* issued by the East German Churches around the same time which argued for outlasting Communism rather than dying under it. But the Open concept for me came first from Bonhoeffer, and from the gathering war-time Ecumenical Movement.

Whilst all Churches in the town are, of course, open to visitors, Deryck Collingwood saw Trinity as open for membership to all Christians and 'seekers' whatever their views. He felt that Trinity should express John Wesley's teaching as set out in his Sermon on the Catholic Spirit: 'Is thine heart right as my heart? Then give me your hand', not 'be of my opinion,' or even 'embrace my mode of worship,' but work with and along side of me; in Charles Wesley's words 'Serving the present age.'

This approach was to speak to two families already mentioned, amongst a number of others, all of whom were looking for a church in Penarth which could meet their aspirations and the needs of their young families. Harold and Margaret Williams had come from Edmonton, Canada, in 1950. Although born and brought up in Canada, Harold was the grandson of Mary Ann Morgan, Mrs Lewis Williams, who had brought Methodism to Penarth. Initially, Harold and Margaret came for a year to Wales, but they stayed on as Harold became Chairman of the family firm of John Williams of Cardiff. Their two daughters were born in Penarth.

Howard and Olive Ponsford are third generation Salvationists, and Olive's grandmother was in charge of the Penarth Corps in the 1880's. The family began to become involved in the life of Trinity during 1960 – the last year of the Rev'd. Percy Watkinson's ministry. Olive, who had had considerable experience of drama in her work with the Salvation Army, was attracted to the Church through work on a production of *Toad of Toad Hall.*. She joined the sewing group and her two daughters became part of the chorus. Howard, who had been a conductor of various musical groups, was asked to help with the children's chorus. After the play had completed its run, Deryck Collingwood asked the children to sing in Church on parade services. Thus the Junior Choir came into being and sang hymns adapted for their age group for many years.

These two families became deeply involved in the life of Trinity. Harold Williams was soon invited to become a Poor Steward, a post which carried a seat on the Leaders Meeting, and Howard and Olive

Trinity Choir and Drama Group present E. Martin Browne's *The Story of Christmas in Mime* in the Church, 1962.

Ponsford committed their outstanding musical gifts to the Choir and Drama Group. Shortly after forming the Junior Choir, Howard Ponsford became the choir master for the whole choir.

Deryck Collingwood visited widely throughout the town during the week and reckoned to call on every church member at least once a quarter. His close contact with his people and his knowledge of them meant that after two years he found it possible to carry the Leaders Meeting with him on almost any issue. When he said: 'I know you want to do the right thing', it was difficult to resist his suggestions.

One of his first acts was, with the help of the chapel steward of the day, to remove the names from the pews. By this time, only three people were paying pew rent and he discussed his proposal with each of them before he took any action. All were entirely in agreement with him.[1]

There was scarcely a facet of life at Trinity that was not affected during Deryck Collingwood's ministry. The changes were most easily seen in the structure of the Church premises: the Trinity Hall area was redesigned, the stage and the floor in the Hall were relaid, classrooms were demolished to provide space for lavatories and a foyer. The narrow entrance from Woodland Place, through which prams and pushchairs were negotiated only with the greatest difficulty, was enlarged and an entrance hall created.

But there were also other changes which were equally important though less immediately striking. For example an office was established with voluntary helpers to handle the much increased paper work which kept the congregation, and the town, informed of developments. The Trust was renewed, this time with four women members and Arthur Hosegood, after reading in the *Methodist Recorder* that people held on to office for far too long, retired from the Secretaryship – a post he had held for forty-two years.

Arthur Hosegood had made two visible contributions to worship in the Church: the Cross and the illumination of the East Window. In 1949, he had wanted to give a silver Cross for the Communion table in memory of his wife, Katherine Frances. He approached his fellow Trustees in the proper way, and although the Church, in company with most other Methodist churches at that time, had not had a Cross on the Table his gift was accepted, the more easily, no doubt, because of the respect in which he was held by the Society.[2] The presence of the school-building had prevented light reaching the East Window, and from 1962 on, encouraged by Arthur Hosegood, various attempts were made to ensure that a system of artificial illumination compensated for this. It was not until 1989 that an adequate system was devised.

The Trustees tidied up some matters which had been unresolved for many years. Pagemont, 1 Victoria Avenue, became the property of the Circuit in 1963. A realistic scale of charges for letting various parts of the premises was fixed. 'Outside' bookings, such as sales in aid of the Cheshire Homes, were sanctioned. Smoking, previously permitted throughout the whole of the ancillary premises was restricted to certain areas. A coffee bar was created on the balcony in Trinity Hall, and a 10.00 pm closing time for the church premises was fixed, with the possibility of extensions if previously arranged with the chapel keeper.

There were a number of changes in the pattern of worship and the experience of visiting Trinity. For example, the morning Service was moved to 10.30, and a rota of 'hostesses' – later to include men – was arranged to ensure that visitors attending services were welcomed in the porch. A verger's gown was purchased for the chapel keeper to wear at weddings and funerals. At some evening services, a table was placed in the chancel so that the minister could celebrate from the eastward position and face the congregation. Communicants moved forward and stood in a circle. However not all new proposals were implemented: the possibility of removing the choir stalls and of moving the organ console to the south transept so that the chancel area could be redesigned was considered, but no alterations were made. There were distinctive changes in the appearance of the choir. The women members wore red gowns with white jabots – made by the Drama Group, and later, after some resistance, the men were provided with blue gowns. Percy Watkinson was the last Trinity minister to wear a suit and dog-collar when preaching: the Ministers who followed him wore either black or grey cassocks, with Geneva bands.

In 1963 the Sunday School became Junior Church, and met, not at 3.00 pm as previously, but at 10.30 so as to coincide with the Morning Service. There were two main reasons for this: firstly to link the Sunday School more closely with the life and worship of the Church so that the children felt part of the Church – not members of an organisation that happened to meet on church premises, and, secondly, to encourage families to worship together. The established practice was for fathers to drop the younger children outside the Woodland Place entrance to Woodland Hall at 3.00 pm and to collect them at 4.00 pm. Bringing the Sunday School and Morning Worship together meant that

168

Remembrance Sunday 1962. Deryck Collingwood places the wreath on the Trinity War Memorial after the Service.

there was, at least, nothing to stop families worshipping together. The arrangement whereby the children sat, if they wished, with their friends in the front pews and in the south aisle and transept meant that there was a considerable and visible Junior Church presence for part of each service.

Two practical considerations affected this rearrangement. Sunday school teachers were increasingly loath to give up their Sunday afternoons to take Sunday School classes, and, linked with this, there was the general secularization of Sunday. Church families wanted to do things together on Sunday afternoons, and an increasing variety of family activities was available to them.

The pattern which evolved was one in which the Junior Church members worshipped with the rest of the congregation for the first twenty minutes or so of the service and then left to continue their worship and learning in groups with others of their own age. A disadvantage of this system was that Junior Church teachers were denied the opportunity of joining in the full service of morning worship, except when there were enough teachers to share the teaching. Some adult members of the congregation might regret the sight of empty pews after the children had left, but, on reflection, they would probably have accepted that needs are best met in different ways at different ages. There were, in any case, exceptions, for example at Parade Services, the older children remained for the full Service, which usually took their presence into consideration. On Communion Sundays a number of the children might return for the final act of the Service.

In the process of changing from Sunday School to Junior Church, from afternoon to morning provision for children, a number of children severed links with the Church. This was, of course, a pity. However, one has to ask how long the numbers would have kept up in an afternoon school, and to note that gradually many families began worshipping together. The Church could be seen to be the whole People of God.

During the whole of Deryck Collingwood's ministry the Drama Group and the Youth Club continued to thrive. An occasion on which they pooled their resources in a circuit presentation which made a contribution on the national scene was described by Kelvyn Johns for *Contact*. The following appeared in July 1965.

Twenty years ago the first M.A.Y.C. London Weekend took place. This year the Youth Clubs of Trinity, Albert Road and Dinas Powis Methodist Churches had the honour of presenting *The Thirty Eight Witnesses* by James Gibbs as the final mime in the display at the Albert Hall. The final mime has always been regarded as one of the main events of the weekend.

At 5.00 p.m. on Friday, 28th, two coachloads of Club members left Penarth, and six hours later arrived at Queensbury Methodist Church. After a late supper several members went off to spend the night in the homes of church members but most slept on the premises.

Early the following morning, the coaches took them to the Albert Hall for the final dress rehearsal, where considerable practice was necessary in carrying on and erecting the set. This made it impossible for the performers to attend the M.A.Y.C. Congress at the Central Hall, Westminster, where the Rev. Tom Davies, of Cwmbran, was inducted as National President for 1965-66. At this Congress Angela Scriven captivated the assembly with a speech on the proposed union with the Anglicans.

In the afternoon or evening those at the Congress were able to witness the Albert Hall display. On the whole this was excellent, although one or two items were a trifle unsatisfactory. Very impressive was the item where cyclists with fairy lights rode around a darkened arena; similarly a beat group proved very popular. On the other hand a parody of the election of a Welsh M.A.Y.C. president, though amusing in places, was too long and relied too much on traditional Anglo-Saxon images of the Welsh. A surprise guest was the redoubtable David Frost.

Lastly came the *Thirty Eight Witnesses*. Over a darkened arena a voice with an American accent – actually it was James Gibbs – began to tell the story. Before the eyes of the audience on rushed the stage crew with the 'houses' and then disappeared in seconds. Janice Baker, the murder victim, and Philip Newman, the murderer, were most accomplished and the others, witnesses, police and stage crew, filled the parts satisfactorily. The effect on the audience was wonderful. They were absolutely silent, although previously they had tended to applaud at the wrong times.

On Sunday everyone went to the Albert Hall again for the annual service, which is the focal point of the whole weekend. It was conducted by the new president, the Rev. Tom Davies, and following well chosen hymns and readings, his sermon stirred the congregation deeply. A collection was taken to raise £600 for two Sterilization Units for the Ivory Coast Hospital. A total of £1000 was reached.

After the Service members of the three Clubs lunched at various restaurants near Marble Arch and then departed homeward in the buses, spending an hour at Hampton Court on the way.

Trinity Youth Club, 1963.

*The Thirty Eight Witnesses* was based on an incident which occurred in New York: a murder witnessed by thirty-eight ordinary people none of whom was prepared to be involved even to the extent of calling the police. The closing prayer attempted to provide a Christian response:

> O God help us to recognise our neighbour when we see him whether he be in the Ivory Coast, in New York or in the street where we live. May we be ready to serve him even at the expense of our comfort, our ambition or our reputation. Help us to get involved in the name of Jesus Christ, our Lord, who became involved for our sakes. Amen.

The 1960's were the heyday of Methodist Youth Clubs. The Trinity Club had not only a very able leader but also a number of assistant leaders, and it was fed by a well-led and well supported Junior Club.

Trinity Youth Club: Members' Committee, 1964.

In 1970, however, Neil Thomas, a member of the Chivers family and the Club's new leader, wrote in *Contact* of a perceptible decline in commitment and numbers as the decade progressed. He looked back to the beginning in 1956 when 'all the members came together on

173

Tuesday, Saturday and Sunday evenings when the privilege of being a member of M.A.Y.C. was appreciated and when happy days and gay times demanded an extra effort and commitment.' He reported that: 'By 1969 the regular attendance had dropped to about fifteen members who were growing older together.' By this time the South Glamorgan County Youth Service had started a fully-equipped and staffed Youth Centre at Stanwell School which could offer an attractive alternative to Trinity – without requiring such commitment as a church-centred club required.

Philip Newman, who was to take over the Club on Neil Thomas's retirement, painted much the same picture. He did not feel that the members of Trinity were as prepared as those in the 1950's and 1960's to involve themselves as helpers in the Club and that the membership itself seemed to be changing. Recreation was becoming individualised: square dancing and barn-dancing had been replaced by dances which involved no set moves and little or no physical contact. Self-expression was all important. The enthusiasm for shared creative effort was being replaced by the 'personalised' entertainment which became the growth industries of the late eighties: computer games and video hire. The local comprehensive schools, too, were providing many of the activities previously the province of the voluntary youth clubs.

During the 1960's there were, however, many opportunities at a national and international level for young people to attend conferences and to travel. *Contact* is full of reports of young people going to Italy, and Greece, or to Taize in France, of attending conferences of European Methodist Youth, the Young Adults Assembly, Youth Missionary Conferences and the British Conference of Christian Youth at Leicester.

A keen group of young people, ecumenical in membership, but based at Trinity and known as 'The Diggers', organised a number of week-end conferences at Llangynidr, reviving a pattern which had been familiar to a previous generation.

Since its formation in 1945, the Young Wives Group had arranged some good interchurch garden parties, including one at which Mrs Rosamond Fisher, the wife of the Archbishop of Canterbury, spoke. Conscious that they were growing older, several of the group whose children had grown up, filled the role of 'childminders' for the Young Mothers' Group which was started in the 1960's. Sheila Gibbs wrote a nativity play for this group – with an all female cast. This was later developed and published under the title *Blessed Among Women: a Play for Christmas and Easter.*

The Women's Hour continued, now under the Presidency of Dilys Collingwood. The Minister was a firm believer in the soundness of the judgement of members of the Women's Hour and used some of the redoubtable regulars, such as Doris McArthur, as a sounding board when considering projects.

Briefly, following the publication of John Robinson's *Honest to God*, theology became a front-page issue. In some circuits and districts, parishes and dioceses, the controversy was divisive and was conducted with a certain bitterness. At Trinity, however, there had never been a strong fundamentalist or literalist tradition and, guided by Deryck Collingwood, in the course of a series of meetings, the Society came to terms with the main issues raised by the book.

The Methodist Church was struggling to 'Restructure' itself during the decade. In *Contact* for November 1967, Deryck Collingwood introduced 'The New Church Constitution' to Trinity. 'A great cry has gone up from Methodism: free us from the shackles of our organization, release our ministers and laity from the treadmill of meeting after meeting.' The minister and the Trinity Leaders' Meeting embraced the idea enthusiastically. Indeed so keen were they that they outstripped Conference legislation in abandoning the Leaders' Meeting and had to back pedal and reinstate it.

At this time Sheila Gibbs was a member of both the Connexional General Purpose Committee and its Executive. And, following on his enthusiastic implementation of the new Church Constitution at Trinity, she nominated her Minister to be a member of the Connexional Restructuring Committee.

In addition to all that was being undertaken at Trinity, Deryck Collingwood exercised his responsibilities as Superintendent of the Circuit. The Albert Road and Dinas Powis Societies were under the pastoral care of one minister, but the needs of the two Churches were very different. The area around Albert Road had not altered in character very much over the years, but Dinas Powis Church, designed by the same architect as Trinity albeit on a much smaller scale as befitted a village, was in the centre of an area in which much new building was taking place and where there was little other free church provision. The leaders of this Church, caught up in the same enthusiasm for youth work as Trinity and Albert Road, but with minimal premises, proceeded, in 1964, to erect a large Youth House. With the help of Methodist trusts and Glamorgan County, they put together financial backing for its erection and for the provision of a youth worker. The Circuit felt that there was a great potential for growth in the Church and that a resident minister would be able to develop a Society which could support a minister financially. A scheme for the stationing of three ministers in the Circuit was worked out. When Joe and Stella Bowles gave Murch Farm, a three-hundred year-old farmhouse, for use as a manse the plan became possible. The Circuit approached the Stationing Committee with a request for a third minister in the Circuit and in September 1966, a young minister with a qualification in youth work was appointed. The initial project envisaged a five-year appointment, at the end of which the arrangement would become permanent. However, the scheme put a considerable financial burden on the Churches. Albert Road and Dinas Powis were stretched by each having to support a minister.

Increasingly, inflation made the arrangement more and more difficult to sustain. The membership at Dinas Powis did not substantially increase and the climate for youth work, especially the running of an open club within a church framework, was very different from that of the early 1960's. The Circuit was aware that, when the five years were up, a different solution might well have to be found.

Although Trinity coped with its share of the increased financial burden caused by having three ministers in the Circuit, steps had to be taken to set the Church finances on a firmer footing. During the Autumn of 1964, Trinity embarked on a Christian Stewardship Campaign. The emphasis was on members of the Society as stewards of 'Time, Talents and Treasure' – with the emphasis on time and talents. This was just as well for high rates of inflation were, unbeknown to the congregation, lying in wait for the third of the 'T's – Treasure. The realistic pledges made by members led to the collection increasing to £60.0.0 per week and this solved the financial problem for the moment. It was however, through the great release of commitment and enthusiasm, as a result of the emphasis on the first two 't's, that the campaign succeeded. Not having to raise money for the Church meant that energy could be directed to three important fields which were opening up as the decade unfolded: relationships with the community, with other churches in the town and with other nationalities.

The campaign, directed by Peter Nurcombe of the Methodist Stewardship Organisation, demanded a great deal from the sixty church visitors, with Ernest Vokes as their Chairman. He had recently moved with his wife from Bristol and devoted his retirement to Trinity and the District. Every member and adherent was visited and all were invited to a family dinner at the Paget Rooms, at which three of the new Trustees, Sheila Gibbs, Allan Davies and Harold Williams shared their commitment for the future with the guests. Ernest Vokes reported in *Contact* that as a result 'additional help was volunteered for every Youth Activity and offers of practical assistance with transport, carpentry, tape-recording, and baby-sitting were made.' Class meetings were re-started and one led by Joyce Wells, at that time a midwife at the Royal Infirmary, still meets in 1993.

Joyce, the daughter of a local preacher of Connexional standing, and of a mother who was devoted to Trinity and missions, was herself a local preacher. In 1964, she was the first woman at Trinity to become a society steward. At a Leaders' Meeting in February 1967, she was, as membership secretary, able to report that the Society had increased from 252 in 1961 to 350 members.

In 1966, for the second Review of Stewardship, Trinity took the Paget Rooms again, and sponsored an exhibition of the work of the voluntary organisations in the town. In his contribution to the stewardship campaign dinner speeches in 1964, Allan Davies had recalled how he had visited a Church which had paintings of present day people on its walls, people who were living and working in the village. He felt that Church was part of the daily life of its community. In another Church, there were clear glass windows so that people could look in and the congregation could look out. At the exhibition, Trinity put this vision into operation.

The third Stewardship Review met in groups in thirty different houses and was not a success. Although there were new offers of time and talents, it was proving too embarrassing for the visitors to continue soliciting for financial pledges. The decision was taken not to hold a review in 1969, and by 1970 financial problems had to be faced again. In retrospect it can be said that the Stewardship Campaign was a success – even if the original expectations were not fully realised. Without the campaign, Trinity would not have been organised for its wider role.

In 1966, when John Kreiger, a member of the Church, was Chairman of the Penarth Urban District Council and Deryck Collingwood was his Chaplain, an elderly Penarth resident died and her body was not discovered for several days.  The Medical Officer of Health, the Council, the Churches and the voluntary agencies were deeply concerned, and a committee, on which Deryck Collingwood became an influential member, was set up to consider improvements in the care of the elderly, especially those living alone.  It was proposed that a Day Centre where lunch would be provided should be set up, and, when the Urban District Council was loath to take a decision, Deryck Collingwood, supported by his Church, committed Trinity to include a room, with a kitchen and lavatories, in its further redevelopment plan. The room would be equipped with suitable furniture and could be used on weekdays as a Day Centre.

In 1964 the Penarth Council of Churches took part in a nationwide project: 'The People Next door', which proved to be a great venture in fellowship.  During Lent, groups made up of members of different Churches were briefed and, in pairs, visited places they would not have gone to in the ordinary way; places as diverse as betting shops and night clubs, and places of worship of other faiths and denominations.  Then they met again and discussed their experiences.  Trinity members entered into this with enthusiasm, and also into supporting, with other Churches, the Freedom from Hunger Campaign and the Bread and Cheese Lunches – a form of self-denial given an ecclesiastical dimension by being held in Penarth during Lent.  Christians in Penarth were getting to know one another better.

The third way in which Trinity explored new ground was in its relationship with other countries and peoples. From the mid-1950's onwards, more students from overseas, many of them from former colonies, were attending British universities and colleges, and there was deep concern within Methodism that they should be properly received and housed.  An International House had been opened in London in 1950 and Maldwyn Edwards, the Chairman of the District, hoped that it would be possible to build a house either in Cardiff or Swansea – the two university centres in the District.  It was not possible to find a site in either of those two cities and Penarth provided an acceptable alternative.

In the 1930's Penarth House, the former home of Philip Morel, was empty and for sale with some four acres of land.  John and Sheila Gibbs bought the property and, in 1938, built their house on what had been a tennis court. Although they had sold some of the ground, there was enough space remaining on which to build an International House for fifty residents.

Although not specifically a Trinity venture, members of the Church were to be much involved in it; first, collecting the money to meet construction costs and, later, in the administration of the House. John Gibbs was the Appeal Secretary and later the Secretary to the House. The £120,000 required was raised from the British Council, Charitable Trusts, Industry in Wales, the Welsh Church Funds and the Thompson Foundation. Harold Williams as Treasurer was able to use his contacts in the business community in South Wales, and Howard Ponsford, as Auditor, brought not only his financial skills but also his practical knowledge of the building industry. Trinity was also strongly represented on the Management and House Committees, and Audrey Whitefield was the Office Secretary.

For Trinity, the opening of the Methodist International House of South Wales (M.I.H.) in 1964 meant that instead of long distance relationships with people overseas, members were able to develop friendships with visiting students and invite them to their own homes. The Women's Work Committee welcomed this; they had been taken aback to realise that their December Bazaar in 1964, the culmination of their year's sewing, would be their last. In future the Church Finance Committee would make an inclusive gift from the Church to missions. As an alternative to a Bazaar, the Women's Work Committee arranged, for some years, missionary occasions when young people who had returned from working overseas spoke about their experiences. The pattern of 'overseas work' was changing.

On one occasion an Indian Doctor staying at M.I.H. organized a 'Taste and Sound of India' evening, during which she not only spoke, but cooked curry for the whole gathering. Another produced an element of shock. After Dr Frank Davey had spoken about introducing a cure for leprosy to the Hospital he had been working at in Nigeria, one of the residents present mentioned casually that when he was at school one of his class mates left suddenly and he heard later that his friend had leprosy.

In the light of the great growth of Methodism in Korea in recent years, the visit of Dr. Oh from the Wonjo Union Christian Hospital, in Kangwon stood out. Because of his limited English, Dr Oh left the Service each Sunday and joined the Primary Department in the Junior

Church.  For several years after he returned to Korea, the children wrote to him and he sent them brightly coloured postcards.

But if Trinity had hoped that its congregation would be greatly enlarged by residents from M.I.H., it was to be disappointed.  Few of the residents followed Dr. Oh's example and attended Trinity.  Indeed, sometimes it seemed that students were more anxious to decry former colonial exploitation than to proclaim international amity.  However, it was a case of bread upon the waters: members of Trinity working abroad have since encountered past residents of M.I.H. who look back on their time in Penarth with affection and with appreciation of the qualities of those who set up and ran the House.

Some of the factors which brought more people from overseas to Penarth, also contributed to more Penarthians travelling abroad.  Especially had relationships been forged with the USA, partly as a result of visits of American ministers and choirs.  Above all was the visit of Jack and Maureen Moody remembered, and in 1965 another exchange was arranged, this time between them and the Collingwood family.

By this time, Jack and Maureen had two young daughters, Martha and Christine.  The children had been told about the Britain of 1954, including, for example, the gypsy encampment on the Penarth Road.  However, in 1965 the only painted caravan the Moodys could find was in the Folk Museum at St Fagans.  The local people had been aware that changes were taking place, but, as is so often the case, the eyes of visitors register differences particularly quickly.  Maureen, writing to the congregation of their Gay Street Methodist Church in Mount Vernon, Ohio, about the gypsy caravans, continued, perhaps a little over-dramatically:

> This was only one evidence of the amazing changes that have occurred in eleven years.  If as a tourist you want to visit the quaint villages of Britain you had better hurry for in the new found affluence which Britain appears to be  enjoying they may disappear.

Jack and Maureen noticed that there were many more cars parked in the streets around Trinity on a Sunday morning than there had been in 1954 – but remarked that the congregation was about the same size.  However, they were still able to write home about 'a depth of dedication – in British Methodism – that is inspiring.'

The Collingwood family had a very successful ministry at Gay Street, where the Church had a membership of 1500 and a Sunday School of 900. Gillian's comment illuminated the difference between being a Christian in the United States and Britain, when she said: 'At home one keeps very quiet about being a preacher's kid. In America they are proud of it.' Deryck Collingwood reflected on a similar phenomenon when he said: 'The first question a businessman asks his neighbour at a luncheon club or baseball match may well be "What's your church?" It is assumed he belongs to one.'

It is interesting that in comparing the weaknesses of the Church in Britain with those in its United States counterpart, Maureen Moody should conclude with: 'How blessed we are in terms of our Church's strength and work. How fortunate in terms of Ministry and outreach. Perhaps our very success, at times may hinder our faith.'

The Baptism by Deryck Collingwood of Sian James, the daughter of Shirley and Ian James; the Trinity Choir, 1964.

The United States, after decades of crowded churches, success and expansion, was beginning to feel the first chill wind of recession. Deryck Collingwood told them, on a subsequent visit, 'all my ministry I have known nothing but failure, but I can tell you, God is in failure as well as in success.' In the June number of *Contact* written just before he left Trinity, Deryck Collingwood enlarged on the theme of failure:

> Looking back over my ministry in Penarth, I am only too well aware of the failures. Here are some of them: An almost total failure to enlist young men in the educational work of our church . . . An equal failure with respect to young fathers who permit their families to come to worship but will not accompany them . . . A failure to persuade young members that 8 a.m. Holy Communion is the best time of all for personal worship . . . And Sunday Evening Services! I consider that much of my best work has been done on Sunday evenings, but few would know it. We really *must* decide whether we want an Evening Service or not and if we do, give it support.

He listed, on the other hand, the ways in which Trinity had witnessed a remarkable renewal of life in the post-war period, before concluding: 'No complacency! There is much failure to challenge us all. Life succeeds in that it seems to fail. When man fails, so often God prevails.'

# CHAPTER 17

## The Rev'd Arnold Morris 1969-1975

To invite a minister to Trinity to follow Deryck Collingwood was a formidable task. As Circuit Steward it was John Gibbs' responsibility to recommend a name to the circuit meeting. Fortunately, he had travelled widely in Methodism in his Vice Presidential Year and had got to know a large number of ministers. On his visit to Cambridge he had met Arnold Morris and was subsequently to meet him from time to time at Connexional Committees.

Arnold Morris was the Minister of Wesley Church in Cambridge when the Methodist Society, which worshipped there, was the largest student society in the University, and both Professor Basil Willey and Professor Herbert Butterfield, two distinguished historians, were members of his congregation.

John Gibbs asked Arnold Morris whether he would consider an invitation to the Penarth Circuit. To serve in Wales was not altogether an attractive proposition to one whose ministry was well established in England and in 1967 Arnold Morris was in Purley, a typical London suburb. Nevertheless, there were certain blandishments that could be held out. Arnold Morris, the son of a Methodist Minister, had been born when his father was stationed in Caerphilly. Ever after, because of his itinerant upbringing, he had identified Glamorgan as his county cricket team. Ninian Park and Cardiff Arms Park were additional attractions to one who, unashamedly, gave his 'Recreations' as 'Cricket and other Games'.

When Arnold Morris came to Penarth, Trinity was to have a pulpit ministry granted to only a few Methodist congregations in the 1970s. Initially, however, when he came to Trinity in 1969 he was at once precipitated into a crisis.

By the June Quarterly Meeting of 1968, the Circuit had recognized that it had overstretched itself by having a third minister. There had been 'miscalculations in forecasting' and the situation had been aggravated by 'cost of living increments'. The meeting decided to reduce the staff again to two ministers when the five year period came to an end in 1971.

This decision was accepted with relief, but left unanswered the difficult question of where the ministers were to live and for which Churches they should have responsibility. There was no question but that the superintendent minister should remain in Penarth at 1, Victoria Avenue. The other two manses were both suitable houses for ministers, and there was little opposition to the recommendation that the second minister should live in Dinas Powis so that a ministerial presence could be manifest in the Village.

When it came to the ministerial oversight of Churches, however, there was less accord. In the autumn of 1969 the Circuit Stewards, John Gibbs and Cyril Smith, with the support of the General Purposes Committee, proposed that the Superintendent Minister should have pastoral responsibility for Trinity, Eastbrook and International House, and the second minister, resident in Dinas Powis, should look after the Societies at Albert Road and Dinas Powis and Headlands School. This made sense in terms of members; Trinity and Eastbrook had 372 members and, between them the other two Churches, with 244 at Albert Road and 107 at Dinas Powis, had 351, and also in the related matter of pastoral coverage. The Quarterly Meeting of December 1969 rejected the proposal by 30 votes to 12, recommending instead that the Superintendent Minister should be responsible for Trinity and Albert Road and that the second minister should have the responsibility for Dinas Powis and the little society of Eastbrook with its 16 members.

This rejection of the Circuit Stewards' proposal brought about the resignation of the two Stewards, Cyril Smith voicing the feeling that the adverse vote showed that 'The meeting had no confidence in its appointed officers.' In later years Arnold Morris was often to refer to this occasion when he lost his two Circuit Stewards in the first months of his Ministry in Penarth. In fact, the allocation of ministerial oversight is the responsibility of the superintendent minister and the Quarterly Meeting's recommendation would ultimately have had no binding effect. Arnold Morris, not wishing to be dictatorial but needing to secure the rescindment of the resolution, visited each of the Leaders Meetings of the Societies with the result that, at an adjourned meeting in January 1970, the original recommendation of the Circuit Stewards was accepted. It was difficult for Albert Road and Dinas Powis to come to terms with not having their 'own' Minister and the initial vote reflected their deep felt concern. The episode shows that the circuit system is capable of dealing with retrenchment as well as advance and the crisis passed. However, it was not possible to persuade Cyril Smith to withdraw his resignation and a new Circuit Steward was appointed.

The Albert Road Church was to develop in the 1970's as a Church and Community Centre with great emphasis on ministry to the whole community. The Dinas Powis Church has made a distinctive contribution to its rapidly growing 'village' community.[1]

When he came to Trinity, Arnold Morris was distressed to find there was no fellowship meeting, the women's Afternoon Fellowship having come to an end in 1961. At once he started a Wednesday evening meeting which continued throughout his Ministry and was long remembered by the thirty or so members who attended; together with his finely wrought sermons, they were perhaps the outstanding features of his Ministry. He did not drive a car but this became a positive element in his Ministry as he developed friendships with those who drove him.

Preparation Classes for new members continued to be held. In 1970 twelve members were received and four and five in the two following years. The number of members remained around 360, but in 1975 when the new Membership Committee was inaugurated, a separate Community Roll was created on which the names of all connected with Trinity, who were not in membership were placed. 29 names of those who 'had ceased to meet' were transferred to this, leaving a more realistic membership of 336.

Arnold Morris was deeply concerned at the small number of people who attended Communion Services. In one of his few articles in *Contact* he wrote:

> One of the things that puzzles me about Trinity is the relatively small number of members who regularly share in Holy Communion. The plain fact is that, according to my records, the attendances are the lowest that I have known in any church of which I have been Minister.
>
> At Communion Services we do all that we can to stress that there is one act of worship. We give opportunity to those who wish to do so to withdraw before the climax, but it is always disappointing to see church members go. The Eucharist is not something reserved for great saints. It is the drama, splendidly set out in our New Order, that gathers up the past and the unimaginable future into one present moment of faith and of fellowship with our common Lord and with His people. It is for sinners. It is for us all.

Trinity had been using the Experimental New Order but as Arnold Morris put it in the same article 'the idea that the Communion Service is something tacked on to the end of a Service and is intended for the particularly holy, dies hard.'

At this time the major Churches brought out Alternative Services in consultation with each other.

In 1975 the Methodist Sunday Service which integrated the Lord's Supper with the Main Service was published and has been used in Trinity ever since. In this Service the Preparation, the Ministry of the Word and the Lord's Supper are one. Holy Communion is celebrated three times a month in Trinity. Once at an 8.a.m. Service, once at the 6.p.m. Service and at the 10.30.a.m. Service when the whole congregation stays to the end and shares in the Holy Communion as a matter of course.

In 1969 the New Room was still a shell. The Penarth Urban District Council had been dragging its feet and if a Day Centre was to be opened in it in the New Year of 1970, preparations would have to be made by Trinity members. Visits were accordingly made to existing Day Centres to see the facilities provided. These were often basic; at one Methodist Church in Cardiff the voluntary workers were washing up in a bowl of hot water on a table. Trinity, with the kitchen at International House as an example, had very different ideas, and a modern kitchen was fitted out with the Penarth Urban District Council contributing some equipment. Chairs, designed for the elderly, were bought with gifts from individuals and Penarth organisations, such as Rotary, the Chamber of Trade, the Grammar School, and the Trades Union Council, in sympathy with the project. Not everyone in the town was in favour. Some considered that the Centre was unnecessary, others that it was in the wrong place. They agreed in saying 'No one will come'.

In the event, the Day Centre was opened by the Chairman of the Council on January 20th 1970, with a full complement of members.

At the beginning the lunch cost 2/6 per head, which covered the cost of the ingredients of the meal. The Council paid the wages of the Cook and Deputy Cook and £2. a day for lighting, heating and caretaking. No rent was received for five years. Arnold Morris, as Chairman of the Management Committee, came to know many of the Day Centre members well and was delighted when as many as fifteen at a time attended the Intercession Service held in the Choir Vestry on a weekday morning.

Within a few months of the opening, meals were having to be rationed to two a week per person, there was a waiting list and the idea of a second Day Centre was being advocated. One Trinity member, Myfanwy Davies, who was deeply involved in the planning of the Centre and later in catering for it, qualified at Barry Technical College, and after planning the kitchen at the Albert Road Day Centre she became in 1973, a part-time Day Centre Organiser, employed by the Penarth Urban District Council.

The New Room was used as a Day Centre on weekdays and by the Church in the evenings and at weekends. The smooth running of this arrangement was greatly helped by Marie Parish, wife of the Chapel-keeper, being the Deputy Cook.

In 1974 the Penarth Urban District Council was taken over by the Vale of Glamorgan Borough Council, which had an established policy on Day Centres and wished the Trinity Centre to be open five, instead of four, days a week. In coming to an agreement on this, the Trinity Trust was at last able, in 1976, to arrange a realistic and inclusive rent. The Council also took over the transport of handicapped Day Centre members which had been previously undertaken by volunteers. All this meant that in effect after 1974 Trinity ceased to have responsibility for running the Day Centre. It continued to be served by voluntary helpers from Trinity and the other Churches and Esme Mason (Marsh) has continued to be the chief link between Church and Day Centre for the last twenty years. From the very beginning, coffee has been served by volunteers on weekday mornings, not only to the Day Centre members, but to all meeting or working on the premises.

Meanwhile, there were developments relating to other parts of the buildings. In June 1971 the Glamorgan County Council who had rented the Woodland Hall in order to provide accommodation for extra pupils and music tuition, announced that it no longer needed it and would terminate its tenancy in November. Trinity having the New Room and the renovated Trinity Hall decided that by using all the accommodation, all the children could meet in the main buildings on a Sunday. This meant that the Juniors would no longer have to cross to the Woodland Hall each Sunday morning which was becoming increasingly dangerous.

The Trust decided to sell the Woodland Hall. This was not an easy matter as Arthur Parish, as Chapel-keeper, had a flat in it. In the event, a most suitable buyer came forward and the Woodland Hall became the Education Office for the Church in Wales. This was a most convenient arrangement for the Trust as there were covenants on the building which restricted its sale. Number 66, Grove Terrace was purchased in its place and turned into two flats, one for the Chapel-keeper and one for a member of the Church in Wales Staff.

Originally Arthur and Marie Parish were Baptists, but Marie had long been a member of Young Wives and Elizabeth, their daughter, was a stalwart member of the Youth Club. When in 1968 Arthur became redundant at Price Brothers, Trinity was looking for a Chapel-keeper, and he was appointed, and from then on he and Marie happily became Methodists. After serving the Church as Chapel-keeper he continued to serve it in retirement, as one of the group of retired men who are so often to be found working on the premises.

In 1970 the Penarth Grammar School became 'Stanwell Comprehensive School', and the recently built Secondary School became 'St. Cyres Comprehensive School'. At this time, Huw Johnes was Headmaster of the former. He and his wife, Anna, came from Llangollen where they were members of the Welsh Methodist Chapel but they chose to attend Trinity, partly because they wished to worship in the town where he worked rather than to travel to Cardiff to a Welsh-speaking Chapel – 'but perhaps more than that; we understood Trinity was an active and lively Church with a Sunday School in which Geraint could get involved and get to know children of his own age.' Huw and Anna became actively involved in Trinity and International House and Geraint joined the Drama Group, Junior Church and Youth Club.

Referring to the years between 1944 and 1954 when his School held weekly assemblies in Trinity, Huw Johnes writes 'Penarth Grammar School had, over the years, established an affiliation with Trinity and this was continued throughout the time that I was Head, with Stanwell Comprehensive School holding Annual Carol Services in the Church.' In 1970 when Thelma Williams, daughter of Harold and Margaret, was Head Girl, she arranged for the VI Form to serve meals, during the Easter holidays, at the Day Centre.

On April 12th 1970 the Morning Service from Trinity was televised by the B.B.C. with Arnold Morris as the preacher. He received many letters of appreciation from all over the world and one viewer even sent collection money. On the other hand, two adverse viewers had switched over to I.T.V. and heard 'an excellent message from another Church.' Arnold Morris had preached at the Television Service from the oak lectern, which had been placed at the front of the Church in 1969, as was his wont. He refused to use the pulpit because of its 'triumphalist associations,' as we have noted.

The success of the Service undoubtedly affected the decision by the B.B.C. to use Trinity again, and three Radio Services followed: on 20 December 1970, and on 28 November and 5 December 1971. All the services were conducted by the Minister, who also preached the sermons on the second and third occasion.

On Sunday 3 January 1971, the Methodist Covenant Service, which had been recorded at Trinity, was transmitted by the B.B.C.

The Choir, with E. Macmillan Ewens as Organist and Howard Ponsford as Choir Master, was a feature of the Television Service as of all Services. Members of the Junior Choir, which numbered 35 at one time, were growing up and being integrated with the older Choir members. Two extra choir stalls were introduced. Not only did the Choir lead the congregational singing but also the Responses which were becoming increasingly important with the use of the New Sunday Service.

Every Sunday morning the Choir sang an Introit and an Anthem chosen from Novello's *Book of Anthems, The Oxford Anthem Book* or Francis Jackson's *50 Anthems for Mixed Voices* and there was always special music for Easter and Christmas. Maunder's *Olivet to Calvary* and Stainer's *Crucifixion* had been in the repertoire of the Trinity Choir from the earliest days, but now were added *The Nativity* by Eric Thiman, *The Saviour* by Andrew Lloyd Webber and the American, John Peterson's *Night of Miracles*. Well established was the 'Service of Nine Lessons and Carols.' David Ponsford, son of Howard and Olive, would make a point of returning to play the organ, however distant he might be. The introduction of candle light gave the Service a special dimension as the gothic features of the Church dissolved into the darkness. A week-night Concert 'Carols with the Choir' became a feature of the Christmas Celebration, and was attended by a number who were not prepared to attend a Service of Worship in a church.

At Easter, the Maundy Thursday, Good Friday and Easter Day Services were the climax of the Christian Year and on Palm Sunday the Junior

189

Arnold Morris in discussion with the Programme Director of the B.B.C. Televised Service, 12 April 1970.

Church processed within the Church with palms. An Easter Service of Nine Lessons and Hymns was devised on the model of the Christmas Service.

Not needed on these evening occasions when the Church was full, were the screens which were introduced in 1969 to bring the small evening congregation forward and to close off the back pews.

A Family Church pattern of worship was now well established with the children and young people joining in the first part of the Service and then leaving to follow Partners in Learning devised by the Methodist Division of Education and Youth; this, as its name suggests, involved teachers and taught exploring together an integrated syllabus. Such experiential-centred teaching was followed in all departments of the Junior Church, at their appropriate levels, and could form the basis for the adult sermon as well, although the Lectionary provided a basis for themes and subjects throughout the Christian Year which preachers normally followed. The children's promotion through the departments of the Junior Church was marked each September by a ceremony within the Morning Service. Arnold Morris never regarded the Junior Church as a separate institution but made it clear that it was always an essential part of the family and the life of the whole Church. Two groups of boys from Headlands School had been attending the Morning Services and Junior Church at Trinity; however, in 1971 it was decided by the Headmaster and Staff that it would be better in future to hold their own evening service when the boys, who were increasingly going home for weekends, would be back at the School. Those Managers who were also Junior Church leaders regretted the loss of opportunity of meeting the boys each week.

In various Minutes the numbers of Church members are recorded, and they remain, on the whole, remarkably constant. However, it is only at the March Quarterly Meeting in 1970 that there is a breakdown into age groups, which gives a revealing profile of the Societies within the Circuit.

Joyce Wells presented the Circuit Membership in the following terms:

| Church Members | | Over 60 | Between 60 & 30 | Under 30 |
| --- | --- | --- | --- | --- |
| Trinity | 362 | 28.7% | 48% | 23% |
| Albert Road | 206 | 25% | 70% | 5% |
| Dinas Powys | 117 | 40% | 50% | 5% |
| Eastbrook | 15 | | | |

Of the 23% under 30 at Trinity, 44% of these were living for most of the year, away from home. This percentage included University students and those who were in their first jobs who had not transferred their membership to another Church.

Although the Youth Club was not as well attended during this period, partly because the new County Youth Club had opened, there were still highlights. One was the Methodist Association of Youth Clubs Welsh weekend held in Sophia Gardens Pavilion to celebrate the Investiture of the Prince of Wales in 1970. As well as contributing items from their production of *1066 and All That* Trinity provided stage management, production, lighting and sound. Two years later Club member, Elizabeth Parish, became Miss M.A.Y.C. Wales. Ex Youth Club members formed themselves into Folk Groups which played at Services, first 'Faith, Hope and Clarity' and then 'Twice Trinity'.

Another was their participation in the London Weekend in 1974. The Sunday Morning Service in the Albert Hall was televised by the B.B.C. and Trinity took part in the presentation on the stage of 'The Testimony of the Ages.' Trinity Drama Group provided the two narrators, Elizabeth Parish and Geraint Johnes, and actors to play twelve notable Christians: Mary, Paul, Perpetua, Hilda of Whitby, St. Francis, Martin Luther, John Bunyan, Susanna Wesley, John Wesley, David Livingstone, Martin Luther King and Mother Theresa.

The party travelled to London by road. The part of Martin Luther King was taken by a student from Natal who, with his wife, was staying at Methodist International House. Stopping at a Service Station off the M4 for a meal they were quite unable to believe that they would be allowed to enter the restaurant and that they would not have to collect their food from a window and eat it outside. Even though they had been in the United Kingdom for some months in a completely integrated environment, they still expected to be confronted with apartheid practices as they would have been in South Africa.

In 1972 the Youth Club became an Inters Club for boys and girls between eleven and thirteen. They joined in wider activities especially those of the Welsh Association of Youth Clubs, which seemed better to suit their needs than M.A.Y.C.

The members of the former M.A.Y.C. continued to meet as a Young People's Fellowship after evening service on Sundays.

It is not unusual for a church to blame broken windows on the members of its Youth Club. However, it is most unlikely that the members of the Trinity Youth Club were responsible for a number of attacks on the stained glass windows in the North aisle of the Church. After a year these were repaired and the windows were protected with wire mesh guards which are still in place and are not obtrusive.

In the Connexion during the whole of Arnold Morris' Ministry the Methodist Church was involved in restructuring itself. This involved devising a way of altering, should it be necessary, the doctrinal basis of the Church, fixed since 1932, and of making the local church into a more sensitive instrument for fulfilling the spiritual and evangelistic purpose for which it existed.[2]

Links between Trinity, International House and the town were strengthened. The Thompson Foundation with its Course for overseas journalists had been one of the first supporters of International House. Each year it ran two Courses of three months each in Cardiff. After returning home a journalist, Stephen Supiya, from Southern Rhodesia, now Zimbabwe, wrote to thank Arnold Morris 'for his Thursdays' visits to International House for evening prayers. That, in itself, has interested part of the residents there, including myself . . . My being with you, even for the ten Sundays only, has helped to give me a vision of what Christians in this part of Britain are.'

In 1973 when Britain entered the Common Market there was a 'Sign in' in all the Churches in Penarth, declaring that the needs of the Third World should not be overlooked at such a time. The petition was presented to James Callaghan, the Member for Cardiff South and, at the time Foreign Secretary, in a ceremony at International House, by John Webber, the Curate of All Saints, Church in Wales.

During vacations the House was being used for Conferences and as a holiday centre for the handicapped.

Despite the failure of the Anglican Methodist Conversations there was a continuing search for unity between the Churches. This found expression at the Faith and Order Nottingham Conference of 1964 where schemes for 'Covenanting for Unity' was launched both in England and Wales. The Methodist Districts in Wales joined with the Anglican Church in Wales, the recently formed United Reformed Church and the Presbyterian Church of Wales in a Commission of the Covenanting Churches for Wales, of which John Gibbs was a member.

193

The Commission made rapid progress – for an interdenominational body – and in 1975 was ready to make a formal Covenant for Union.

*Contact* in March 1975, reported:

> On Saturday, January 18th, in Seilo Presbyterian Church of Wales, Aberystwyth, a National Service of Thanksgiving for the making of a Covenant by the Four Denominations, was held. The Presbyterian Church of Wales, the United Reformed Church, the Church in Wales and the Methodist Church covenanted to work and pray for Union. Good wishes were brought by the Baptist Union of Great Britain and Ireland (South Wales Area) some of whose congregations desire to covenant, and by the Union of Welsh Independents, a few of whose Churches are in favour of the Covenant.
>
> There were also present representatives of the Roman Catholic Church, the Society of Friends and the Salvation Army, and good wishes were brought by them on behalf of their members.
>
> Part of the Service was in Welsh; part in English. The singing, which was splendid, rose above all difficulties of language, in true worship.
>
> John Gibbs was one of the three Methodists who affirmed in the name of the Methodist Church:
>
> 'We have entered into a solemn Covenant before God and with one another, to work and pray in common obedience to our Lord Jesus Christ, so that by the Holy Spirit we may be brought into one visible Church to serve together in mission to the Glory of God the Father.'

The climate in Wales was particularly favourable to a closer relationship between the Churches.[3]

At the same time that interdenominational issues were being discussed, the Drama Group remained active. Following a production of *Noah* by Andre Obey in 1972, a considerable number of the Group was involved in a District Production of the musical, *Ride! Ride!*, based on an incident in the life of John Wesley, Howard Ponsford being responsible for the music. After a week's production in Cardiff's Sherman Theatre, *Ride! Ride!* was taken to the Wyvern Theatre in Swindon and the

Redgrave Theatre in Clifton to coincide with the Bristol Methodist Conference of 1974. This was the second Conference production and, as a result of both, Conference recommended that the play should be presented as widely as possible throughout Britain. To enable this to happen, a Production Company was created, Aldersgate Limited, which arranged for a professional cast to take the play to most of the larger provincial theatres ending with an extended run at the Westminster Theatre in London. Aldersgate Limited continued in existence after the close of the run, mounting some ten professional productions, of which *Sentenced to Life*, a play about euthanasia, by Malcolm Muggeridge and Alan Thornhill, was the most controversial and an adaptation of C. S. Lewis's *The Lion, the Witch and the Wardrobe*, the most successful.

*Ride! Ride!* signalled the end of the Trinity Drama Group. After thirty years the enthusiasm of the original production team, which year by year had presented religious and classical plays, was spent, and there was no one to succeed them.

The years following the end of the 1939-1945 War were ones in which the Drama Group and the Youth Club flourished. Life styles and leisure activities, especially television, required the Church to re-think its communal activities and by the 1980s a different pattern was emerging.

Other changes were taking place. Ever since Percy Watkinson had expressed his initial disapproval of the Manse, the Circuit Stewards had wished to replace Pagemont. In the summer of 1974 a suitable house, 71, Stanwell Road, came on the market and was purchased for £20,750.

Ministers and their wives moved houses frequently and it was no small matter for Arnold and his wife, Noreen, to move for the last year of Ministry in Penarth before going to Nicholson Square, Edinburgh. They very graciously did so and enabled the change of houses to be made, no easy matter at the best of times. Pagemont was on the market until August 1976, when it was sold for £18,000.

The change of Manses was a matter of great satisfaction to Sheila Gibbs. She was Secretary of the South Wales District Manses Committee for thirty years, during which time the standard of Manses in the District, as of housing in general, greatly improved. She knew that her great grandfather, a Primitive Methodist Minister, at a time when they moved stations each year, had arrived at a two-roomed Manse, at Stanton, near Ashbourne in 1831 to find it almost unfurnished. In effect, in her concern for the Ministry she spent the thirty years trying to provide and furnish a suitable Manse for him and his family.[4]

This chapter is concluded with the printing of the Order of Services, including the text of the Televised Sermon, and Newsnotes for the week commencing Sunday, 12th April 1970.

## TRINITY METHODIST CHURCH, PENARTH

### Sunday, 12th April, 1970

10.30.a.m. Morning Service, B.B.C.1. Rev. Arnold Morris, B.D.

The Congregation rises as the Choir enters.
Procession and Introit:

Let all mortal flesh keep silence.  (Hymns & Songs No.38.)
Prayer:
Hymn 228: Hail Thou once despised Jesus.  Hyfrydol  (380)
The General Confession:
Declaration of Forgiveness:
    If we confess our sins, He is just, and may be trusted to forgive our sins, and cleanse us from every kind of wrong.
Gloria in Excelsis: (said by all).
Prayer:
The First Lesson: Psalm 65 (N.E.B.)
    read by J.M. Gibbs.
Hymn 871: In our work and in our play.
The Second Lesson: Philippians 2 v. 1-11 (N.E.B.)
    read by Shelagh Greenland.
Anthem: Dear Lord and Father of Mankind. (Parry)
Dismissal Prayer for Beginners and Primary.
Beginners and Primary leave.
Hymn 273: Come Down, O Love Divine.
Ascription.

Sermon – Part One

We preach not ourselves but Christ Jesus as Lord . . . unto Whom be glory.  Amen.

You saw the children go out of the Church.  They have gone to have their own lessons in their own rooms.  Some of them will be thinking about 'things that we treasure.' I suppose they will include some of the odd things that may be quite precious to a small child, even if it's a ball of string or a saucepan lid. All this is for those children the first step towards a very great idea – the idea of the gracious gifts of God. We here are to think about God's gift of His Spirit.

The Christian life is not just a matter of keeping rules and regulations. It is a matter of being led by the Spirit of God. But this raises a very big question. How do we know when it really is God's Spirit that is leading us?

Like all other good and true men in these parts I am a whole-hearted supporter of Cardiff City. When I am carried away with enthusiasm, or when I am expressing my feelings about some decision by a referee, am I being led by God's Spirit? When teenagers are 'sent' by pop music, are they?

When students revolt, are they? How much that you and I do in an average day really is done by the guidance of God's Spirit?

I call heaven and this congregation to witness that I have not tried to answer those questions. I've only thrown them out because I think that they are examples of all that tells us that we need tests that we can apply. In his first letter to the Corinthians, in Chapter 12, St. Paul gives one to us.

He was writing to a church that had its problems. One was the people who claimed that they had special spiritual gifts and would begin using unintelligible language. We call it 'speaking with tongues.' The question was, were they inspired by God or were they merely hysterical? St. Paul's test is that if anyone says 'a curse on Jesus' it cannot possibly be inspired by God.

Would anyone wish to curse Jesus? I'm afraid the answer is 'Yes'. Years ago, in the old Birmingham Bull Ring, I stopped to listen to an open-air speaker commending the Christian faith. Suddenly, a man in the crowd shouted out just about the most blasphemous words about Jesus that I have ever heard. THAT man was not inspired by God.

But St. Paul goes on to say that when anyone says 'Jesus is Lord', then, undoubtedly, God's Spirit is at work. 'Jesus Christ is Lord' is one of the oldest Christian confessions. I would say that the best definition of a Christian is that it is anyone who says it and lives by what it means.

It means, I believe, that, whether we can define it exactly or not, Jesus lived in a unique relationship with God. It means that He suffered and died and was raised from the dead. It means that His living spirit is always at work in the world and can never be totally and finally defeated. It means that He is the Lord of the Church. It means that He is the supreme authority for every individual Christian.

And St. Paul is saying to us that you can never come to believe that all by yourself. There has to be a moment of inspiration in which you abandon yourself to what you can't logically prove. And you may be assured that you are being led by God when you are impelled towards Jesus Christ and His Lordship.

I do hope that you won't dismiss all this as being merely academic. It certainly is not. It leads to some very great challenges about our Christian lives, about what must be supremely important for us, about how we should make our everyday judgements, and so on. Before we go on to think about some of them we shall sing one of Charles Wesley's great hymns, the one in which he says –

No man can truly say that Jesus is the Lord
Unless Thou take the veil away and breathe the living word.

Here follows Hymn 363: Spirit of Faith, come down.

Sermon – Part Two

Before we sang that hymn I threw out some questions. Let's return to them. One was 'What is the distinguishing mark of a Christian?' Some people always seem to want to answer that in terms of moral standards and behaviour. They want to tell us that the genuine Christian always lives a better life than non-Christians do. They remind us of all the good causes pioneered by the churches and kept going by faithful Christian folk.

Of course I don't deny all this but if you take it too far you've got problems. So many people who have no formal religion and don't go to church live very good lives and do quite a lot of excellent social service. Instead of denigrating this, isn't it better for Christians to be glad of the good that such people do, and to recognise that the difference is not always one of morals and social service. It is one of obedience. The genuine Christian has a personal obedience to the living Lord Jesus Christ.

In the course of my Ministry I've known many young people who could have gone all out for careers of material success and power but who didn't. They went off to do things like teaching in mission schools or working in hospitals in faraway places. If you asked them why, they wouldn't talk easily about it and they wouldn't be pompous but it would come through that it was because of an obedience to their Lord.

Their call isn't the way for all of us. Each of us must work out what ours is. For you it might very well be to stay where you are and do what you do and do it as a believing Christian.

I also mentioned our day-to-day decisions in what may well be difficult and perplexing situations. The Christian has familiar and well tried exercises, such as Bible reading, prayer, reason, talking it over with wise friends, and so on.

There is something else that we can do. We can ask ourselves NOT which course of action would be easiest or most profitable or even most pleasurable BUT which would best show that for us Jesus is Lord. Would it be, for instance, to go after a better job or not to do it, to write that letter or not to write it, to interfere in someone else's life or to let them be – or whichever it is? I don't say that doing this leads to quick and easy answers. So often, all that we can do is just do our best and leave it with God. I do say that it means putting first things first and beginning in the right place. Try it, and see what happens.

There is one more word that I want to say to you. I remind you again of what St. Paul said. 'No-one can say Jesus is Lord except by the Holy Spirit'. That may have had a very special reference. In those early days of the Church, when Christians were being persecuted by the Roman Empire they could have saved themselves from death by denying that they were Christians. They could make a sacrifice before an image of the Emperor and say 'Caesar is Lord'. They might even be required to go further and say 'And Jesus is accursed'. Then, when it really was a matter of life or death, 'the Noble Army of Martyrs' stood firm and suffered and died for it. They did it not just by screwing up their courage but by the power of the Spirit of God. One early writer said that their blood was the seed of the Church. The same sort of situation has faced innumerable other Christians in other times and other places. I suppose you and I may never have to face anything like that but we may sometimes be in situations where everything seems to make us want to deny our faith and deny our Lord – and want quite desperately to do it.

Some time ago, a friend was giving me a lift to a station. As we drove along we talked about a mutual acquaintance who had been through an experience that was an agonizing test of his faith. The driver said 'I wonder what I would do if I had to face something like that'. He was silent for a while and then he said 'I suppose what they say is true – strength would be given'. He used those simple old words but you and I know what they meant – the strength of the Spirit of God that enables the Christian to say in the most desperate circumstances 'Even in this, although I don't understand it, Jesus Christ is Lord'. And we came to the station and I got a train and went home.

The Intercessions:

O God, our Father, grant us the help of Thy Spirit
in our prayers for the salvation of mankind.
(After each petition:-
　　Minister: Lord in Thy Mercy.
　　People: Hear our prayer.)
The Lord's Prayer. (said by all)
Hymn 249: In the Name of Jesus (Beaumont)
(During the singing of this Hymn the Offertory is received and presented at the Communion Table.)
The Grace (Minister only).

# ORDER OF SERVICE AND NEWSNOTES

## Sunday, 12th April, 1970

Newsnotes

| | | |
|---|---|---|
| Mon. | 3.0.p.m. | Women's Hour – Speaker: The Minister. |
| | 6.0.p.m. | Brownies. |
| | 7.15.p.m. | Guides. |
| | 7.30.p.m. | Youth Club Badminton. |
| Wed. | 6.30.p.m. | Inters Club. |
| | 7.30.p.m. | Church Fellowship Meeting in the New Room, led by the Minister . . . open to anyone who cares to come. |
| Thur. | 11.0.a.m. | Intercessions for the Sick. |
| | 7.0.p.m. | Choir. |
| Fri. | 6.30.p.m. | Cubs. |
| | 7.30.p.m. | Scouts. |

Christian Aid Week – 13/18th April.

Sunday, 12th April at 3.0.p.m. in All Saints Church. Annual Dedication Service.

Monday, Inaugural Lunch at Stanwell Road Baptist Church at 12 noon.

Tuesday, Bread and Cheese Supper from 7.30.p.m. in Trinity Day Centre.

Coffee Mornings daily at Christchurch: 10.a.m. – 12 noon.

Penarth Children's Art Display continues until 18th April

Daily at Stanwell Road Baptist Church Hall 2.30.

---

6.30.p.m. Evening Service and Holy Communion.
The New Order.
The Minister.

---

Members of other Churches are welcome at the Lord's Table with us.

Introit:  'We love the place, O God,
Wherein Thine honour dwells:'

Prayer:
Hymn 670:
First Lesson: John 11 v. 1-16 (N.E.B.)
    read by H.W. Ponsford.
Hymn 631:
Second Lesson: John 11 v. 17-27, 32-44.
Prayer and The Lord's Prayer
Hymn 309:
Ascription:
Sermon:
Hymn 269

| | |
|---|---|
| 24. | Those who leave shall do so now. |
| 29. | The Peace. |
| 30. | The Creed. |
| 31. | The Offertory for the Poor. |
| 33/35. | The Thanksgiving. |
| 37. | The Breaking of the Bread. |
| 39. | The Prayer of Humble Access. |
| 40/45. | The Communion. |
| 46/50. | The Final Prayers. |

---

Sunday, 19th April.
10.30.a.m.    Family Worship and Holy Communion.
                 Rt. Hon. George Thomas, M.P.,
                 Secretary of State for Wales.
6.30.p.m.    Youth Service.
                 The Minister.

---

# CHAPTER 18

## The Rev'd Leslie Craze 1975-1981

Arnold Morris had been a student at Handsworth College in the late 1930s with Leslie Craze and he suggested to the Circuit Stewards that they should consider inviting him to Trinity for 1975. This they did and when they arrived, Leslie and Marion Craze brought a new dimension of ministry to the Church.

Leslie Craze had been a missionary in the Bombay and Punjab District of India from 1938 to 1945. He then moved to the Trichinopoly District and Diocese and worked there, greatly enjoying the first years of the new Church of South India in spite of its early problems. In 1937, Marion Marshall had gone to India as a Women's Work Missionary to be Vice-Principal of the Methodist Girls High School at Trichinopoly, and she subsequently became Principal of the Women's Educational Work at Dharapuram. She and Leslie were married in 1943. They returned to England with their two daughters in 1953. Marion Craze was the first minister's wife at Trinity to be a professional woman and a car driver, although by the time they came to Penarth she had retired from teaching. Leslie Craze had served on the Connexional Overseas Committee and was to serve on the Connexional Homes for the Aged Committee when he was at Trinity. The Churches at Redhill, East Grinstead and Hastings which he served when he returned to Britain, were similar to Trinity and with his South India experience he was able to make a distinctive contribution to the Welsh Covenant, not least in the South-west Glamorgan Covenanting Committee where he was alternatively encouraged and depressed by the fluctuating rate of progress in the growing together of the churches.

Trinity during his time, was somewhat exhausted by its efforts at ecumenicity, by the Conversations with the Anglicans and the Welsh Covenant, and by its own Methodist Restructuring. 16 April 1977 was the appointed day under the terms of the Methodist Church Act 1976 when all that had been prepared for in the previous years actually came into effect, but it took a number of years before the new terminology was adopted by the older members; 'Church Council' replacing the 'Leaders Meeting' and 'Circuit Meeting' the 'Quarterly Meeting'.

There were changes, too, in the life of the Church. The Junior Church, although smaller than in previous years, was stimulated by the study outlines in *Partners in Learning*. This provided themes which could be expressed musically and dramatically at Junior Church Anniversaries. On one occasion the Battle of Solferino was enacted to show the birth of the Red Cross, and on another a large model of Trinity Church was built and the growth and outreach of the Church was enacted around it.

Leslie Craze was impressed by the way the Junior Staff carefully prepared expression work and gathered informative material before their classes and the encouragement they gave to the boys and girls when in the Church, to join in the worship. Their encouragement, too, of the children's achievement by preserving their drawings and models for others to see. Trinity was indeed, becoming a family church.

The commonly experienced falling away of boys and girls in their early 'teens was staunched by the coming of Douglas and Sheila Harris to Penarth in 1976. Douglas Harris was appointed Professor and Head of Department of the Electrical and Electronic Engineering Department of the University of Wales Institute of Science and Technology in Cardiff. He had grown up as a Baptist but after marrying Sheila, a Methodist with an Ex-Primitive background, they attended, in various places, Methodist, Baptist and United Reformed Churches before settling at Trinity. On arrival in Penarth with their three children they made the rounds of the Churches and then asked their children to decide. They said 'Trinity'.

Douglas and Sheila Harris took over the leadership of the Young People's Fellowship, with as many as twenty members, half of whom had grown up in the Junior Church. They met regularly on Sunday mornings; on Saturday evenings they opened a Coffee Bar in the New Room with music and games – observing strict instruction to close by 10.30.p.m. – and on alternative Sunday evenings the group would meet in one another's homes, often the Harris's. They organised weekend residential conferences at Llangynidr and each year a small number attended the M.A.Y.C. weekend.

But the Harrises were not to settle permanently at Trinity or, indeed, in Penarth. Douglas Harris took early retirement from the U.W.I.S.T. and served two universities overseas, in Papua New Guinea and in Bulawayo for periods of three years, with mid-term leave so that they could keep in touch with their family. Their eventual and final retirement is eagerly awaited by Trinity.

The condition of the Youth Club at this time was not so happy. Philip Newman, the qualified leader, was financially supported by South Glamorgan, but was not supported by voluntary helpers from Trinity, except for Rosemary, his wife, and the strain of running a Senior Club was considerable. He reported in September 1979 that, although there were 70 on the books, there were only about 15% with any Trinity connection and, at times, oversight was difficult. He added:

> Since many of the older ones – 16 to 17 years old – seem to divide their Tuesday evenings between the Club and the bar at the Railway Hotel – we are losing the commitment that every organisation needs.

Visits to Butlins in Minehead and to the ice-skating rink in Bristol were arranged and a sponsored walk, organised in conjunction with the Welsh Association of Youth Clubs, raised £40. But an attempt to combine with the Albert Road Youth Club to attend the M.A.Y.C. London Weekend only succeeded in interesting one member and had to be abandoned.

Accordingly, from January 1980 the Club reverted to its younger group of 12 to 15 years and allowed only limited membership to non-Trinity youngsters with the result that they had 35 members, most of whom had some connection with Trinity. The Club arranged a Service each year on the Tuesday of Holy Week alongside the other Church Services.

The public house alternative to the Youth Club, – The Railway Hotel – here first mentioned, was to become an increasingly popular venue with young people, including the children of Church Members, and has added to the complexity of running a traditional M.A.Y.C. Club.

In contrast to the decline of the Youth Club, the success of the Play Group run by Philip's wife, Rosemary, with Elizabeth Gillespie and Sheila James, was remarkable. Meeting on Tuesday and Thursday afternoons, a membership of 44 mothers with 60 to 70 children was reported, with 19 mothers and 26 children on the waiting list. There were evening meetings in homes of the members and later on church premises, as more room was needed. The Group raised considerable sums for charities, such as the Leukaemia Unit at Llandough Hospital, and fed the younger end of the Junior Church. Increasingly the young mothers came to Services, whilst their babies were looked after in the creche, and, even more significant, into Church membership.

Leslie and Marion Craze were concerned that the months of July and August were particularly empty, apart from Sunday worship and Marion mobilized the Women's Work Committee to put on coffee mornings at the Manse each Summer to raise money for special projects. One year they supported a resource centre that William Gibbs was instrumental in setting up at the David Livingstone Teacher Training College in Zambia. People were thus brought together at what was otherwise a quiet time in the Church year.

Leslie Craze was also as concerned as any of his predecessors by the fact that many in the Trinity congregation seemed not to know those whom they worshipped alongside, so he and Marion, set about introducing the congregation to one another. Each month they invited those whose birthdays fell in that same month, and their spouses, to an evening in the Manse. In consequence, they gathered together a cross-section of the congregation each month and were encouraged by the response they received.

Class Tickets were now distributed by the class leaders to the members on a yearly, rather than quarterly, basis. This meant that contact between leaders and members was less frequent.

On his visits, Leslie Craze met a great many people who insisted that they were members of the Church but who did not attend Services. It was as if Trinity was their Church, in the sense that it was the one they stayed away from; their connection was a loose one even if they were technically members. A time came when, their absence being so extended, they had to be considered as having 'ceased to meet.'[1] The Church was, however, maintaining the size of its congregation. Throughout the connexion a church family count was instituted on a normal Sunday with the results for Trinity:

| 1974 | Those attending Morning Service | 136 |
|------|--------------------------------|-----|
|      | Those attending Evening Service | 30  |
|      | With 69 in Junior Church        |     |

| 1978 | Those attending Morning Service | 183 |
|------|--------------------------------|-----|
|      | Those attending Evening Service | 31  |
|      | With 76 in the Junior Church    |     |

The poor attendance at the Evening Services was a matter of concern. In 1975 the time of Service was changed to 6.p.m. and the venue to the New Room. It was thought that a Service 'in the Round' would be liturgically acceptable and encourage a greater feeling of fellowship and involvement. This arrangement was partly also to save heating costs, but as the Church needed to be heated for the Sunday Morning Service the saving was not significant. After a period of experimentation, the Evening Service returned to the Church in 1976, where it is still held. Numbers have not improved.

This is a pattern experienced by the other Penarth Churches, with the exception of Tabernacle Baptist Church, which draws large congregations to a full service of evangelical Worship and Fellowship on Sunday evenings.

Leslie Craze had continued the Tuesday evening Minister's Fellowship. He noted in *Contact* that 'it was a small and diminishing group but that it should be the most important meeting in the week'. When the ecumenical Lent Groups organised by the Penarth Council of Churches began, the Fellowship was closed as most of the members were involved in the Lent Groups. During Summer and Autumn 'Open House' meetings were held each week in the homes of different members for Bible Study, discussion and hearing about various aspects of Christian work. Groups arising out of the need for older Young Wives to meet together, such as 'Meeting Point,' emerged, lasted for a number of years and then gave place to other groups. Joyce Wells' Class continued to meet, but Trinity was not a Society whose members met in class during the week as well as on Sundays for public worship. Fellowship and service were centred on the work in the Day Centre, at International House and the new Methodist Home for the Aged, Morel Court.

International House continued to serve the international community studying or working in Cardiff. Some of the residents, for example, in 1980 Stella Selvadurai, a Christian from Sri Lanka and a World Council of Churches Scholar, identified themselves strongly with Trinity and made many friends in the Church and the town. On her return to her war-torn country, Stella kept in touch for a time but since 1987 no communication has been received from her, one example of the sadness which involvement in the international scene entails.

With their particular background, Leslie and Marion Craze enjoyed especially the chaplaincy at International House, sharing meals with the residents and conducting prayers in the Chapel on Wednesday evenings when as many as seventeen might be present. At one time a Jesuit

Leslie and Marion Craze, with Betty Field and residents of International House, 1978.

Priest and a Nun were staying in the House and they used the Chapel to celebrate Mass daily.

In the summer of 1975, the members of Trinity had a new sphere for service and friendship. With the other Churches in the South Wales District, they welcomed a Methodist Home for the Aged. 'M.H.A.' had been founded in 1943 and already had a Home in North Wales; now it was to have one in Penarth. A suitable site adjoining International House and near to the sea was offered and accepted. The purpose-built House had thirty pleasant rooms, personally furnished, for single people and married couples, 'freeing them from day-to-day worries, providing privacy and dignity and creating a safe, stimulating environment for their old age . . . Methodist Homes have made a continuing commitment to provide high quality Christian care for those in need'.

Trinity members became involved with the Home; in its administration, and in service to its residents, by, for example, providing transport to Church Services, to entertainments, for hospital visits or just for shopping, and by welcoming them to their new home in Penarth. Mebe James, widow of Donald, was one of the first residents and did much to make others feel at home in the House, her Church and the town.

Several distinguished Methodist Ministers have lived in Morel Court, including Colin Roberts, Secretary of the Home Mission Division, an Ex-President, who said on arrival 'What has God got for me to do here?' Also Wilfred Doidge, at one time a Secretary of the Youth Department. He was already well established in the Circuit having moved, after his retirement, to a flat belonging to the Methodist Ministers' Housing Society in St. Maeburne. After his wife's death, he moved to Morel Court.

During 1976, Leslie Craze lead the celebrations to mark the seventy-fifth anniversary of the opening of the Church; it was a Festival Year for Trinity. He was particularly anxious to increase the membership and appealed particularly 'for the number of people I meet who used to come to Trinity but do not come now – somehow they have slipped out for no particular reason – to return.' As one of the money raising efforts the Society had recourse to a Bazaar with the object of supplementing the weekly giving of the Church.

To indicate the activities in the Church, here follows a list of stalls at the Summer Bazaar held in June 1976.

| | |
|---|---|
| Women's Hour: | Cake Stall. |
| Choir: | Jewellery. Objects d' Art. |
| Junior Church: | 'We made it' and halfpennies. |
| Guides: | Soft drinks, ices. |
| Scouts: | Games. |
| Neighbourhood Committee: | Cordon Bleu Recipe Book. |
| Property Committee: | Greengrocery and Garden. |
| Youth Club: | Groceries. |
| Meeting Point: | Needlework, knitting, baby clothes. |
| Women's Work: | Teas. |

There were changes made in Morning Worship; these were not revolutionary but contributed to the sense of order and reflected on the growing concern for dignity in worship. The congregation continued the Trinity tradition of standing as soon as a hymn was announced and also rose as the offertory was received.

The collecting plates, which had always been used in the Church following American practice, were found to be too small due to inflation and in 1976 were replaced by alms bags, made by the members. These were received on a new alms dish. This was given in memory of E. Macmillan Ewens, who had died soon after retiring as organist. He had served for thirty years, so, for a period covering nearly sixty years, Trinity had been served by only two organists.

The traditional counting of the collection by the stewards at the close of each Service gave place in 1976 to its being counted and banked by the office staff, a group of retired members, on the following Monday.

In 1976 the Junior Church Anniversary took the form of a Family Communion.

At a Circuit Meeting the concern was voiced that Christian Education was increasingly lacking in the schools and within Methodism generally. The Churches were encouraged, on the American model, to meet for two hours on Sunday mornings, with one hour for worship and one hour for Christian education and fellowship. Trinity members were unprepared to depart from the traditional one hour's Service on Sunday mornings. However, it was decided to serve coffee after the Morning Service on Parade Sundays, and this has continued providing an opportunity for fellowship.

At Morning Communion Services, if a second minister was not available, local preachers, both men and women, were invited to share in the Service, to read part of the Great Prayer and to distribute the Bread or the Wine. To emphasise that the Communion Service was for all, it was decided that the words in the Order of Service: 'Those who must leave do so now' be omitted from the printed and spoken Order. The music and the Choir continued to be a very strong feature, especially of Morning Worship. In 1980 the Choir attracted an average attendance of over twenty-eight for choir practice on Thursday evenings; during the year they sang fifty introits and fifty one anthems.

Christmas Eve Communion was becoming an accepted Service in Methodism and in 1976 Trinity extended an invitation to Stanwell Road Baptist Church to hold a joint Service alternating between the two Churches. In March 1981, however, the Church Meeting decided that, because attendance had increased so markedly, Trinity would hold its own Service in future. Trinity members wanted to worship in their own Church at this time of the Church year; but it meant that one of the few Services that Trinity shared with another Covenanting Church was discontinued.

Two liturgical innovations, for Methodism, were made. As Easter approached, the Great Cross, built for the production of *Blessed Among Women* was erected in the north transept and hung with appropriately coloured cloths, green, purple, black and, lastly, white. On each of the four Sundays of Advent, during the Service, a large red candle was lit and on Christmas Day a white one, in an appropriate ceremony, using prayers, readings and a hymn.

Mothering Sunday was marked initially by the children distributing flowers to all the women who were mothers in the congregation. This was quickly seen to be divisive and so all women received posies. They were also delivered to those who could not be present.

Trinity was becoming a popular Church for weddings, partly as the Methodist Church permitted the marrying of divorced people, following due enquiry and in consultation with the Chairman of the District. All couples received appropriate preparation, and the seriousness of the rite was made clear. Especially happy occasions were those marriages involving Church members and those who had grown up in the Sunday School or Youth Club.

211

The number of Baptisms in Trinity increased likewise. In the Statement on Holy Baptism at the Methodist Conference of 1952 it was laid down that normally the Sacrament of Baptism should be administered in the Church by an Ordained Minister at a Service of Public Worship. From 1975, Trinity established this practice, using the Service set out in the Methodist Service Book. After preparation of the parents and god-parents, the baptismal parties would attend Morning Service, often in large numbers. The children were received 'into the congregation of Christ's flock' and the whole Church 'promised to maintain a common life of Worship and Service' into which the new members could be received and grow.

Some members of the congregation were distressed that, following on the Service, the members of the baptismal parties did not attend Trinity again. There were, however, instances when coming to Trinity for this purpose led to the taking up of membership. As the parents had sought out Trinity for this purpose, they would have had some personal or family connection with Trinity.

Inevitably, in a church the size of Trinity, deaths occur of members at the height of their powers and of service to the Church. Such a one was Glyn Marsh, who died suddenly in June of 1980. As we have noted he had followed his father to work for the Penarth Urban District Council. He had been employed in the finance department, and he brought his financial skills to Trinity, serving as Church Treasurer for many years. He was involved in every aspect of the Church's life, especially the Choir and Drama Group. As Leslie Craze said 'he might be said to have been born in Trinity, he grew up there, was married there and a succession of ministers knew him as a friend who could always be relied on.' He had married Esme Bryant who, with her sister, Daphne, had also grown up in the Church. It was their grandmother, who, when her husband became caretaker of Victoria School, nurtured them in the Church. Esme's long-standing commitment to the Neighbourhood and Catering Committees is outstanding. Daphne has been society steward and a very acceptable local preacher – they are both at the heart of Trinity.

It seemed that it would be difficult to find a successor to Glyn Marsh but good fortune had brought Glyn and Iris Davies to Penarth – and Trinity – in 1976. They had both been born in Swansea, where Glyn had attended the Welsh Independent Chapel and Iris the English Baptist Chapel which became their church after their marriage. Glyn held a succession of appointments in British ports, and while at Fleetwood they became Methodists. Glyn was then posted to Willerby and when, finally, he became personnel manager for the South Wales Docks, the family chose to live in Penarth. Glyn Davies willingly took over the Treasurership of the Church on Glyn Marsh's death and has subsequently become the Treasurer of the Covenanting Churches in Wales.

At this time another experienced administrator, Leslie Harmer, with his wife, Anne, was moved with his government department to South Wales and he, too, willingly took up office in Trinity, becoming Church Council Secretary. He had had wide experience of Methodism, having been Circuit Steward of the Chislehurst Circuit.

The Trinity 6th Penarth Scouts and Guides celebrated their 50th Anniversary in 1976. With one or two lean patches, they had thrived during the whole of this period, producing their own leaders from amongst their members and establishing a position in the forefront of scouting practice. They were one of the first to develop a Company of Venture Scouts, a mixed group of former Rovers and Rangers, and they travelled widely, for example, to Canada in 1980. Some scout and guide companies sit loosely to their sponsoring churches: at Trinity they are closely integrated into the ongoing life of the Church and the Church has sought to provide for their needs – even allowing them to dry out their equipment in the Church itself after a wet camp.

The condition of the structure of the Church and Trinity Hall was monitored faithfully and regularly by the property steward and committee. The property steward was loath to recommend major repairs owing to the financial position. Signs of damp were noticed in Trinity Hall, and in 1980 it was reported that severe frost had damaged some of the coping stones and flashings, and that the finials on the roof were in a poor state. The finials were removed. The louvres in the Tower, which had had to be taken out because they were unsafe were, however, replaced.

The Church Council was encouraged to hear that 'generally speaking the building is in good heart, except for some of the masonry which is deteriorating.'

It was during Leslie Craze's ministry that a second Trinity Member became High Sheriff of South Glamorgan. Harold Williams, O.B.E., had been President of the Institute of British Foundrymen, Chairman of the Confederation of British Industry for Wales and a Member of the

European Iron and Steel Community.  In addition, he was a member of the Court and Council of Cardiff University of Wales.  In 1979 he invited Leslie Craze to be his Chaplain and during the year they were involved in a number of functions and Services both in Penarth and in the County.  Harold was not to miss out on his Trinity commitments and he continued to fulfil his lectern rota appointments, reading with the Canadian accent which he has never lost.

A quiet piece of service by a Trinity member which continued was the regular sending out of 'Letters to the Housebound' by Jean Dewar, herself increasingly handicapped, but determined to keep lonely Methodists in the District in touch with the Church.

The Circuit Meeting continued to meet quarterly in the four churches in the Circuit and, on occasions, had difficult issues to consider.  The Methodist Conference was deeply concerned with exploring Christian understanding of Human Sexuality and remitted a consideration of this to the lower courts of the Church, both to the Circuit Meeting and the Church Councils.  In September 1981, Sheila Gibbs, as Secretary of the Circuit Meeting, had the responsibility of reporting on the discussions in the Penarth Circuit.  She could report no consensus, especially on the question of the acceptance of active homosexuality amongst members.  The discussion was particularly fraught over the issue of active homosexual candidates for the Ministry and the majority opinion came down heavily against accepting them.  It was remarkable how many 'ordinary' Methodists were prepared to discuss these issues frankly, openly and compassionately.  Those with responsibilities for young people were particularly concerned.  After a lull, the issue was again before the Church ten years later.

When the time came for Leslie Craze to leave Penarth, there was an ecumenical flavour to his farewell. The September *Contact* reported that:

> 'At a Circuit Garden Party held at Sea Roads on July 18th 1981 a fond goodbye was said to Leslie and Marion Craze.  In addition to the tributes from representatives of each of the four Churches in the Circuit, an appreciative contribution was made by the Reverend Ralph Holtam, Rector of Sully and the current Chairman of the Penarth Council of Churches, who stressed the part played by Leslie Craze in the ecumenical life of the town.'

Leslie and Marion have retired to Wedmore in the Cheddar Valley Circuit. In addition to their life in the village and in Wells nearby, where they have acted as Welcomers to the Cathedral for a number of years, Leslie became the Circuit Steward of the Circuit, almost a unique occurrence and an Indian Summer for a man who began his Ministry in India itself forty-five years before.

# CHAPTER 19

## The Rev'd John Ashplant 1981-1989

The Circuit Stewards had invited a sector minister, the Rev'd Raymond Trudgian, who was in a teaching appointment, to follow Leslie Craze in 1981. But, unfortunately, he suffered a breakdown in 1980. Not until the early summer of 1981 did it become plain that he would be unable to come to Penarth in the Autumn. Trinity was faced, in June, with not having a minister for September.

The Conference Stationing Committee met at intervals during the year and the great majority of invitations were arranged well before the September in which moves are made to a new circuit. There is a final meeting during Conference to fill stations which, for differing reasons, remain open. It might be because men – and, since 1973, women and men – were needed elsewhere for immediate appointment, as in the case of Stanley Dixon in 1937. It might be through illness or because the circuit stewards had been unable to persuade any minister to accept what was considered to be a particularly unattractive appointment.

John Ashplant was at this time the Superintendent of the Cheddar Circuit living in Churchill. He had had a distinguished ministry as Superintendent of the Edinburgh Mission and later of the Plymouth Central Hall, where he was adviser to Westward TV and TSW. When he moved from Plymouth to Churchill in 1972, it was in response to a request from Westward TV that he be allowed to remain in the West Country. From there he was able to travel weekly to Plymouth to continue his TV ministry. But after staying there for nine years, he felt it was time to move on.

On the first list of stations he was 'put down' for St. John's, Glasgow. He had always left himself 'in the hands of the Stationing Committee' but he was distressed by Glasgow's distance from Plymouth and his work there.

John Gibbs was a member of the Stationing Committee and he was able to assure John Ashplant and the Committee that he would be more than welcome at Trinity, immediately. The opening in the Penarth Circuit was heaven sent; with the development of the M4 and the M5 the travelling time, if not the distance, between Penarth and Plymouth was not great.  So, Trinity had a new Minister and 'Westward Television could retain its religious programmes' adviser.

John Ashplant had been born in Bideford in 1920 and served in the R.A.F., having been enrolled, as we have noted, in the Woodland Hall. On demobilisation in 1945, he went on leave to his home town of Bideford.  There he found that the Minister of High Street Church had suddenly died, and he was asked to be the Minister of his home church for the rest of the connexional year – an unusual pre-collegiate appointment.  He then went to Didsbury College in Bristol for his ministerial training.

Trinity welcomed the new Minister and his wife, Barbara, with real warmth and with relief that their problem had been so satisfactorily solved.  They learned to watch him leaving Penarth for Plymouth after Sunday evening Services, aware that he had a long drive in front of him, but secure in the knowledge that he would be back in Penarth the next day to fulfil his Ministry at Trinity, and so that his wife could preside at the Women's Meeting. Trinity was not apprehensive about his being a 'mission man' – they had appreciated Percy Watkinson with a similar background in the 1950s, and, even if John Ashplant was inclined to 'lead from the front,' his style was never overbearing and he listened to his people.

The congregation on his first Sunday was perhaps somewhat apprehensive; but an adherent, not yet, quite a Methodist, voiced the general feeling: 'Where on earth do you Methodists get all these wonderful Ministers?'

Barbara Ashplant shared in his Ministry, greeting the congregation in the Porch each Sunday and, as a bonus, their brother-in-law, Gordon Baker from Ely Methodist Church, joined Trinity and brought his professional skill as an ITV Scenic Carpenter to the service of the Church in many practical ways, as in the making of visual aids, and as property steward.

John Ashplant had recently brought out a book, based on his TV talks, *Faith for Life*, which he used to good effect in his pastoral ministry.

On becoming acquainted with the church life in Penarth, he was appreciative of the work done during Christian Aid Week but surprised by the slow growth of inter-church co-operation in the town in other respects.  He had been used to working closely with ministers of the other Churches when in previous appointments. The absence of any joint Communion Services, such as he had experienced in England, he found particularly distressing.

The Churches in Wales had theoretically moved further towards unity than those in England by virtue of having signed the Welsh Covenant. Armed with this, he was able to persuade the Anglican Church that on occasions such as the Octave of Prayer for Christian Unity it would be both fitting and right to hold Services of Concelebration, for which the Covenanting Churches had drawn up an Order of Service. The first Joint Communion Service was held in Trinity on 1 February 1985. This arrangement has continued in Penarth and, in rotation, the Services are held during the Week of Unity in the Churches which have signed the Covenant.

In 1982 there was the need to designate a new Chairman for the Cardiff and Swansea District of the Methodist Church – soon to be known as the South Wales District. The Chairman's role is an administrative one for the District, which has some twenty-one circuits, and a pastoral one for one hundred and fifteen ministers and a number of lay people. The Chairman also has to play a representative role in relation to the other Churches and to Local Authorities in the area.[1]

Donald Knighton was appointed Chairman at the 1983 Conference, and in September 1984 he returned to Wales from Selly Oak in Birmingham, where he had enjoyed a concentrated Ministry, to the oversight of the dauntingly large District that stretches from Ross-on-Wye in the East to Fishguard in the West, and from the Bristol Channel in the South to Hay in the North.

Donald and Anne, with their two younger children, Ben and Rachel – their elder son, Daniel, remaining behind in Birmingham – moved into the Chairman's Manse in Cardiff. This soon bore the stamp of Anne's taste upon it, nurtured, many years before, by Kathleen Hughes, her Headmistress at the Penarth County School.

In addition to covering a huge area, the District has within its boundaries four Universities – or University Colleges as they are known in Wales – and, because of the separation of Wales, ecclesiastically, from England, the Chairman of the Methodist District has to relate in terms of Church leadership with the Archbishop of the Church in Wales and the Roman Catholic Archbishop of Cardiff, as well as with the leaders of the Free Churches in Wales.

The Induction Service for the new Chairman was held at Trinity on 31 August 1984. Donald's mother, Evelyn Knighton, had recently died at Cedar Lawn M.H.A. at Stratford on Avon – the town to which she and her husband, George, had retired. George Knighton, his father, was able to be present and so was his sister, Mary, who has contributed so many vivid memories to these pages. After taking a Science Degree at Bedford College, London, Mary married Derek Jefferson, whom she had first met in Llangynidr when she was a school girl. Stanley Dixon officiated at their wedding at Trinity in 1952. Beside being the supportive wife of a busy minister in Lincoln, Worcester and Sheffield, Mary has taught in various schools and recently, besides obtaining her doctorate at the University of Sheffield, has lectured in Environmental Studies. She is deeply involved in Network and is a member of the Stationing Committee.

Donald Knighton's Induction Service was conducted by the Secretary of the District, the Rev'd Tom Davies, and Trinity Choir, under their new Conductor, Edgar Watkins, led the singing. Laymen and laywomen led the prayers of intercession. In addition to the Methodists, several from Trinity, who took part, the Archbishop of Wales, Bishop Mullins for the Roman Catholic Church, and the Rev'd Lesley Jones, a former Moderator of the Presbyterian Church of Wales, welcomed Donald in English and Welsh on behalf of their Churches. They promised to work with him and pray for him, as did Mrs. Jeane Jones, on behalf of the United Reformed Church and the Rev'd Herbert Price on behalf of the Baptist Church. The Charge was given in a fine address by the Rev'd Dr. John A. Newton, Past President of the Conference, who also inducted the new Chairman. Methodists came from the far ends of the District and there were representatives from all the Circuits in which Donald has served with the result that Trinity was full for the occasion.

The International House of South Wales had become a valued part of Penarth life; however, the international and national scenes were changing. During the 1960s and 1970s accommodation at International House had been in very great demand, but by the 1980s there was an increasing number of empty rooms. In the autumn of 1984: at the start of the new academic year the House was full, but there were soon empty rooms – the overseas and U.K. students having got to know each other, some had moved out into flats which they rented. It proved impossible to fill the empty places and with only partial occupancy the House was not financially viable. The decision was taken to close the House at the end of August 1985.

A Service of Thanksgiving for the twenty-one years of the House's Ministry and Service was held at which all the Trinity Ministers who had served as Chaplains were present. The Lord Lieutenant of the County, Sir Cennydd Traherne, K.G., who had supported the House from its inception, paid tribute to the contribution it had made. Donald Knighton, as the new Chairman of the District and the Chairman of the House wrote:

> The closing of the Methodist International House is a sad occasion, but we have much to thank God for in its twenty one years of caring ministry to generations of residents.
>
> The House will be remembered with gratitude all over the world and its ministry has had a tremendous influence under God upon many people. Changed circumstances now make inevitable the closing of the House, but the money, released by its sale, will be used in a wider way 'for work among students – especially overseas students'.

Here is included part of the Warden's address in which Kenneth Field described life in the House:

> We give thanks for the opportunities and privileges of the past 18 years – that have been filled with strangers that became friends and then part of the 'family'.
>
> The Thomson Foundation scholars from Courses 17 to 43 – 440 of them in groups of 12, arriving on a Friday afternoon wondering how they would manage to become 'students' again – to live through our winters – to have their evening meal at 6.15. in the middle of the afternoon to them.
>
> The British Council scholars and the Teaching of English courses, the engineers – how difficult the Japanese, Balinese and Thai found our language and the one from Jordan who walked in the road so no one should jump on him.
>
> The Doctors on the Tuberculosis and Chest Disease courses – first at Sully and then at Llandough Hospitals. Many of these took part in the life of the town in Rotary and the Churches.
>
> The trainees who filled their rooms with car engines and spare parts, the electronic wizards whose spiders web of wires made

room care a hazard, the musicians who added so much to the pleasures of the House, especially at parties.

A special privilege has been the 17 couples who came, met and married – the three babies who arrived whilst their mothers were here and, in a different way, the two people who have died here and who to the end were happy and contented.

Not only the residents from home and overseas. We think of the many elderly, handicapped and deprived holiday makers. The deprived children from Birmingham who came every year until their funds ran out – particularly the little horror who climbed out of one of the top floor windows into the next room.

We think of the Red Cross groups, of the dedication of their helpers. Betty and I count ourselves fortunate to have been able for 11 years to have Penrose and Moorcraft mentally handicapped groups for a week's holiday.

Throughout all these years Methodism has been the ground of our Christian faith and it has been a great joy to share 'Our House' with Church Committees and District Committees, Superintendents' meetings and Presidential lunches and to host the District Women's Luncheon Club.[2]

Since it is now a Nursing Home, a new type of resident of the building is able to enjoy the views over the green, the Cliff Walk and the Bristol Channel to the Somerset coast and beyond.

In this chapter, young parents and their children will have increasing mention. The Tribute to Robert Bond in 1905 was signed by parents and their children and underlined his Ministry to the whole family 'the playmate of the children, the guide and confidant of the young people, the trusted friend and companion of the parents.' Some seventy-five years later, Trinity Ministers still strive to fulfil this ministry. Continuity with an earlier stage in Trinity's history is demonstrated by the three sons, Samuel, Matthew and Nicholas, of Elaine and Alan Hooper, who, although living in Wenvoe, are members of Trinity. Elaine is the great grand-daughter of the Miss Mary Anne Morgan who brought Methodism to Penarth.

The Youth Club, now very much a junior club, made little contribution to the life of the Church, although it did provide activities for a comparatively small number of young teenagers. Philip Newman retired as leader in 1984. He and his wife, Rosemary, had grown up in the Youth Club and, after leading it for a long period, they continued to be closely involved with money raising activities for the Church. The club leaders who followed him were not supported by the Church to any degree, in spite of requests in *News Notes* for help, and they were not known generally to the congregation.

On the other hand, the Scouts, using this term to include all those involved in the Scout and Guide Movement, continued strongly and the monthly Parade Services were well attended. On those occasions the lessons were read and the offertory was collected with dignity by the Scouts and Guides. Coffee and soft drinks served after Parade Services provided an opportunity for the members of the Church to meet together, although only a small proportion of the congregation, perhaps 50 or 60, took advantage of this.

Not only did the Scouts grow their own leaders but it made a strong contribution to the ongoing life of the Church and the Junior Church.

Edward and Sheila James both moved to Penarth; Edward came in 1950 at the age of four, and at eleven joined the Trinity Scouts. At fourteen he joined the Youth Club and went with the Rev'd Tom Davies to the Plas-y-Antur Methodist Adventure Centre in North Wales, after which he became a member of the Church. He joined the Merchant Navy as an electrical officer. Sheila Bloomer came to the town when she was eleven and joined the Youth Club at 13. In 1971, whilst Edward was on leave, he got to know Sheila whom he had first met as a very young club member at a 'Bar-B-Q' at Lavernock Point in 1962. They married in 1972 in Trinity, and now, with their daughter and son, Bethan and Owen, are deeply enfolded in the life of the Church. Edward is a hardware engineer with South Glamorgan with the responsibility for maintaining the traffic lights, and Sheila is a medical receptionist. They have made a substantial contribution to the life of the Church initially through the Scouts and Young Wives'. Edward has specialized on the lighting of Trinity, and, in 1981, Sheila became a Church Steward. She continues the tradition of women in this role which Trinity has fostered, and the family shows how, in addition to incoming families, Trinity produces its own members, and their children grow up in the Church.

The Cubs were joined by an even younger group in 1988, a Beaver Colony, and in 1989 a Rainbow group of younger girls was formed which completes the coverage over the whole age range.

The whole Scout Group is particularly in evidence before Christmas when, joined by the Y.P.F., the Youth Club and some senior members of the Church, they run a postal service, delivering Christmas cards in Penarth. Stamps are sold at a competitive price, two of the rooms in Trinity Hall are taken over as a sorting office for a month and by Christmas Eve all the letters, in 1992 some 45,000, have been delivered. By this and other means the Group and the other youth activities made a considerable sum, £4,500, for their funds and for their contribution to the Church.

Baptisms were by now almost always held during the Sunday Morning Services, and were not infrequent: John Ashplant baptised over 130 babies in Trinity during his Ministry. Practices changed in various ways and from 1982, lighted candles were presented to the parents of the child within the Service with the words:

The Minister:

'I give you this sign, for you now belong to Christ, the Light of the World.'

The Congregation:

'Let your light so shine before men that they may see your good works and give glory to your Father who is in heaven.'

Each Baptism represented hours of the Ministers' time in preparing the family, which invariably had some contact with the Church, either through having been involved in the Sunday School, youth club or scouts, or through having been married in the building. Often couples were returning to their parents' Church for the baptism of a grandchild.

Attempts have been made within Trinity to keep the parents, and the children, in touch with the Church by means of a Cradle Roll Service to which baptised children are invited. Some families choose to attend, and their children join the Beginners' Department of Junior Church when they are three. Others choose not to and a number leave Penarth for one reason or another.

There was good support for the Junior Church and the departments were usually fully staffed. In 1984, Bert Scriven retired as superintendent – the term with its authoritarian overtones was still in use. He was followed by a young teacher, Tony Farmer, who had grown up as a

223

Methodist in Walsall and Aldridge but did not get involved with Trinity until some years after taking up an appointment in the art department at St. Cyres Comprehensive School. His wife, Mary, had been born in Penarth, and was the grand daughter of Dick Evans, one time Circuit Steward, but she had moved away with her family as a baby. On her return to Penarth she attended some evening services but without enthusiasm. Only after their first child was born and she had taken him to the Play Group did they became involved in the life of the Church. She and Tony began coming to Church regularly and Tony joined the Choir. In time and as the children of the original leaders grew up, Mary took over the leadership of the Play Group, and she is now also leader of the Beginners Department of Family Church. Mary, Tony and their children, David, Jane, Sarah and Christopher, are one of the key families in the Church.

The pattern of Junior Church that had been established continued, even to the extent of celebrating Anniversaries with visual aids. On one occasion a Super skyscraper, – the Tower of Babel – was built up laboriously within the Church only to be destroyed and superseded by the Pentecost Experience. On another a Lighthouse, which lit up, was built.

Children participating in services were sometimes inaudible. The situation improved dramatically in 1989 when the new amplification system, which incorporated a loop system, was installed.

There was one break with tradition: some of the staff found the preparation for the *Partners in Learning* syllabus too demanding and, in some cases, felt that the lessons were not explicitly Bible-centred. They changed to the Scripture Union Course, more traditional, and less adventurous than *Partners in Learning*.

It was in 1981, that Bert Scriven started the Trinity Social Club, at first to provide opportunities to play badminton, and later, with its activities extended, to become a social meeting point; an equivalent of the Guild. In addition to being an honoured local preacher, Bert Scriven has been determined also that the Church shall remain healthy and strong in fellowship. That this is so is due in no small measure to what he has brought to it ever since the days when he returned from the Forces and settled in Penarth in 1946.

Trinity entered enthusiastically into two projects sponsored by the Penarth Council of Churches. An evangelical 'Jesus for Life'

Campaign in 1983 and, four years later, 'The Bible Come to Life' was mounted in All Saints Church and portrayed the background to the Bible by means of models and dramatic presentations.

Trinity is a Church in which Americans feel particularly at home. Because of Penarth's proximity to the industrial estates in Barry, a number of American families with Lutheran backgrounds who work there have chosen to live in Penarth and attend Trinity. Two of the stars of the Welsh National Opera, Jaques Trussel, who sang Don Jose in *Carmen*, and Richard Finck, Rigoletto in *Rigoletto*, have been part of the Trinity congregation from time to time and their voices, when they have chosen to give them full rein, have added a remarkable dimension to the Trinity sound.

The position with Class Meetings in the Society has remained much the same, but Trinity has continued to support the Lent Ecumenical Groups in very good numbers and has supplied more than its quota of leaders.

At Barbara Ashplant's prompting, Trinity hosted a Daffodil Rally which continued regularly over the years. Not a normal festival of the Christian Year, this brought together the women of the Churches and enabled them to celebrate the passing of winter and the coming of spring; a modern example of taking over a non-Christian festival and incorporating it within the Christian Year.

Barbara also started the Young Women's Fellowship at Trinity and, like the Women's Meeting, it has continued as one of the most significant meetings in the Church.

Young people from the Church continued to go away for weeks or shorter periods but now, rather than to traditional M.A.Y.C. events, it would be more likely to be the Greenbelt Festival or Youth Makes Music, Dance and Drama. The Church had an 'Away Weekend' on the Gower.

With the final retirement of Howard Ponsford as choirmaster in 1987 and the retirement of a number of long-standing choir members in the next two years, the musical side of Trinity had to take another direction. The formation of a Council of Churches Choir to sing on ecumenical occasions also distracted somewhat from the appeal of the Trinity choir, and Trinity, accustomed to full choir stalls, was distressed. It has not been possible to restore the choir to its previous strength from amongst the members of the congregation. However, the volume and quality of the congregational singing has been maintained; a combination of Welsh and Methodist traditions.

On E. Macmillan Ewens' retirement, there had followed a succession of able organists, but it was not until 1983, when June Poley was appointed, that continuity was again achieved. She was joined by Evelyn Careless at Christmas in 1989, and Trinity is now served by two very competent organists who share the Services between them. Evelyn Careless has taken responsibility for the small choir which remains.

By the 1980s, Trinity was no longer a stewardship church and in 1981 rejected the suggestion that it should again become one. The annual deficits in the Church accounts were met by gift days, the Sunday collection and covenanted giving. Inflation continually altered the financial situation, and, in 1982, the Treasurer, Glyn Davies, urged the Society to increase its giving by £20 a week. By the following February it was clear that this was no longer sufficient. It was not only the need to pay the rising Circuit Assessment for the support of the Ministry and the Methodist Church as a whole that caused concern, it was the cost of heating, lighting and maintaining both the Church and the Hall. Further, although the buildings had been repaired forty years earlier after War damage, there was considerable deterioration in both structures, as Derck Dowdeswell, a professional surveyor and member of the Church, warned the Property Committee.

The Committee was despondent. There was even talk of demolishing the Church and the Hall, as was to happen in 1989 to the United Reformed Christchurch in the centre of the town. However, it was estimated that it would probably cost £750,000 to demolish the present premises and build new profit-making structures on the land, and so this draconian solution was rejected. The problem, however, remained.

The Church Council was faced with a major decision; should things be patched up, some decoration undertaken and immediate faults treated, none of which would attract any grant, or should a major scheme be initiated? The condition of Trinity Hall was aggravated by the fact that, with the demise of the Drama Group, the stage area, the lighting box and the scenery store had become increasingly dusty and untidy. As can happen only too easily on church premises, all kinds of unwanted articles, rejected jumble, broken chairs and torn curtains had been dumped in these areas. As a result the image of the Church as a pleasant place in which to meet and work had became increasingly obscured.

At the same time as the premises were crying out for attention and clearly required considerable expenditure, the Conference launched a stirring appeal for money for 'Mission alongside the Poor'. Trinity had to set her claims against appeals for assistance for churches and organisations in run-down areas in Britain, particularly in the Inner Cities. Nor were Methodists allowed or inclined to forget the needs of the wider world and of the overseas outreach of the Church.

At Church Councils in 1983 a number of the members voiced the opinion that nothing should be spent on Church buildings; in effect, on ourselves. This view was sympathetically received, but John Ashplant pointed out that, unless the church base in Britain was maintained and in good heart, it would be impossible to respond to similar demands from elsewhere in the future. The members of the Church Council found this dilemma almost overwhelming: they decided to try to meet, as best they could, demands from outside as well as to proceed with a scheme for the renovation of Trinity Hall. This became known as 'Trinity 2000', the year by which it was hoped it would be in good enough shape to meet both the needs of the Church and appeals from outside.

A wide consultation was set in motion and ideas for the best use of the ancillary premises were canvassed. There were suggestions for a larger foyer for the Church and for a replanning of the Chancel area, but these did not gain support; it was felt that there was enough to do without redesigning the inside of the Church. Nevertheless, a library of contemporary religious books for adults and children was established in the South Transept. The needs of the various organisations using the premises were listed and use by outside organisations was envisaged. It seemed impossible to compass the total requirements within the space available until a scheme was proposed to insert a concrete 'table' within the Hall which would, at a stroke, double the space available.

With this proposal the scheme took off and the needs of all the potential users of the premises could be met. There was sufficient height within the former Hall area to create a new space on the first floor with adequate headroom to permit badminton to be played and to create, in effect, a new Hall with pleasant proportions and of Victorian appearance, incorporating the delicate wrought-iron pillars and the large leaded window in the South wall.

'Trinity 2000' was presented to the Church Meeting in October 1985 which was attended by 150 members at the end of a three course meal prepared by the women of the Church. 85% of those present voted in favour of the project and a fundraising committee was appointed, with Sheila Gibbs as chairperson and Audrey Whitefield as secretary.

*Contact* December 1985 reported:

> The idea of making the premises fit the requirements of the new century was warmly endorsed, having in mind that our forefathers had planned the Church and the ancillary buildings one hundred years ago for our use and to the Glory of God.

An Appeal brochure, describing Trinity from 1890 to 1986 was produced with a striking cover which showed the Church on the corner of Stanwell Road and Woodland Place – 'Where many ways meet'.

The Church rose to the financial challenge. A successful Gift Day, at which £20,000 was raised or pledged, followed in February, and from this point on every section of the Church was involved in money raising. However, even in 1986, when fund raising for 'Trinity 2000' was at its height, £4,000 at least was given by the Church for other causes, in part fulfilment of its pledge not to allow other needs to go unsupported. The work began on 9 June 1986 and was to cost £150,000.

Stanwell Road Baptist Church provided hospitality to the Junior Church whilst the work was in progress.

John Ashplant wrote in the commemorative Brochure.

> No unforeseen structural difficulties have been encountered, and the work has progressed on schedule. By the end of 1986, Trinity will have an excellent suite of premises – a beautiful Church in which to worship, ancillary premises comprising a splendid large multi-purpose upper hall, a series of rooms of varying sizes on the ground floor, including ample storage space, a lift by which to reach the upper hall, a new entrance off Woodland Place into a large foyer, a Church office, and a little prayer chapel which will be open to all. The scheme includes the rewiring of the electrical system, a modern gas-fired heating system for the new Trinity Rooms, and a new boiler for the heating of the Church. In addition, a certain amount of remedial work has been done on the structure itself, which we would have had to do in any case.

Our community involvement will be significantly enhanced by the advent of our new premises. Not only will they provide our own organisations and activities with better facilities, which is important, they will also enable us to work out the role of the Church in response to community needs. We must foster the closest possible relationships between local community groups and the Church, making it clear that such groups can rely on our moral and practical support. At the same time – and this is very important – we are convinced that the Gospel has a unique contribution to make to the well-being of the whole person. The community needs the Church and the Church needs the community. Each is part of the other. Both belong to God.

Towards the £150,000, the sale of 66, Grove Terrace realised £41,000 and grants from Methodist and other Trusts contributed £40,000 including a generous contribution of £10,000 from the Rank Trust, thus illustrating the in-church joke that, 'Methodism is supported by the Rank and File'. Fundraising activities produced £16,000 and gift days £43,000.

A final gift day was held when only £10,000 remained outstanding and, at a Morning Service in February 1988, John Ashplant was able to announce that this had been raised.

In 1983 Tim and Ruth Coward moved to Penarth bringing with them their children, Martin and Caroline, when Tim got a job at the Cardiff Institute of Higher Education.

Tim Coward had been an Anglican, but became a Methodist on his marriage to Ruth Slater who came of strong Methodist stock. She had an uncle, who was a China Missionary, her father and aunt were local preachers, and she herself started to preach at sixteen. Following two years at Southlands Teacher Training College, she spent another two years as a missionary teacher in a new school on Grand Bahama Island. She then returned to London where she and Tim were married in Chelsea Methodist Church by the Rev'd Tom Davies, who had been the minister at Albert Road Church. When he heard that they were moving to South Wales, Tom Davies was anxious that they should join Albert Road Church. However, the two children became members of the Trinity cubs and brownies and, as they family lived in Stanwell Road and did not consider it was right to pass one church to go to another, they came to Trinity.

Since Ruth was a member of the Connexional Local Preachers Committee and had been a member of Synod in London and Sheffield, she brought a new connexional slant to Trinity and new strength to the group of circuit Lay Preachers. She is head teacher of a multi-racial nursery school in Grangetown.

Tim is now Head of the School of Design at C.I.H.E. and his expertise in design has enabled him, as Chairman of the Property Committee, to make an outstanding contribution to both 'Trinity 2000' and to the Spire and Restoration Project. The Circuit has appointed him to follow Howard Ponsford as Circuit Steward, so in this important office in the Circuit there is a succession of leadership by men originally from outside Methodism who now are closely identified with it.

On 2 March 1987 Tim Coward announced that the premises were in use and a fortnight later they were officially opened by Trinity's own Anne Knighton in her Year of Office as Vice President of the Methodist Conference.

In the years since she had left Penarth, Anne had moved beyond circuit, and more recently, District, responsibilities into wider Methodism. She had become Chairwoman of the Connexional Young Wives Committee., and from that committee it was a natural step to involvement in Women's Fellowship and Women's Work as it came together in Network. She was on the General Committee of the Overseas Division and represented the British Conference at the Nigerian Conference and at the Irish Conference. It was as a representative from the Irish Conference that she attended the British Methodist Conference in 1985 and was designated as Vice-President for 1986. When she opened the newly designed Trinity premises she had just returned from the World Federation of Methodist Women at Nairobi and had been one of the few white Methodists at the Black Methodist Conference in Britain.

John Ashplant was expecting to leave Trinity in the September of 1988, but no minister had been secured to follow him and at the Circuit Stewards' request he agreed to stay at Trinity for another year.

He was happy at Trinity and looking forward to a further year when, in June 1988, he suffered a severe heart attack. He was unable to fulfil his duties but Gerald Stoddern, the Second minister in the Circuit, stood in for him and took over the responsibilities of Superintendent Minister as well as helping him in the taking of Services, as he gradually recovered his strength.

There were retired laymen to help and there were supernumerary ministers in the Circuit. In particular Deryck Collingwood, who had retired to Penarth in 1987 took an increased number of Services. In the Autumn of 1988, John Ashplant was back at work part-time and by Christmas he was full-time. He was fully able to enjoy his last few months 'in the active work' as the Minister of Trinity.

In Trinity's early days there were very few marriages. In 1902 there were only two; one was of John A. MacArthur and the other of Christine Nance, both of Trinity families. In the three spring months of 1989 there were ten, not one of which had an easily recognised Trinity connection. Each would have represented hours of pastoral counselling, and many would be in the difficult field of the re-marriage of divorced people. Also during this period, and as a token of his recovery, John Ashplant received twenty-two new members, including five married couples, into the membership 'of the World Church and of the Methodist Church.'

John Ashplant's final message to Trinity in Contact was headed 'Permission to sit down,' an honoured Methodist phrase for retirement. He wrote about his last minute decision to come to Trinity made within 24 hours in June 1981: 'Nothing has happened to cause us to regret that decision'. And he wrote of the warmth of fellowship in the Church and the Circuit, the imaginative alteration to Trinity Hall and especially the Services of Holy Communion. 'I am glad,' he continued, 'that my final Service at Trinity will find us together at the Lord's Table.' And concluded:

> And so to Hall Green Birmingham . . . I trust I am not 'worn out', but even if I am, it has been in a good cause. If I were given another life to live, I would still wish to be a Methodist Minister.

# CHAPTER 20

## The Rev'd Albert Jewell 1989-

Albert Jewell came to Trinity from a background different from those of the previous ministers. He had been born in 1936 in St. Albans and from a non-church background had joined the Methodist Youth Club there – that club being the most attractive in the town. This first contact with Methodism was to lead to his becoming a Methodist Minister in 1960. He had a distinguished academic career, an M.A. from Oxford, a B.A. from Cambridge and then an M. Phil. from London University. He married Gill Fytche, daughter of a leading St. Albans Methodist family and a member of the Youth Club. In 1962, he had been an Assistant Tutor at Didsbury College, and later chaplain at Ashville College and to Leeds University and to what was then the Polytechnic. He had been National Chairman of the Samaritans.

It was from Leeds, where he had responsibility for four churches and was Superintendent of a large circuit, that he came to Trinity, looking forward to the concentrated ministry that appointment offered.

Towards the end of John Ashplant's Ministry, Howard Ponsford had become Circuit Steward, in addition to being one of the treasurers for the Methodist Conference which was to meet in St. David's Hall in Cardiff in June 1990. For one to whom a Salvation Army Company and later a single and largely self sufficient Church, Trinity, was the natural unit for mission and in which he felt very much at home, the assumption of Circuit and, indeed, Conference responsibilities was an illustration of the way in which Methodism extends and stretches its members.

The Conference had recently introduced a new way of stationing ministers and this made good sense to Howard. In place of the haphazard methods of the past, under the new system circuits set out their needs and ministers set out their aspirations, and the hope was that a marriage of the two could be brought about. A job description for the Trinity appointment was prepared and circulated by the Chairman of the District, and a list of ministers who would be 'free' at the appropriate time, together with brief C.V.'s and statements expressing their aspirations, was made available to the Penarth Stewards. The system laid down the date on which the Circuit Stewards were able to approach the Minister of their choice.

If the minister to whom the circuit stewards wrote – or telephoned – as their first choice did not feel 'happy' with the circuit after a visit had been made, or the circuit stewards and the church stewards of the particular church or churches did not think that the minister would be 'right', negotiations would begin again with their second choice. Problems sometimes occurred at this stage since some might well have already accepted an appointment by this time.

The Penarth Stewards, after a number of negotiations, did not find a minister who they thought would suit Trinity, and as we know from the previous chapter, they asked John Ashplant whether he would postpone his retirement for one year, and this he did.

At the appropriate time in the following year the Stewards began their search again, this time for an appointment in September 1989. They were soon to be successful and Albert Jewell accepted the invitation to Trinity and is the Minister at the time of writing.

For the first time, the Manse drive holds two cars as Gill needs one for her own work as a part time teacher of children with special educational needs.

Trinity's involvement in the work at Headlands continued as Gill Jewell became the Chair of the Home soon after her arrival in Penarth. The National Children's Home's pattern of care for disadvantaged children has reflected changing thinking and social conditions. Headlands continues to provide education, training and support for a number, howbeit reduced, of seriously damaged and disturbed children in an atmosphere of caring and affection.

For Albert Jewell one of the attractions of the appointment had been the knowledge that an elaborate scheme for the updating of the premises had been undertaken and paid for, and that he would be free from property worries and able to concentrate on a pastoral ministry. However, this was not to be. Within six months of his arrival in Penarth a windstorm caused evident damage to the spire of the Church, and, after making an extensive survey of the whole premises, Derek Dowdeswell presented a daunting list of work that needed to be done: the repairing of the coping stones, the replacement of the rain water 'goods', repointing and attending to the Bath Stone and replacing defective stone work. The following major items needed immediate attention: the renewal of the whole roof, the rebuilding of the north gable end and the removal of the chimney stack in the Hall, and the repairing of the Church Spire. There was also a considerable area of dry rot in the floor of the new foyer and in the chapel – which had only recently been relaid.

The Church was resilient enough to take all this in hand: a fundraising committee was again set up with June Elias in the Chair, and Harold Williams taking responsibility for the appeal to Trusts and grant-making bodies. June Elias had come to Trinity with her family in the 1960's from a Welsh-speaking Valley background and since that time had become deeply involved in the life of the Church and the National Children's Home. The members faced the challenge of what was, at this stage, an open-ended commitment: they began work aware that other defects might well present themselves once repairs to the hundred-year old buildings got under way.

This time the Church was able to centre the appeal on its well known and well loved feature, the Spire. Support was forthcoming from the town, determined not to lose a distinctive feature of its townscape, and contributions from outside normal church sources flowed in. Stimulated by the wide interest, Cadw, the Welsh equivalent of English Heritage, responded to the appeal and offered financial help and specialist advice.

One of Cadw's requirements was the appointment of an architect. This, Trinity was at first loath to accept – churches are aware that this involves extra expense – but the appointment of Noel Architects in 1991 has brought nothing but good, both in their supervision of the work and in the introductions of funding they have been able to make. Trinity will soon be restored to its appearance in 1901 – finials and all – and will be the Victorian Church its founders desired. Cadw recognised the quality of the building and the careful restoration by giving both the Church and the Hall a Grade II Listing. The Church is already sited in a Conservation Area.

The Committee for the Spire and Restoration Appeal see their way to raising all the money required. Of a total of £170,000, Graham Wilson, the new Church Treasurer, estimated that £120,000 would have been received by the end of 1993 through Grants (£43,000), Gift Days (£25,000), Donations (£24,000) and Fund Raising Events (£23,000). With a further and final Gift Day for this purpose, additional Grants and Fund Raising efforts, he was confident that by 1994 the whole amount would have been raised. The Church would then be able to move towards meeting some of the other financial needs pressing in on it from the world and the wider church.[1]

In the first fourteen months of Albert Jewell's Ministry, two events which were unusual in the life of Trinity took place: Cardiff, and more particularly St. David's Hall, welcomed the Methodist Conference, visiting South Wales for the first time, and Trinity offered hospitality to the Penarth Company of the Salvation Army whilst their Citadel was being rebuilt.

Many homes in the Circuit provided hospitality for the Representatives and, because of the happy experience of overseas students at International House, Penarth was made the centre for the Representatives of the World Church. Trinity Hall was the venue for the meetings of the Stationing Committee and one of the four Ordination Services, was held in the Church on 24 June. Relatives and supporters of the Ordinands began arriving in Penarth in the early afternoon and 'Trinity Friends', helped out by the Circuit, provided a tea and a supper. The Church filled up, indeed it was packed some half an hour before the Service was due to begin. Hassocks were put down in the front of the Church for the Ordinands to kneel on and the Choir Stalls were filled by the Ministers who were to take part in the Ordinations. This involved the Laying-on of hands by senior Ministers and by Ministers who had helped the Ordinand through his candidature. The Charge was given by Rev'd Dr. Gordon Wakefield, one time Principal of Queen's College, Birmingham.

After their Ordination, first the nine Candidates and their families, and then the whole congregation, some six hundred of us, took Communion. There were three points from which the Elements were distributed and the three lines were unobtrusively stewarded so that there was no confusion. The Service prompted thoughts of the great Communion Services recorded in John Wesley's Diaries. Trinity provided a fitting setting for the Service – united in spirit with the other three, less elaborate, venues in the District. In all the same feeling was present and the Services communicated a similar message to all taking part in them, 'Go ye into all the World and preach the Gospel.'

While the involvement with Conference was brief, Trinity's welcome to local Salvationists was offered over an extended period. The Company joined the Sunday morning Services, swelling the numbers considerably, and, on occasions, bringing their band to accompany hymns and, sometimes, lead the worship. Trinity was not taken aback

235

by the hand clapping, which seems to be part of all charismatic worship these days – and on the charismatic scale the Salvation Army is more conservative than many. A number of the members joined in, but it was not really Trinity's style of worship. It was interesting to see that a number of the Salvation Army members would join in the Service of Holy Communion, although it does not fall into their pattern of worship.

On Sunday evenings, they held their own Services in Trinity Hall, which was far enough away from the Church for their band not to cause any distraction. Inevitably one was prompted to wonder what a visitor from Mars – or for that matter from Iran – would have made of two Christian bodies worshipping the One God in different parts of the same building.

In view of the history of the Salvation Army it was appropriate that a Methodist Church should offer the Penarth Company such hospitality. There was concern that their departure would leave empty places but the winter congregation filled the Church well after they left.

In 1991 Trinity celebrated its Centenary. During the year, Trinity decided to look forward rather than back and engaged in a review of its Church life, beginning at the Annual General Church Meeting in April 1990, and continuing through Away Weekends at Llangynidr, to establish a number of possible priorities which were evaluated by the seven house Groups which met during Albert Jewell's sabbatical. In addition to the continuation of the House Groups, objectives were established and are being pursued vigorously. There were other celebrations: a Flower Festival, an Exhibition of Photographs from 1880, a Gala Dinner Dance, at which surprisingly few of the young couples present danced, and a final Service on 28 April. This was led by Donald Knighton and the preacher was Dr. Donald English, the President of the Methodist Conference.

Albert Jewell took his sabbatical leave in the early summer of 1991. Methodism has now adjusted to this institution and Circuits are beginning to take their ministers' absences for a period as a matter of course. Gerald Stoddern temporarily took over as Superintendent Minister and the Trinity laymen and laywomen were much in evidence.

Women have traditionally given much of their time to the church. Increasingly, men, who have taken early retirement, find their role in the day to day care of the church, and not only when their minister is away.  Two such in Trinity are Stanley Roberts and Leslie Evans, who together are to help the Minister in the administration of the Society.

Stan Roberts, a Welsh speaker, was brought up in North Wales as a Calvinistic Methodist, and Bronwen, his wife, in Dinas Powis as an Anglican.  They came to Trinity with their two sons and their foster daughter in 1981, having become Methodists in Swansea through the influence of neighbours.

Leslie Evans was brought up in Cardiff Docks and was apprenticed as an engineer.  After he retired from his position at Distillers Chemicals in Barry – where he had often had to work on Sundays he began to come regularly to Trinity with his wife, Margot, and their two sons.

In a previous generation, Bronwen and Margot might well have been deeply involved in Women's Work, but patterns have changed.  It is significant that Bronwen worked devotedly as the first organiser for Traidcraft from 1982, both in the town and the Church, and that Margot has been organiser in Trinity for Christian Aid for the last seventeen years.

That there is only one Class meeting regularly in Trinity is regrettable, but the position is compensated for to some degree by the success of a number of house groups which meet for a specific purpose and for a set time.   In the November of 1991, six house groups met to study St. Mark's Gospel using a study guide drawn up by Albert Jewell. When he was on Sabbatical Leave in the summer of 1991, over one hundred members met in groups to plan the 'next ten years at Trinity.' There is always, too, involvement in the ecumenical Lent Groups. Perhaps these should be seen as the present-day equivalent of the traditional Class Meeting.

To compensate for Classes not meeting, the class leaders decided to visit each of their members once a quarter and deliver *Contact* to them personally, thus establishing and maintaining a network of relationships within the Society.   The relationships have in some cases been cemented in Away Weekends such as that held at Lindors in 1992 and the Away Day at Atlantic College in 1993.

Each year the staff of Junior Church and their families have spent time at Llangynidr preparing their programme – particularly the Christmas and Anniversary Services. A young choir under Janet Pedwell took part in a number of services and for such services, she, with Albert Jewell, produced an alternative Hymn Book entitled *With all my Heart*. Janet Pedwell, with her daughter Amy, as one of the dancing/singing group, her son Simon, as Joseph and Tim Reith, as Pharaoh, produced *Joseph and his Amazing Technicolour Dream Coat* for the Junior Church Anniversary in the Church in June 1993.

Whilst the Spire was being repaired, the Cock was taken down and kept in the Church. During this time, the Minister arranged for all the Junior Church to step over it – so that when restored to its position they would be able to say they had 'stepped over the cock.'

Trinity was able to make a contribution to the Christian Arts Festival organised by the Penarth Council of Churches during 1990, especially to the Art Exhibition. As part of the Festival, pictures collected by Douglas Wollen and John Gibbs in the 1960s were hung in the Turner House Gallery. The collection, which belongs to the Methodist Church, represents a significant collection of contemporary Religious Paintings and one of the most striking works has been used on the cover of this book.

The report to the Annual Members Meeting in 1992 yielded some statistics for this period which provide comparison with former years.

The average attendances at Church Services over four weeks were:

|                | 1989 | 1990 | 1991 |
|----------------|------|------|------|
| Morning        | 172  | 195  | 181  |
| Evening        | 31   | 30   | 32   |
| Junior Church  | 61   | 66   | 60   |

and the number of members:

|     |     |     |
|-----|-----|-----|
| 310 | 316 | 289 |

The Women's Hour was much reduced, having only some 30 to 40 members.

The Play Hour was attended by 40 mothers and 50 children.

The Young People's Fellowship had 15 members.

The Scout Group, one of the largest in the District, had 165 members comprising all ages, and 20 leaders.

The Social Club had between 25 and 35 members.

The Young Women's Fellowship had been meeting fortnightly on Tuesday evenings for 7 years and had some 15 members.

In addition to the Church activities on Church premises the following 'outside organisations' benefit from them:

| | |
|---|---|
| Day Centre for Elderly | Therapy Club |
| Weight Watchers | Penarth Society |
| Keep Fit and Tap Dance | Methodist District |
| Penarth History Society | Women's Luncheon Club |
| Salvation Army | Stroke Club |
| Ballet Classes | Arthritic Society |
| National Child Birth Trust | PODS: Penarth Operatic & Drama Society |

This list may impress, but the figures bring us down to earth; so much effort over the last hundred years put into the service of Christ and His Church and so little to show for it.

There are signs of new life, and of widening and deepening involvement. Albert Jewell's imaginative project to help elderly people to live in their own homes and retain their dignity and independence; the 'Live at Home' Scheme under the auspices of the M.H.A. The Easter number of *Contact* in 1993 drew attention to the problem of homelessness which is found even in Penarth.

Perhaps the Church does indeed only exist for others and, if we attempt to save our life and concentrate on building a large and thriving Society at Trinity, we shall lose it. The Society, however, has been heartened by the arrival of a family who have recently joined Trinity.

In 1992, Dr. Dayalan Clarke, with his wife, Dr. Vino Clarke, moved to Penarth, and took up appointments in hospitals in the area. After a period of uncertainty, they, with their young son, Dushyant, have chosen to worship at Trinity, being drawn by its friendliness and the Junior Church. The parents felt that the type of worship offered was similar to that found in the Church of South India in which they had been brought up, and in which Dr. Dayalan Clarke's father is a Bishop.

When Trinity first opened its doors in 1901, it felt that it was largely on its own; now, in Archbishop Temple's phrase, the Churches 'plan to do nothing separately that they cannot do together.'

As Trinity takes its place in the strong and effective local Council of Churches there is no room for an exclusive witness or ministry: the Churches complement each other, with their particular strengths and weaknesses. As the Minister of Tabernacle, with its traditions which are different from those of Trinity, said in 1992 during the Exchange of Pulpits: 'Tabernacle needs Trinity and Trinity needs Tabernacle.'

Some of the Churches in Penarth may be within a stone's throw of one another, but throwing stones at each other has no part in their united Ministry to Penarth. The stones are not cast, but are built up into the Church whose one foundation is 'Jesus Christ her Lord.'

The interior of Trinity with congregation after the Sunday Service August 1993.

# CHAPTER 21

## Anne Mary Knighton 1934-1991

This history of Trinity ends with the Celebration and Thanksgiving for the life and witness of Anne Mary Knighton.

Anne Knighton was not a minister of Trinity and indeed, she was not ordained, but she can be considered as a missionary sent from the Church into the wider church – and into the world.

Anne Knighton, before she was married, Anne Evans, first appeared in this history in Chapter 13 and reappeared in Chapter 19 when, as Vice-President of the Conference, she opened the new Trinity Rooms.

On May 14th 1991, Anne died after a short illness. This was a great shock not only to the Methodists in her beloved Wales, but also to Methodists throughout the world and to members of other Christian Churches who had got to know her after she was Vice-President and became, in a sense, a World Christian.

The Funeral Service was held at Trinity on 23 May 1991. The Church was full to overflowing and the Service was relayed to Trinity Hall where a second congregation was gathered. All the major Christian Churches in Britain were represented by their leaders at the Service.

It is impossible to describe the sense of loss mingled with gratitude for Anne's life which was almost palpable on that occasion, but below is the Order of Service and the Address by the Rev'd Dr. John Newton.

A Service of Celebration and Thanksgiving
for the life and witness of

Anne Mary Knighton

Welcome:     The Rev'd Tom Davies.

Hymn:        Meet and right it is to sing, H&P 501
             John Wesley.

Prayer:      Mrs. Rosemary Wass,
             Vice President of the Conference.

Anne Knighton: from the cover of *Now* magazine, July/August 1991.

Old Testament
Lesson:           Isaiah Chapter 61, v. 1-3  10-11.
Rev. Dr. Donald English,
President of the Conference.

Psalm 118

Hymn:            God is Love: Let heaven adore him, H&P 36,
Timothy Rees.

Epistle:          Romans Chapter 8, v 28, 31-35, 37-39.
Rev. John Atkinson, Secretary of the Synod.

Anthem:        Good Christian Men, Rejoice and Sing.
Ernest Bullock.

Gospel:         John Chapter 14, v 1-6, 27.
Rt. Rev. George Noakes, Archbishop of Wales,
President of Cytun.

Address:        Rev. Dr. John Newton,
Chairman of the Liverpool District.

Prayers:        Rev. Brian Beck, Secretary of the Conference.

Hymn:            Love divine, all loves excelling, H&P 267,
Charles Wesley.

Blessing:       Rev. Dr. Donald English,
President of the Conference.

## Address

'For I am sure that neither death nor life . . . nor anything else in all creation, will be able to separate us from the love of God in Christ Jesus our Lord'. (Romans 8:37-38).

That was Anne Knighton's faith, and she lived it to the utmost. As we give thanks to God for Anne now, we each have our own vivid recollections of her faith in action. I think, for example, of the evening of Palm Sunday in 1987, when she preached as Vice-President of the Conference at St. James', Woolton, in south-east Liverpool. Her text was, 'We preach Christ crucified . . . the power of God and the wisdom of God'. (1 Corinthians 1: 23-24). Her message was of God's power in weakness, of life through death, of hope and resurrection breaking through in the direst circumstances of our lives. It came all the more powerfully from one who was no stranger to suffering, in her own body and in her family life.

In the morning of that Palm Sunday, she had told the people of Prescot Methodist Church that, from her Welsh upbringing and experience, she had known communities which had experienced suffering, and a kind of death, through economic decay and mass unemployment. Yet, in their midst, Christian people had stood as a sign of hope and resurrection, striving to renew the life of their neighbourhood. It was the same essential message as Paul gives us in Romans 8 – life overcoming death by the grace of God, and breaking out into resurrection.

You could say of Anne what John Bunyan said of his own sermons, 'I preached what I felt, what I smartingly did feel.' She knew the meaning of suffering and loss. She was born here in Penarth in 1934, the youngest of four children, one of whom died in infancy. Her father was a Welsh miner, her mother a nurse. The father, deprived of his work during the lockout of the 1920s went from one hazardous occupation to another and became a deep-sea trawlerman. He died when Anne was only ten, but he and his wife had given their children the best start in life: a caring, loving family; a living Christian faith; and a profound commitment to social justice and the needs of the poor.

Anne was educated at Penarth Grammar School and at Cardiff College of Domestic Arts. She had done a year as a trainee pharmacist, but left College qualified to teach Home Economics. She taught for five years in Cardiff, and continued to teach part-time through many years of married life, and not only in schools. In Birmingham, she taught English to unemployed school-leavers, and, as a second language, to housebound Asian women. She was a fine teacher – not just technically proficient, but with a rare ability to relate, pastorally and personally, to those she taught. Her gifts also found expression in eight years' service as a Domestic Bursar in the Selly Oak Colleges.

In 1960, she and Donald were married, and Anne began a more than thirty years' demonstration that it is possible to be a superb home-maker, and fulfil oneself professionally, and make a major contribution to the life of Church and community. Many will know the open-hearted hospitality which she and Donald practised. I first experienced it when they were newly married, and living in a tiny flat in Oxford. Myself and another college contemporary of Donald's from Wesley House paid a friendly call on them while we were on holiday. Anne not only gave us Sunday lunch, but pressed us to stay the night. Somehow, food and bedding and space were found to accommodate the unexpected guests; and it was all done without fuss, and with laughter, so that any diffidence we had vanished away like the dew in the morn. And many here will have known that same quality of hospitality – in Droitwich, in Selly Oak, in Wimbledon and in Cardiff. In every place, Anne filled the Manse with joy. She had all the Welsh charm of voice and manner. She had Methodist warmth, without a trace of sentimentality. She was full of joy: joy in her husband and children; in her many, many friends; in her garden, her music, her love of France and its people; in her work in Church and community. And at the heart of it all, the deep undertow of all her joys, was her joy in God, in the renewing power and love of Jesus. She was a living advertisement for the Christian Faith, a vivid illustration of Charles Wesley's lines:

> How happy the man whose heart is set free,
> The people that can be joyful in Thee;
> Their joy is to walk in the light of Thy face,
> And still they are talking of Jesus's grace.

Anne not only had the gift of joy; she had the capacity to bring out joy in others. When she came to Liverpool as our Vice-President, and I took her on her round of engagements, I was reminded of John Henry Newman's motto, 'Heart speaks to heart.' As the Recorder report put it: 'Wherever she went, her words, her winning manner, and her joyous faith, spoke directly to the hearts of the Methodist people'.

Yet there was nothing sugary or sentimental about Anne. In speech, as in character, she was direct, open, forthright. In her public utterances, her words searched and challenged those who heard her. She grew into the office of Vice-President in a quite astonishing way, becoming an able and impressive ambassadress for her Church. She didn't mince words. In an interview with Judith Edwards of the Liverpool *Daily Post*, she replied to one question in her crisp, clear style: 'I find this money-orientated society nauseating. We should value people for themselves. Even if you are 'nobody' you still count. You still matter and you are still valuable to the community, to yourself and to God'.

If she had the Welsh charm, she also had the authentic Celtic fire. She could be angry and indignant – like her Lord – at the injustice and crass stupidity which hurt people and stunted their development. Hence her work for Amnesty International, for Mission Alongside the Poor, whose committee she chaired, for the Women's International League of Peace and Freedom, and for her beloved Labour Party. She was a pillar of Network, the Methodist Women's movement, and worked tirelessly for the full participation of women and young people in the life of the Church and the world. But she was never shrill. You never felt Anne was riding some personal hobby-horse. You recognised a patent, clear-sighted sincerity, a passion for truth, for people, for the Gospel that sets us free. At the root of her character, her motherliness, her love of home and family, her public service and leadership in the Church – at the root of it all was the love of Jesus Christ. And nothing in life or death separated her from that.

Not all will know that, in her earlier married life, Anne sustained serious head injuries, as a pedestrian involved in a road accident. It was the kind of blow that would have broken some people; or at the least, convinced them that they must now lie low, lead a quiet life, and restrict themselves to domesticity. Not Anne; she not only surmounted the setback. She went from strength to strength in service and discipleship. I was privileged to know her, as a dear friend, for over thirty years; and I see her as standing in a fine succession of distinguished Methodist women: Grace Murray, Elizabeth Ritchie, Nancy Bolton, and others of that ilk. She was a highly gifted person, and could chair that unpredictable assembly, the Methodist Conference, with just the right blend of humour and firmness. She walked the world Christian stage too, representing British Methodism in numerous overseas conferences, and being designated as area president, for the British Isles, in the World Federation of Methodist Women. Other Christian Churches recognised her calibre, and she was a Vice-President of Cytun, the new ecumenical instrument for Wales, as well as Moderator of the Steering Committee of the Council of Churches for Britain and Ireland.

All these high offices she fulfilled with great dignity, with complete naturalness, and without a trace of pomposity. On that Palm Sunday of her Vice-presidential visit to Liverpool, between preaching engagements, she came for an afternoon walk with our family, in Sefton Park. As the Recorder report expressed it: the Vice-President 'under the influence of the warm Spring weather, was . . . observed kicking a football in a minor league game sponsored by the Chairman's youngest son.'

That was absolutely typical of her youthful spirit, her ability to relate to anyone and everyone – young and old, rich and poor, bad or good,

Christian or pagan. She had found in Christ the springs of a universal humanity. She embodied the true catholicity of Methodism and of the Christian Faith; because she loved and served a Lord,

> '. . . whose mercy is divinely free
> For all the fallen race – and me'.

And the 'me' really did come last with this splendid Welsh Christian woman, for whom we devoutly thank God. As Vice-President, she took as her patron saint, Barnabas, the son of consolation, the great encourager. She encouraged us then, and she encourages us now, by her faith and goodness, and because she has gone ahead of us, eager as ever, to that Kingdom where, as St. Augustine says, 'We shall see and know; we shall know and love; we shall love and we shall praise'. To Donald, Daniel, Rachel and Ben, to Anne's brothers, and all her loved ones, we offer the assurance of our love and prayers. We commit Anne confidently to the mercy of her Creator, and the love of her Saviour; and we claim for her the promise that, 'neither death nor life . . . nor anything else in all creation will be able to separate us from the love of God in Christ Jesus our Lord'. AMEN.

Joyce Wells wrote in *Contact:*

> Throughout the world there are numberless people who are grateful – and, yes, better Christians – for having known Anne Knighton, amongst them many at Trinity, which she called 'home'.

This last chapter of the Story of Trinity channels the stream of the worship and service of the Church through one particular life, raised within that Church, and in giving thanks for the Life and Witness of Anne Mary Knighton it gives thanks also for all that has been good and strong and life-affirming within Trinity Methodist Church.

# NOTES

## Chapter 1   Penarth

1     The Plymouth and Windsor-Clive Family

Along with much of the coastal land in Glamorgan, Penarth was owned by the Plymouth Windsor-Clive Family.  The Earls of Plymouth and Barons Windsor had been ground landlords of most of Penarth since the marriage of Other, Third Earl of Plymouth, to the Lewis heiress in 1730.  The exploits of Robert Clive, a clerk in the East India Company and later Victor of Arcot and Plassey added a new dimension to the family's reputation, and the victories are commemorated by street names in the town.

The Earldom of Plymouth became extinct in the early nineteenth century but in 1855 the abeyance of the barony was terminated in favour of Harriet Windsor-Clive, Baroness Windsor.

2     The Church and Chapel Buildings in Penarth

| | |
|---|---|
| 1859 | Llandough Baptist Chapel. |
| 1861 | Sardis Calvinistic Methodist Chapel, Plassey Street. |
| 1863 | Arcot Street Wesleyan Methodist Chapel. |
| 1866 | The Parish Church, St. Augustine's rebuilt. |
| 1870 | Tabernacle Baptist Chapel, Plassey Street. |
| 1877 | Penuel Welsh Baptist Chapel, Plassey Street. |
| 1877 | Gospel Hall Brethren, Plassey Street. |
| 1877 | St. Joseph's Roman Catholic Church. |
| 1879 | Bethel Welsh Congregational, Annibynwyr, Plassey Street. |
| 1883 | Free Methodist Chapel, Cogan. |
| 1885 | Stanwell Road Baptist Church. |
| 1890 | Trinity Wesleyan Methodist Church. |
| 1890 | Bethania Welsh Presbyterian Chapel, Hickman Road. |
| 1891 | All Saints Anglican Church. |
| 1894 | Holy Nativity Anglican Church, Plassey Street. |
| 1897 | Christchurch Congregational Church, Stanwell Road. |
| 1904 | Hebron Hall Brethren, Cogan. |
| 1906 | St. Paul's Anglican Church moved to Arcot Street. |
| 1906 | Albert Road Wesleyan Methodist Church. |
| 1915 | St. Joseph's Roman Catholic Church, Wordsworth Avenue. |

# NOTES

1954     St. David's Presbyterian Church of Wales. Joined by the congregation of Christchurch United Reformed Church in 1985 to form Elfed Avenue United Church.

1990     Jehovah's Witnesses, Kingdom Hall Plassey Street.

1991     Salvation Army Citadel, Plassey Street rebuilt.

3    'Chapel' or 'Church'

Methodist terminology has varied in its use of these two terms. The announcement of the building of Trinity in the 1899 Annual Report of the Wesleyan Chapel Committee described the new building as a 'Church,' whereas the illustration in the same publication was headed 'New Wesleyan Chapel.'

Chapel is the term normally used for a place of Worship for a gathered and defined group or society, for example Llandough Baptist Chapel, Leys School Chapel, King's College Chapel, Wesley's Chapel in City Road, when it was built in 1778, or for a building in which not all the acts of Christian Worship are performed. Church is used for the place of Worship of the Community, for example All Saints' Parish Church, the Norwegian Church in Cardiff Bay.

As Methodism became a Church at Methodist Union the term Church tended to be used more and more, thus proclaiming that its buildings were places of Worship for the whole community.

Chapel is too restrictive a term to describe a Methodist Church of today with its outreach into the community, but its overtones of warmth and togetherness are elements which it should be loath to lose.

## Chapter 2   Methodist beginnings in Penarth

1     Benjamin, E. Alwyn. *Penarth 1841-1871*, Cowbridge: Brown, 1980.

2     Frederick J. Jobson. *Chapel and School Architecture*, Hamilton, Adams & Co., 1850. Reprinted by the Methodist Property Division.

# NOTES

3      Rupert Davies, *Proceedings of the Wesley Historical Society,* Feb. 1992.

## Chapter 3   The Building of Trinity 1899-1901

1      James Munston. *The Nonconformists in Search of a Lost Culture,* London: SPCK. 1991.

2      Jobson, ibid.

3      John B. Hilling. Cardiff and the Valleys, London: Lund Humphries London, 1973.

4      John Morel Gibbs. Morels of Cardiff. The History of Family Shipping Firm, Cardiff: National Museum of Wales, 1982.

5      James Cubitt. A Popular Handbook of Nonconformist Church Buildings 1892 The Builder.

6      *The Methodist Recorder* of 12 October 1899 carried the following report of the stone laying under the headline 'The President at Cardiff':

Probably no other town in Great Britain has shown more rapid progress in population during recent years than Cardiff. And, as is very well known, Methodism has kept pace with the population, and is still the foremost church. The Penarth Circuit, in its brief history, has shown much enterprise and liberality. Ten years ago, before its division from Wesley Circuit, there was only one minister where today there are four. And five new churches have been founded within these few years. Penarth is a beautiful residential town just three miles from the Welsh Metropolis, and on Sept. 27 there was a large company assembled to greet the President of the Conference, and to witness the laying of six memorial stones.

The stonelaying ceremony was commenced by the Rev. J. Jenkin, superintendent of the circuit who was assisted by the Trinity minister (the Rev. S. Yelland Richards), the Revs W. Maltby

(Chairman of the District), James Bridge, Russell Maltby (formerly minister at Trinity), J. B. Blanch, and J. H. Watson. The first stone was laid by the Mayor of Cardiff, Alderman Sir Thomas Morel, who was one of the founders of the church eight years ago. Other stones were laid by Major Wyndham-Quin, M.P., Miss Andrews, Mr. Parsons, Mrs Humphrey Wallis, and Mrs T. E. Morel.

The evening meeting was held at Arcot Street Chapel, under the chairmanship of Mr. R. W. Perks, M.P. The chairman's speech was an able and forceful review of Methodism – historic, modern and future. The President followed with an eloquent speech on the position of present day religious systems, and the due place of Methodism. His final appeal to the young people of Methodist homes was most telling.

## Chapter Four   The Rev'd Robert Bond

Dr. Bond – List of signatories of the Tribute.

| | | |
|---|---|---|
| obert J. Hancock, ock Chambers. | Annie E. Hancock, Dock Chambers. | Maud Hanwell, Rathveal, Stanwell Road. |
| hn Evans, , Wood Street. | J. Sandford, 22, Wood Street. | Mrs. Martin, |
| A. Powell, , Cornerswell Road. | E. Moxey, St. Maeburne, Marine Parade. | G. Blight, |
| J. Cox, , Arcot Street. | D. Hicks, 39, Albert Road. | F. B. Tudball, 10, Sully Terrace. |
| J. Tudball, , Sully Terrace. | Francis P. Scriven, 100, Stanwell Road. | I. F. Scriven, 100, Stanwell Road. |
| ank P. Scriven, 0, Stanwell Road. | Clem Scriven, | W. H. Woolcock, 9, Cornerswell Road. |
| A. Hallums, | A. Hicks, | L. Stamp, 7, West Terrace. |
| Stamp, West Terrace. | G. Cocks, | Alfred J. Frazer, 1, Beach Road. |
| urtnay Frazer, Beach Road. | D. E. Lewis, | M. J. Adams, |

# NOTES

Gordon G. Gordary,

Ann Evans,

W. Ford,
46, Arcot Street.

Ivor Hatton Evans,
6, Cwrt-y-Vil Road.

Mansel Hatton Evans,
6, Cwrt-y-Vil Road.

Ralph Hatton Evans,
6, Cwrt-y-Vil Road.

Henry Frazer,
1, Beach Road.

Annie Frazer,
1, Beach Road.

Joseph Frazer,
1, Beach Road.

Donald Frazer,
1, Beach Road.

R. T. Hinde,
3, Cwrt-y-Vil Road.

S. P. Hinde,
3, Cwrt-y-Vil Road.

K. Powell,

T. Powell,

S. E. Griffiths,
76, Stanwell Road.

Percy Griffiths,
76, Stanwell Road.

F. V. Hancox,
10, Earl Road.

S. H. Hancox,
10, Earl Road.

A. Rosewarne Chenhalls,
66, Plymouth Road.

J. E. Chenhalls,
66, Plymouth Road.

Dorothy C. Chenhalls,
66, Plymouth Road.

Margaret Chenhalls,
66, Plymouth Road.

Lily Sloggett,

Nellie Tiller,
2, Rudry Street.

Daisy Slogett,

Ada Stamp,
7, West Terrace.

Winifred Evans,
23, Wood Street.

Fannie Rees,

Marjorie Gordon,
15, Station Road.

Madeline A, Kennard,
28, Ivy Street.

Alice Evans,
Wood Street.

Ada Jenkins,
111, Glebe Street.

Mrs. Martin,

Rose Hallett,

Eva M. Tuckfield,
Monkton House,
Holmesdale Place.

Mrs. Vicker,
4, Grove Terrace.

Emily Summers,

Alice E. Venn,
7, Ivy Street.

E. Edmunds,

M. Sampson,

Mrs. McArthur,
24, Ivy Street.

E. Price,

Elizabeth J. J. Evans,
23, Wood Street.

Annie Lewis,
33, Plymouth Road.

J. Hitchings,

Emily R. Bleby,
13, Clive Place.

Mary G. Kneebone,

M. I. Parsons,
7, Wood Street.

Emma Edwards,

Ethel Howell,

Edna Parsons,
7, Wood Street.

Mary Frances Jones,

Alice Mitchell,

B. Pritchard,
14, Victoria Square.

# NOTES

R. M. Gay,

Maggie Ashford,

Gladys Biss,
4, Church Place South.

Lottie Jones,

Dorothy E. Wood,
16, Clive Place.

Lily M. Evans,
64, Glebe Street.

Sarah Evans,
23, Wood Street.

Gertrude Sandford,
22, Wood Street.

Elsie Tudball,
10, Sully Terrace.

Kathleen Barnes,
2, Roseberry Place.

J. Marsh,
48, Plassey Street.

P. Allen,

Gertie M. Thomas,

Charles Tonkin,

Edw. H. Ede,
17, Victoria Square.

H. Stanley Ede,
17, Victoria Square.

John Morgans,

Emily Gibbs,
8, Cwrt-y-Vil Road.

Winifred Swannell,
Roxburgh, Plymouth Road.

Esther Edmunds,

Sarah A. Garland,
6, Glebe Street.

Annie Sweet,
42, Hewell Street.

Gwen Russell,

Daisy Barnes,
2, Roseberry Place.

Florence Maggs,
9, Sully Terrace.

Jennie Redclift,
14, Cornerswell Road.

L. Parsons,
7, Wood Street.

Louie Griffiths,
76, Stanwell Road.

M. Collins,
31, Redlands Road.

R. J. Gordon,

Annie M. Sandford,
22, Wood Street.

Edmund Pocock,
12, John Street.

Ellen Tonkin,

Mildred M. F. Ede,
17, Victoria Square.

Fiona M. Ede,
17, Victoria Square.

Emma Morgans,

E. W. Pearce,
8, Cwrt-y-Vil Road.

Geo. Garfield Hancock,
Dock Chambers.

Daisy Hare,

Nellie Webber,

Jessie Winchester,
2, Sully Terrace.

Alice Evans,
23, Wood Street.

Muriel Davies,
147, Stanwell Road.

Mary Hind,
Super's Manse,

Olive McArthur,
24, Ivy Street.

Hettie Lipscomb,
33, West Terrace.

Edith Kennard,
28, Ivy Street.

Irene Mardon,

F. W. Weston,

Bella Hindmarsh,

D. H. Evans,

David Evans,

Max C. Ede,
17, Victoria Square.

Mary S. Blanch,
17, Victoria Square.

Emily L. Pearce,
8, Cwrt-y-Vil Road.

G. A. Atkins,

John Hedley Strong,
23, Clive Place.

# NOTES

Avesia F. Atkins,
30, Clive Place.

Charles E. Venn,
7, Ivy Street.

Alice E. Venn,
7, Ivy Street.

Eliza R. Livermore,

G. H. Ramsdale,
3, Earl Road.

Mrs. Winchester,
2, Sully Terrace.

R. Winchester,
2, Sully Terrace.

R. Sandford,
22, Wood Street.

Mrs. E. Sandford,
22, Wood Street.

Hatton Evans,
6, Cwrt-y-Vil Road.

W. J. Kennard,
28, Ivy Street.

H. A. Vicker,
4, Grove Terrace.

Albany Parsons,
7, Wood Street.

I. Broughton,
10, Machen Street.

F. G. Cox,
32, Redlands Road.

H. Williams,
9, Sully Terrace.

H. Tiller,
2, Rudry Street.

Geo. S. Jenkins,

Thomas J. Lewis,
9, Victoria Square.

W. Collins,
Cornerswell Road.

Thomas Good,
46, Redlands Road.

S. M. Parsons,
7, Wood Street.

J. N. Strong,
16, Grove Place.

Thomas Morel,
Roxburgh, Plymouth Road.

E. N. Strong,
16, Grove Place.

R. E. Parsons,
7, Wood Street.

C. V. Scourfield,
9, Dingle Road.

T. H. Griffiths,
76, Stanwell Road.

J. C. Griffiths,
76, Stanwell Road.

A. Hitchings,

R. M. Evans,
39, Grove Place.

A. E. Barnes,
2, Roseberry Place.

C. Adams,

W. Sweet,
42, Hewell Street.

H. Fulford Sanders,
74, Stanwell Road.

Ivor Evans,
West End Stores,
Stanwell Road.

Henry C. Martin,
12, Albert Road.

H. Stamp,
7, West Terrace.

F. R. Thomas,

A. McArthur Senior,
24, Ivy Street.

A. McArthur Junior,
24, Ivy Street.

V. Hatton Evans,
6, Cwrt-y-Vil Road.

O. Hatton Evans,
6, Cwrt-y-Vil Road.

Maggie Hatton Evans,
6, Cwrt-y-Vil Road.

Gwen S. Collins,
Cornerswell Road.

L. H. Allen Pratt,
Mount Stuart Square,
Cardiff.

Irene Winchester,
2, Sully Terrace.

Mabel Skoines,

Alice Parish,

Helena Tonkin,

Grace Rees,

G. P. Griffiths,

Alice Maggs,
9, Sully Terrace.

Hilda Hicks,
39, Albert Road.

# NOTES

Rose Jones,
9, Station Road.

Annie Scourfield,
9, Dingle Road.

H. Evans,

F. P. Scriven,
100, Stanwell Road.

A. Good,
46, Redlands Road.

Hughie Owen Jones,

B. Dobson,
11, Westbourne Road.

W. I. Dobson,
11, Westbourne Road.

Howard Hitchings,
64, Grove Terrace.

E. R. Care,
Monkton House,
Marine Parade.

Thomas Hodge,
11, Victoria Square.

Thomas Stephenson,
44, Stanwell Road.

A. Stephenson,
44, Stanwell Road.

Eliza Mewton,
11, Park Road.

A. E. Brookes,
66, Salop Street.

Clara Strong,
16, Grove Place.

H. Horwood,
40, Maughan Street.

Thomas W. Jones,

Maggie Woolcock,

C. T. Atwell,
28, Salop Street.

I. Evans,
23, Wood Street.

V. Bowen,

T. Bradfield,

William Thomas,
Archer Road.

George Dobson,
11, Westbourne Road.

Lydia Thomas,
Archer Road.

Ernest E. Wood,
3, Westbourne Road.

G. G. Care,
Monkton House,
Marine Parade.

Thomas Hodge,
11, Victoria Square.

Alfred Jenkins,
15, Ludlow Street.

Alice Stephenson,
44, Stanwell Road.

J. T. Ramsdale,
3, Earl Road.

G. W. Hawkins,
39, Dock Street.

W. J. Needle,
157, Stanwell Road.

A. Horwood,
40, Maughan Street.

E. P. Gibbs,
5, Marine Parade.

Blanche Hancock,
Dock Chambers.

B. Hoult,
27, Ivy Street.

L. Barnes,
2, Roseberry Place.

T. Parish,

H. Shepherd,

J. Rowland,
9, Bromfield Place.

R. W. Dobson,
11, Westbourne Road.

Katy Barnes,
2, Roseberry Place.

Ella D. Wood,
16, Clive Place.

R. D. Waller,
33, Victoria Road.

George Hodge,
11, Victoria Square.

William Rimron,
4, Cwrt-y-Vil Road.

W. H. Mewton,
11, Park Road.

A. J. Cox,
30, Redlands Road.

J. H. Turner,
3, John Street.

E. A. Needle,
157, Stanwell Road.

W. J. Isaac,

Elizabeth Gibbs,
5, Marine Parade.

Susan Gibbs,
5, Marine Parade.

J. A. Gibbs,
5, Marine Parade.

R. A. Gibbs,
5, Marine Parade.

R. Lidgett Gibbs,
5, Marine Parade.

Margaret E. Clements,

H. Norwood Atkins,
30, Clive Place.

George Pawley Jr,
21, High Street.

Louisa Parsons,
7, Wood Street.

Mary Jepson,

Emma McArthur,
24, Ivy Street.

Rose James,

Tom James,

S. A. Sandford,
22, Wood Street.

Harriet Sandford,
22, Wood Street.

Marie Toulmin,
6, Victoria Square.

William Toulmin,
6, Victoria Square.

Susan Thomas,

Louisa Pawley,
21, High Street.

Ethel Allen,

Nellie Lipscomb,
33, West Terrace.

Thomas Bishop,
22, Salop Street.

Stanley Parsons,
7, Wood Street.

Minnie Bishop,
22, Salop Street.

William T. Davies,
15, Earl Road.

Gerty Davies,
15, Earl Road.

Ethel Cox,

Lilly Davies,
147, Stanwell Road.

Winnie Davies,
147, Stanwell Road.

Llewelyn Davies,
147, Stanwell Road.

Mrs. Lloyd Evans,
50, Stanwell Road.

Mrs. Price,

A. Parsons,
7, Wood Street.

Edith Morel,
Roxburgh, Plymouth Road.

Susan P. A. Morel,
The Lindens.

S. Gladys Morel,
The Lindens.

J. G. Morel,
The Lindens.

Annie E. Scriven,
5, Marine Parade.

Stanley Hinde,
3, Cwrt-y-Vil Road.

Nellie Hinde,
3, Cwrt-y-Vil Road.

Trevis Hinde,
3, Cwrt-y-Vil Road.

Winifred Scriven

Clara S. Thomas

## Chapter 5  The First World War

1      'The Fallen' 1914-1918

Edwin Chick
William Coney
Frederick Dakers

Henry Essery
Hugh Price Evans
Douglas Farquar Thompson
Osian John Henry Foote
John Angel Gibbs
George Robert Guy
Edward Charles Hookway
Thomas John Lewis
Frank George Pope
Douglas S. George Pettigrew
Thomas Henry Sandrey
Robert Ernest Smith
Frederick Lewis Whittington

## 1914 'They Also Served' 1918

| | | |
|---|---|---|
| George Angel | Philip Angel | Richard Angel |
| Frank Angel | Gordon A. V. Avon | Ivanhoe E. N. Avon. |
| E. Lester Barnes | Charles Batten | John A. Biss |
| Ivor Broughton | Charles H. Bryant | David Bryant |
| Arthur G. Bradfield | H. Kenneth Budgen | Neville D. Budgen |
| Ernest R. Budgen | John C. Chick | William Collins |
| Thomas Coney | Albert J. Cox | Horace Cox |
| Louis Cox | Oswald Cox | William Cox |
| William H. Cox | Henry A. Cranham | William C. Cunningham |
| J. Harvard Davis | Wilfred H. Davies | Ralph L. Dawson |
| Charles S. Dennis | George Dobbs | William J. E. Edwards |
| Max Ede | H. Stanley Ede | Reginald Ellis |
| Alfred W. Evans | Ivor C. Evans | T. Herbert Evans |
| D. Harry Evans | Ivor John Evans | Frank A. Evans |
| Ralph Hatton Evans | Ivor Hatton Evans | Mansell Hatton Evans |
| Alfred Farr | Percival C. Farrell | William S. Farrell |
| Reginald Foote | Thomas H. Garrett | Vivian Garrett |
| R. J. Lidgett Gibbs | John Good | Thomas Good |
| Gerald Gordon | William S. Gould | Arthur R. Grigg |
| J. Charles Griffiths | Thomas H. Griffiths | J. Pearson Griffiths |
| Fred C. Haines | Arthur Hall | Frank E. Hannah |
| Walter W. Hannah | G. Luens Hardie | George W. Hawkins |
| Philip Hibbert | Edward Hill | Fred Hill |
| R. Trevis Hinde | W. Stanley Hinde | John R. Hinton |

# NOTES

W. Henry Hinton  James Hole  Thomas Holland
Ralph G. Holloway  Arthur W. Hosegood  Bert Hoult
David R. Howells  Melville H. Ingram  S. George Jenkins
John T. Jenkins  Charles Jennings  Sidney Jennings
Herbert C. Jeynes  Albert W. Jones  Fred C. Jones
Hugh O. Jones  Robert J. Jones  Edgar C. Kennard
Maurice Kidney  Thomas Kidney  Frederick L. Land
William Lewis  Harry Livermore  Ivor Lloyd
E. George Marks  Albert Marsh  Reuben Marsh
Alewyn Marsh  James Marsh  Arthur R. Martin
J. Andrew McArthur  Gordon McArthur  Bert Alfred McArthur
Thomas H. McArthur  Inez McArthur Miss  Fred Mears
William Mears  James Mears  Ernest Mears
William Maggs  G. Henry McNeil  W. Robert McNeil
James K. Millar  Henry Baden Morris  Charles Oakey
Alfred H. Palfrey  Fred Parrish  Thomas Parrish
George Parrish  Reginald E. Parsons  W. Gwynn Parsons
Stanley M. Parsons  J. Clifford S. Parsons  Alfred E. Pearce Parsons
A. Leonard Pearce  Joseph E. Pearce  Walter W. Perrin
Reginald S. Pitman  L.H. Allen Pratt  Alfred B. Pritchard
George E. Pritchard  M. Ivor Redclift  Herbert Rees
William Rogers  Victor S. Rowlands  Arnold L. Rhys Evans
Richard J. Sandford  Ralph G. Sandford  R. David Sandford
Philip Sandrey  Cyril Scourfield  W. Clement Scriven
F. Pearce Scriven  Bert Sloman  Frank Soderland
Frank Standfield  Thomas A. Stephenson  G. Herbert Stevenson
Albert Stamp  E. Noel Strong  T. Hedley Strong
Ambrose H. Tapper  Arthur E. Thomas  Arthur Thomas
Charles S. Tonkin  R. Vivian Tonkin  Albert E. Tucker
George W. Warren  George Weaver  Albert W. Western
Frank Western  Walter Western  Ivor H. White
John M. Williams  George A. Wilson  Clifford Winstone
Percy Winstone  Bert Yarnton  Frank Yeoman
Foster Yeoman

Red Cross Nurses

Maud Angel  Dorothy C. Chenhalls  Margaret R. Chenhalls
Olive Hatton Evans  Doris Hatton Evans  Susan Gibbs
Dorothy H. Griffiths  L. Eileen Holloway  Doris Watkin Lewis
Beryl Watkin Lewis  Hilda S. Pearce  May Reed

258

# NOTES

## Chapter 7   The Rev'd Percy C. Pegler

1.    Class Structure in Trinity.

Class was affected by various considerations including the kind of work the church member did, and the size of house or the street or road in which the family lived.  Domestic arrangements were also significant, for example, up to the Second World War a household which employed a maid might be considered to be middle-class.  In the first part of this century, the class to which a church member felt he or she belonged had to be taken into account, and there were fine gradations within classes of which only the individuals concerned were aware.  In a situation of rapid social change, status altered from year to year, and the level of education came to count for more and more, so that, by the end of the Second World War, any class differences which remained, were vestigial.  Within Methodist chapels significance was attached to the distance of a pew from the back of the building, the back pew being the most prestigious.  This was in marked contrast to Anglican and general Nonconformist practice.

At the best the taking of 'sittings', leasing a place and having one's name on a family pew, was a way of committing oneself and one's family to supporting the church.   At its worst, it became a status symbol. Kenneth Young wrote:

> The system of paying pew rents began at different times in different chapels.  At Harrold Congregational Chapel from about 1815 onwards, worshippers were asked to choose their seating and paid a quarterly subscription according to their means.
>
> *Chapel*, London: Eyre Methuen, 1972, p. 188.

Information about the availability of pews and sittings is given in a leaflet for the Dedication of Roath Road Methodist Chapel, Cardiff, built thirty years before and in a similar situation to Trinity.

> The rates vary from 1s. to 2s.6d. per sitting, per quarter.  Ample accommodation has been provided for the poor, both below and upstairs.  Strangers will be heartily welcomed and will receive the most courteous attention.

# NOTES

In 1871 the practice was regarded as entirely acceptable and a minister, the Rev'd T. Galland Hartley, looking back from the Jubilee in 1921, told a *Western Mail* reporter: 'I never saw anything like it for sudden success. Family pews were taken and were always filled with some of the leading business men.'

Increasingly the practice of having names on the seats was found to be unacceptable, and was eventually abolished by all churches.

2.    Marriages at Trinity

In the first thirty years of the Twentieth Century some 115 marriages were celebrated at Trinity. Very few of the bridegrooms came from outside Penarth, and in many cases both families were Trinity members. A list of the occupations of the brides' fathers follows:

Occupations of brides' fathers.

| | |
|---|---|
| 1901 | Foreman mason. |
| 1902 | Colliery agent, mason. |
| 1905 | Dock pilot. |
| 1906 | Master Mariner, ironmonger, builder, water bailiff, dairyman, general labourer, gardener. |
| 1907 | Upholsterer. |
| 1908 | Tailor, coal foreman, gentleman. |
| 1909 | Platelayer, shipowner, sea captain, contractor. |
| 1910 | Farmer, grocer, woodman, carpenter. |
| 1911 | Carpenter, coal trimmer. |
| 1913 | General labourer, labourer, coachman. |
| 1914 | Furniture salesman, railway employee. |
| 1915 | Collier, insurance agent, shipowner, dock pilot. |
| 1918-1922 | Coachman, railway-carriage inspector, platelayer, brick burner, commercial traveller, insurance broker, commercial traveller, mason, farm labourer, railway general manager, van driver, labourer, provision merchant, mason, labourer, miller, marine engineer, pierman, commission agent, dock inspector, banksman, caretaker, shipowner, coal trimmer. |
| 1922 | Commercial traveller, mason. |
| 1924 | Fruiterer, cement worker, bootmaker, ships' store merchant, railway clerk. |

| | |
|---|---|
| 1925 | Carpenter, bricklayer, commercial traveller, accountant, dairyman, coal tipper. |
| 1927 | Wholesale ironmonger, insurance manager, police inspector, railway guard, general labourer, railway guard, mason, railway foreman, painter and decorator, painter. |
| 1928 | Smallholder, tailor, chief clerk, marine engineer, shipowner, gas fitter, engine driver, painter, insurance agent. |
| 1929 | Mason, labourer, cement worker, coal trimmer. |
| 1930 | Coal tipper, gardener, chief clerk, quarry foreman, grocer, stationer, transport labourer. |

## Chapter 8   The Rev'd George Charnley

1    The Amendment proposed:

'This Quarterly Meeting, having considered the Scheme submitted to it by the direction of Conference, is of the opinion that the Scheme, however amended, would neither promote nor achieve Methodist Union and might even prove divisive and disastrous.

The meeting declares its belief in the desirability of Methodist Union, but considers that the method adopted in the present proposals is not the best method of approach to union nor does it inspire the hope that real unity will be achieved thereby.

The meeting therefore urges the Conference to suspend further consideration of this scheme until the possibilities of union along other lines have been more fully explored.

The meeting further suggests that during the period of postponement, the Conference recommend:

1    The preparation of a Federal Scheme.

2    A campaign for closer co-operation, increased fellowship and intercommunion between the Methodist Churches and wherever possible a united Evangelist campaign.

The meeting is of opinion that these should be first stages towards ultimate and complete union.

The main Resolution was eventually passed.'

## Chapter 10   A Spring Postponed

1       The Result of the 'Enquiry into Sunday School and Weeknight Activities at Trinity' in September 1937:

There were no Society or Junior Classes.
There was no Guild or Junior Guild.
There were 14 Guides and 3 Scouts.
There were 27 members in the Band of Hope.
There were 33 in boys and girls clubs.
In the Sunday School there were
40 in the Primary Department.
35 in the Junior Department.
30 in the Senior Department.
7 in the over 15s Department.
A total of 112 with an average attendance of 84.

## Chapter 12   The Rev'd Robert Hingley

1       These developments reflected the thinking of the whole Connexion, particularly in relation to youth work.  Inevitably this was the result of planning and preparation.   In 1941, a Conference Committee recommended that the Sunday School and Guild Departments should be merged into a single Youth Department.  The following year Conference itself declared that 'something essentially Christian, positive and inspiring and audacious is demanded from the Church; nothing of value need be abandoned, nothing experimental ought to be condemned.'  New approaches were planned 'to reach and serve the largest possible constituency of young people.'  The result was the setting up, in 1943, of a new connexional department, the Youth Department, with its District, Circuit and Church Councils.  Partnership at all levels of Church life between age and youth was to be the goal,

and all sides of life would be covered so that the growth of balanced Christian personalities could be encouraged.

In 1945, the Methodist Association of Youth Clubs came into being to meet the need, particularly, for those between the ages of fourteen and twenty. Established clubs and those created as a result of the new youth-oriented policy were to be brought together in a single, nation-wide association. 'The highest standards were to be aimed for and the clubs were to be used as a means of Christian evangelism, education and service'. The pattern was of weekly, interdenominational meetings, of clubs offering balanced programmes which promoted physical, social, mental and spiritual well-being. Members were to be involved in the management; there were to be 'opportunities for Christian training and worship', and 'the development of Church loyalties was to be by invitation rather than by compulsion or pressure.'

## Chapter 14   The Rev'd Percy S. Watkinson

1    The Circuit Meeting was, and is, responsible for Methodist strategy over a designated area. It has always been an essential part in a connexional system whereby ministers are stationed by the Conference in a circuit 'with special responsibility' for one or more Churches.

The Circuit Meeting has the responsibility for inviting, paying and housing the ministers, although for a considerable time an anomaly existed in that the ownership of the Trinity Manse, ever since Dr. Bond's day, was with the Trinity Trustees. The meeting's most difficult task is that of fixing the assessment for the different Societies within the Circuit: the amount each is required to contribute to the cost of the ministry and to other connexional expenses, in effect, everything other than the upkeep and ongoing life of the individual Church. The Circuit Stewards, with the help of a finance sub-committee, suggest the assessments and strive to bring the Societies to accept that they are fair and just. It is a measure of the harmony within the circuit and of the standing of the Circuit Stewards whether this is an irenic and stress-free exercise or no.

The Circuit Meeting also considers local issues, for example, the Meeting spoke for the Methodist people of Penarth on a perennial issue

263

in local politics, when it opposed the suggestion that the town be incorporated into 'the Great City of Cardiff.'

Churches take advantage of the meeting together of the circuit, to give publicity to forthcoming events and to report on notable ventures in which they have participated locally or nationally.

By and large, it can be said that the Meeting is required under the constitution of the Methodist Church, but of its existence the ordinary member in the pew is largely unaware.

2    When John Wesley visited St. Ives, he stayed with John Nance. From the Diary of John Wesley April 12th 1744:

> Between seven and eight the mob came and beset John Nance's house. John Nance and John Paynter went out and stood before the door; though they were quickly covered with dirt. The cry was 'Bring out the preacher! Pull down the house' and they began to pull down the boards which were nailed against the windows. But the Mayor, hearing it, came without delay and read the proclamation against riots: upon which, after many oaths and imprecations, they thought proper to disperse.

## Chapter 15   The Anglican-Methodist Conversations

1    Michael Ramsey wrote:

> I know that I am a priest and a bishop in the historic order, referred to in our prayer book as coming down from the apostles' times. I know that Methodist ministers are ministers of the Word and sacrament used by Christ and they have been for many, many years. I know that their ministry is not identical with the historic episcopate and priesthood, but I am unable to define precisely what the relative value of the two is. I am frankly agnostic about a great deal of the Methodist ministry, knowing that it is not identical with my own, but also being perfectly certain that they are not just laymen. I am frankly agnostic. Is there anything wrong in acknowledging that? I have not invented this agnosticism for the purpose of this service. I have all my life

been agnostic about this.  Very well then.  In this laying on of hands with prayer I would be asking God through his Holy Spirit to give to the Methodist ministers what He knows that they need to make their ministry identical with ours as presbyters and priests in the Church of God.  It would be perfectly clear what was being asked for, the equalization of our ministries.  What would be undefined and undefinable is the present relative status. For that there is a great deal of room for variety of opinion.  You might have your opinions, I might have mine, the Methodist minister might have his, but that doesn't come into the service. The service asks God to be good enough to make our ministries equal, giving to them what grace and authority he knows that we need . . .

What would I mean receiving that laying on of hands?  I would mean this.  I believe that I am a priest and bishop in the Church of God.  Nothing can make me more so.  But I do believe that my ministry will have a very new significance and authority as a result of this Anglican-Methodist union, and I pray that God will give me that enrichment and significance through receiving the laying on of hands from the Methodist president and his colleagues.

Owne Chadwick. *Michael Ramsay: A Life* London: O.U.P. 1991, p.339.


## Chapter 16   The Rev'd Deryck Collingwood

1      Pew Rents and Allocated Pews.  The system finally broke down when a supernumerary minister, who had come to live at St. Maeburne was asked by Frank Jenkins to move to the 'Worn-out Ministers' Pew.'

One of the pew owners, William Collins, when asked to relinquish his seat, said he had 'never liked the pew allocated to him, anyway', and would be glad to move.

2      The Cross on the Table.  It would have been considered 'High' in 1949 to have a Cross on the Communion Table.  The puritan strand in Methodism has been wary of the use of symbols for fear that the symbol

might take the place of what it symbolises. However, visual symbols are now accepted as devotional aids: a cross on the Table, or hanging on the wall behind the Table, is now a central feature of almost all Methodist churches.

## Chapter 17   The Rev'd Arnold Morris

1.    Albert Road Church

By 1965, its income of £50 a week was insufficient to do more than maintain its weekly ministry to the northern part of the town, leaving nothing to be set aside for essential maintenance and repairs. In addition, there was a general feeling that it was inappropriate to have two Methodist Churches, offering a very similar pattern of worship and fellowship in a town where the two congregations might well be accommodated in a single building. There was awareness, too, of the many great humanitarian causes in the world crying out for support.

Three courses of action were considered: the demolition of the Church and its replacement with a new development such as Sheltered Housing, amalgamation with Trinity to form a single Methodist Society in Penarth, or adaptation of the present premises by creating a dual worship and general purposes area in the existing schoolroom, leaving the actual Church unused for the time being.

The last was decided upon. By September 1971 the schoolroom had been adapted and opened as a Church, with a sanctuary area at one end which could be closed off while weekday activities were in progress. The former Church did not remain unused for long. A Day Centre was created, similar to the one that had been established at Trinity, to serve the northern end of the town. A suspended ceiling closed off the whole of the upper balcony area of the Church and suitable 'homes' were found for the organ, pews and the stained glass East Window. The premises, now designated a 'Community Centre' were opened in 1974. The number of organisations for which it provided a base was impressive; Centres for the Blind and Handicapped, the Citizens' Advice Bureau, Tenants' Associations, Community Concern and 'Anonymous' groups, and, later, the Penarth Pastoral Foundation. The

Youth Club continued to meet in the basement and by 1975 a full-time Youth and Community Worker had been appointed.

In 1979, the temporary suspended ceiling in the former Church was replaced by a solid floor which provided ample space upstairs for badminton, gymnastics, table tennis and old-time dancing. The usual activities of a Methodist Church continued with Services on Sundays and fellowship meetings on weekdays; the Guides and the Boys' Brigade, those long-established Methodist Youth activities, continued to thrive whilst all the changes were taking place.

The whole of Penarth is served by the Albert Road Church and Community Centre, and it is estimated that over 1,000 people use the premises in the course of a week.

Dinas Powis Church.

Here, the work initiated by the young minister continued, although the maintenance of Youth House was a drain on the financial and administrative resources of the Society, which still in many ways regarded itself as a Village 'Cause'. By assuming responsibility for paying the salary of a Youth, later a Community, Worker, Glamorgan County Council recognised the contribution that the Church was making in creating a community between 'the Village' and the new estates which had been built and which were separated by the main road and a railway line.

The subsequent change of name from 'Youth House' to 'Wesley Centre', indicates the shift of emphasis from open youth work, to service to the community across the whole spectrum of ages and interests.

2      This Restructuring required an Act of Parliament which began its passage as the Methodist Church Bill in 1965 and ended as the Methodist Church Act in 1976. There was considerable opposition, mainly directed against the provision for possible changes in the doctrinal stance of Methodism, but also in defence of the long established rights of local trustees. The Bill proposed the abolition of Trustees as the sole bodies in which the property of the local churches was vested, and the establishment of Church Councils in which the

# NOTES

powers and responsibilities of the Trustees would be shared with the Leaders Meetings.

There was a widespread feeling that the existence of both Trustees and Leaders militated against the implementation of a unified Church policy and that the Trustees were often out of touch with the life of the Society and unsympathetic to its current needs. The Trinity Trustees, however, were not unsympathetic to the idea; on moving away from Penarth, Trustees normally resigned and so there was a gradual change in membership, but they could, as in the case of pew rents, lose contact with the needs of the Society. The Trinity Trustees did not resist their disbandment, although a number who did not move on to the Church Council took umbrage at what they felt to be a rejection of their services.

A number of Meetings were created by the new structure:

The Members' Meeting, held twice a year which can be attended by all on the Church Membership Roll. Chaired by the Minister, it elects the stewards, the Church Treasurer and representatives to the Church Council.

The Church Council, also chaired by the Minister, inherited the duties of the Leaders Meeting and added to those the responsibility of the Trustees. An elected body, it is advised by special interest groups in the appropriate fields. The Minister is an ex-officio member of each of these committees but does not necessarily preside. Indeed, at Trinity, in 1974, with its strong lay leadership, the Chairs of the Finance Committee, the Neighbourhood Committee, the Property Committee and the Committee for Mission were all lay. The Minister chaired the Church Family and the Pastoral Committee.

The new Constitution has gradually been accepted and its strongly democratic character is appreciated. Busy Church members are saved from attendance at unnecessary committee meetings, an overall strategy for the Church can be put into place and a unified control can be achieved.

At the height of the Anglican-Methodist Conversations, it seemed strange to be putting our own house meticulously in order. With their

268

postponement, Methodism in Penarth was in a position to be able to play its role effectively and was prepared to face the challenges of the future.

3       Wales was particularly fertile ground for acceptance of the Covenant.  This was partially because the Anglican Church had been disestablished since 1922; in addition there was the binding factor of the Welsh language used in parts of all the Churches, and a sense of Welsh identity, greater in some areas than others, which already overrode denominational boundaries.  There was also a compassable area in which the Covenant would have to operate.

The proposals for Covenanting were based on the belief that visible unity in the life and mission of all Church people is the Will of God, that such people should 'covenant together to accept each other as true members of the Body of Christ, to recognise each other's ministries, to receive the historic episcopacy, in the case of those who did not yet possess it, and to work towards visible unity.'  For the non-Anglican Churches, acceptance of episcopacy presented some difficulty.  The Methodist Church had discussed this issue earlier and at length in the Conversations with the Anglicans and was prepared to incorporate an episcopal form of ministry based on the assumption that it was already 'episcope' in that Conference exercised this function.

But where Wales pioneered, England was unable to follow. Discussions on the Covenant reached a head in the summer of 1982. The Methodist Church, the United Reformed Church and the Moravian Church accepted the Covenant Proposals, but the Church of England could not raise the required 66% either in the House of Clergy or in the total of all votes cast in the General Synod.  Some Clergy did not feel that the proposals adequately safeguarded 'Catholic Order,' and they were also concerned that the Covenant, if signed, would put back their Conversations with Rome. They were also aware that the Free Churches would present for recognition and reconciliation women ordained ministers as well as men.

As a result there is, as yet, no Covenant in England and this cannot but have a somewhat damping effect on the Welsh situation.  However, although considerably 'mistier' and less challenging than the organic unity which was the aim of Stage Two of the Anglican Methodist scheme, the Covenant has placed Wales in the forefront of international schemes for ecumenical advance. This can be seen in its development of a Communion Rite in 1982 and of an experimental rite for the administration of Christian Baptism for use in all the Covenanting Churches.

The Covenant has added a further dimension to Church relations in Penarth, both alongside and, in some degree, within the Council of Churches and, more recently, Cytun (Churches Together in Wales). Since Stanwell Road Baptist Church has signed the Covenant four Denominations are able to take part in joint Communion Services in Penarth, although they are not, as yet, under a single President. Despite all that is being done together under the Council of Churches, there is sometimes little to indicate that the Covenant has been signed and many Trinity members have little awareness that, with our close neighbours. All Saints and Stanwell Road Baptist Church, we are covenanted 'to work and pray so that by the Holy Spirit we may be brought into one visible Church.'

The emergence of one visible and united Church within Wales, if this meant the breaking of links with wider Methodism, would be serious for Trinity. It would threaten the very grounds for which many of its members and adherents seek out the Church which is the subject of this study. Trinity brings a British and, indeed, a World dimension to the Penarth Churches, and any United Church in Wales must reflect the richness of the contributions that each of its constituent member churches can bring. It will be a measure of the rightness of the Covenant when this is achieved.

4    The following extract is from the Autobiography of the Rev'd William Lea, deposited in the Rylands Library, Manchester:

> When we had got through our journey and were arrived as we hoped at our 'home', when the wearied mother and children hoped to find rest, alas, how were we disappointed. Not that there were no place for us, there was a two-roomed cottage provided for us. On our entering it, lo, how we were amazed. Not at the splendour of its furniture, nor at the beauty of its ceiling; for of the latter there was none at all; and of the former there were only some six or seven pieces, and none of these

appertained to the chamber, not a stick or thread of furniture was there. There was a pantry, but not the weight of a penny-piece of earthenware did it contain, and only one vessel was there for all culinary purposes, and that was the tea-kettle; and of that we could make no use for there was no fire, nor a single article in the crockery line. Hence we retreated with expressions of wonder withal, and repaired to a Public House and gave orders for some refreshment. After a short time we received a message from a Mr. S. giving us an invitation to take up our abode at his house, until our habitation was prepared. On our arrival we received an explanation touching the desolateness of what we had looked for as a home. But it is unnecessary to dwell on these reasons assigned; it may suffice for me to state that I was the first married Preacher appointed to the Station.

I had for a time at least to be furniture broker, and as such attended several sales in Ashbourne and made purchase of sundry necessary articles of furniture for our house. And I also made purchases at Leek of a number of culinary utensils, and which to save carriage and to expedite conveyance, I, in true hawker's style carried them over my shoulder hanging back and front, for twelve miles.

And in this way, by much labour and stringent economy, in a short time, I prepared our two-roomed cottage that we were able to occupy it, and to relieve Mr. S. from our encumbrance; and ourselves also from what was not to us, the most desirable, lodging in the same room where the servant lads bedded.

## Chapter 18  The Rev'd Leslie Craze

1      'Ceased to Meet'.

In the 1909 version of the Methodist Hymn Book the term used for such people had been 'backsliders.' But this picturesque word was already falling into disuse at the turn of the century, and was being replaced by the more general description, one which more adequately covered different categories. There were, for example, the former members who had lost their zeal and ceased to attend services, and there were those who had moved away from Penarth. If such people joined another Methodist Church and notified their minister, then their membership was transferred to that church. If they joined another denomination this was recorded and they could be so listed. A considerable number, however, gradually lost touch with Methodism. There was a tendency to retain the names of such people on the Membership Roll because their parents or friends wanted to be able to feel that they were still members of the Church – however loose the ties.

Douglas Wollen, the Minister at Albert Road in the Penarth Circuit had been the Connexional Church Membership Secretary. In his 'Report to Conference' in 1960 he wrote:

> If we can reduce the number of 'ceased to meet' we shall soon begin to show a steady increase . . . We believe that many of these lapsed Methodists could be saved by better pastoral care. We are constantly hearing of what can only be called cases of pastoral inefficiency – Members never visited by their class leaders though they have stopped coming regularly to church. Members transferred to other churches without any acknowledgment being received and without the transferred members being visited in their new home. Those of us who are Ministers confess that we are sometimes to blame but the final responsibility rests with and is shared by the whole Leaders Meeting.

Maybe he was right to castigate the Methodist people, but he ignored the teaching of the Parable of the Sower in which the pattern experienced by the church is foretold.

**Chapter 19   The Rev'd John Ashplant**

1     The nomination process for a Chairperson of District

The process of appointing a minister as the Chairperson of a District is lengthy. It begins with the appointment of a small panel of ministers and lay people by the Synod, which, after meeting on its own, meets with a Connexional Panel. The Connexional Panel have a knowledge of ministers of the right age who have had appropriate experience, and from this meeting a name or, if there is disagreement, more than one name, is sent to the Synod for consideration.

The Synod then votes on 'the name', or names, and, if it so wishes, it can have a further name added. The Synod's nomination then goes to Conference. The Conference, which also has the right to consider additional names, eventually, votes on the names before it. The Chairperson Designate takes office in the September of the following year, some two years from when the process was initiated.

2    International House

There are a number of causes for the fall in demand on places at International House between 1964 and 1985. During this period, the colleges in Cardiff had provided increasing accommodation for their students. The Thomson Foundation courses were moved from Cardiff to a centre near London, and the hospital courses for overseas Doctors for the treatment of pneumoconiosis were reduced in frequency and length. The requirement that overseas students at British colleges and universities pay 'full fees' and the changing position of the British Council drastically reduced the number of British Council Scholars. Those who now come from overseas have different needs; they are no longer young men and women taking a first degree or introductory course, often they are mature students, married and with children whose needs are better met by self-contained flats.

The number of U.K. Students choosing to live in an international community has not been maintained: it seems that the idealism of the post-war period did not survive the '80s.

The House was well filled during vacations by groups of handicapped adults and children, but they, too, found funding increasingly difficult and the holiday-makers visiting Penarth which the House accommodated in vacations had little effect on its viability.

The House depended on full, or nearly full occupancy, and its charges had to compete with those made by the other student hostels. These were subsidised either directly or indirectly by the providing bodies.

# NOTES

The Penarth Town Council was distressed at its closing and passed the following resolution at its meeting on 7 November 1985.

The Penarth Town Council commemorates the work of the past 21 years which has taken place at International House. This work has become part of the history and tradition of Penarth.

It was begun by Christian people who sought to overcome some of the effects of racial prejudice as it existed in this country in the 1950s and 60s, when overseas students had great difficulty in finding accommodation. In addition, International House played a significant role in providing a venue for holidays for the handicapped and the elderly.

Over the past 21 years the work of the International House was assisted by many Penarth people from every denomination and from all walks of life. They welcomed 'the stranger within their gates' in the true spirit of Christianity, and in so doing made a very significant contribution towards increasing international understanding.

The Penarth Town Council wishes to record this work – and to express thanks to those who were inspired to found the International House and to all those who supported its work over the years.

Mair Coombes Davies,  Town Mayor

E. J. Vick,                       Town Clerk

# NOTES

## Chapter 20   The Rev'd Albert Jewell

1     The Financial position of Trinity Methodist Church.

The financial stability of the Church has been undergirded by it Endowment Fund. In 1993 this amounted to £36, 000 invested with the Central Finance Board of the Methodist Church.

However, the policy of the Church Treasurers and of the Church Council is that income from this sum should not be used to meet deficits on the annual accounts but reserved to provide for the upkeep of the property, which, after one hundred years, requires constant maintenance.

It is by the regular Sunday giving of the Congregation – a considerable amount of it covenanted and, in consequence, attracting tax repayment, that the on-going annual liabilities of the Church can, and should, be met. There is income from lettings, but the Church Treasurer is loath to rely on these to make up any shortfall in the annual accounts because of their fluctuating and uncertain nature.

Over the first thirty Sundays in 1993 the weekly offerings averaged £470.  Here follows the statement of receipts and payments for the year ended 31 August 1992.  These indicate the sources of revenue, and the expenditure both on the Church and as contributed to the Circuit for the support of the Ministry and the Methodist Connexion as a whole.  Some amounts raised, for instance for Overseas and Home Missions and for Christian Aid, are not included in these figures.

# NOTES

## Statement of Receipts and Payments for the Year ended 31st August 1992

### RECEIPTS

|  | £ | £ |
|---|---|---|
| Collections |  |  |
| Envelopes | 4341.67 |  |
| Envelopes (Covenant Scheme) | 10396.35 |  |
| Cash | 7687.11 |  |
| Other direct payments | 7536.49 |  |
| Tax refunds on Covenant gifts | 5063.26 | 35024.88 |
|  |  |  |
| Hire of rooms |  | 2005.90 |
| Day Centre rent etc |  | 4802.01 |
| Donations to upkeep |  | 726.75 |
| Wedding and Funeral fees |  | 1150.00 |
| Collections for Special Purposes |  | 850.82 |
| Junior Church |  | 113.42 |
| Sale of Centenary mugs |  | 195.00 |
| Day Centre Teas & Coffees |  | 92.00 |
| Miscellaneous |  | 72.00 |
|  |  |  |
| Contra Items |  |  |
| Y.P.F. Christmas stamps |  | 185.57 |
| Visit to Ebbw Vale Garden Festival |  | 291.50 |
| Donation for purchase of Lectern Bible |  |  |
| (In Memoriam) |  | 180.00 |
| Malicious damage recovery (Roof) |  | 20.00 |
| Collection: Ebbw Vale Garden Festival |  | 80.49 |
| Total |  | 45790.34 |

# NOTES

## PAYMENTS

|  | £ | £ |
|---|---|---|
| Caretaking (Wages, materials etc) |  | 7688.92 |
| Heating & lighting (Gas & Electricity) |  | 2792.90 |
| Water charges |  | 509.60 |
| Insurances |  | 1321.53 |
| Circuit Assessment |  | 21337.50 |
| Telephone |  | 161.10 |
| Repairs & Renewals |  | 607.47 |
| Organ maintenance |  | 512.32 |
| Organists |  | 400.00 |
| Printing, Duplicating & Stationery |  | 1506.33 |
| Collection for Special Purposes |  | 746.82 |
| Connexional & Other Funds |  | 1345.00 |
| Junior Church |  | 513.70 |
| Lift Maintenance |  | 91.00 |
| Subscription to R.S.C.M. |  | 30.00 |
| Music copyright |  | 112.00 |
| Baptismal & other candles |  | 77.24 |
| Communion glasses & wine |  | 35.01 |
| Hymn Books/Marriage Service Books |  | 223.17 |
| Confirmation gifts |  | 63.37 |
| Loan to Scouts (Purchase of Mini Bus) |  | 1500.00 |
| Miscellaneous |  | 141.11 |
|  |  |  |
| Contra Items |  |  |
| Y.P.F. Stamps Fund |  | 185.57 |
| Visit to Ebbw Vale Garden Festival |  | 291.50 |
| Purchase of Lectern Bible |  |  |
|     (In Memoriam of David Whitefield) |  | 180.00 |
| Malicious damage recovery (Roof) |  | 20.00 |
| Ebbw Vale Garden Festival | 80.49 |  |
| Add: Contribution from Church Funds | 19.51 | 100.00 |
|  |  | 42493.16 |
| Surplus on Years Account |  | 3207.18 |
| Total |  | 45790.34 |

277

# A DESCRIPTION OF THE CHURCH AND THE ANCILLARY PREMISES

## The Church

The first Methodist Service was held in the Tin Tabernacle on 3 August 1890, and services continued to be held there until 1897 when they were transferred to the Schoolroom which had been built alongside. The Tin Tabernacle was removed to Barry and, when re-erected, served as a Moose Hall; it was destroyed by fire in May 1993.

The present Church was opened on 2 January 1901.

The main building material is Newbridge Stone, an excellent weathering stone which was quarried from various sites in the South Wales mining valleys. The spire and window surrounds are of Bath Stone which is vulnerable to weathering.

The Church has been little altered. It has retained its original layout and many of its original features, and adaptations, to enable the Church to accommodate large choirs or dramatic performances have made use of temporary rostra.

The stained-glass windows were designed by H. J. Salisbury, brother of Frank Salisbury, the Methodist artist.

|  | Subject: | In Memory of: |
| --- | --- | --- |
| West Window: | 'Death is swallowed up in victory' | Susan andAnnie Gibbs |
| East Window: | The Ascension | Thomas and Susanna Morel |
| South Transept: | 'Give unto them eternal life' | John Angel Gibbs |
| North Transept: | 'Suffer little children to come unto me' | E. Rabjohn Moxey |
| South Nave: | 'Feed my Sheep' 'Come, take up thy Cross and follow me' | Arthur Dawson Llewelyn and Elizabeth Davies |

| | | |
|---|---|---|
| | 'Except ye become converted and become as little children ye shall in no wise enter the Kingdom of Heaven' | Rev'd Joseph Blanch |
| North Nave: | 'Well done good and faithful servant' | William and Lydia Thomas |
| | 'Thou shall love they neighbour as thyself' | – |
| | 'Be thou faithful unto death' | – |
| Clerestory: | Moses and Elijah | L. H. Allen Pratt |

E. Rabjohn Moxey was the general manager for John Cory, Coal Exporters, when the firm established coaling stations throughout the World. He was a pillar of Roath Road Methodist Chapel in Cardiff, and, on his death, his widow removed to 54, Plymouth Road, Penarth, and worshipped at Trinity. Her pew was in the south transept so that she could see the window in the north transept that she had given in her husband's memory.

Susan and Annie Gibbs were the mother and unmarried sister of Susanna and Martha Morel. They lived in Dumfries Place in Cardiff and never moved to Penarth.

The widow of the Rev'd. Joseph Blanch moved to Penarth and lived with her daughter and son-in-law, the Edes.

William Thomas was an Accountant, who lived with his wife, Lydia, in Brynowan, Archer Road.

The Organ consists of 3 manuals plus full pedal board. It was built by Norman and Beard of London and Norwich, and installed in 1908. Enlarged in 1919, it was renovated and rectified by Rushworth and Dreaper in 1949.

It is considered to be a fine example of Victorian Organ construction; the sounds have warmth and are conducive to a worshipful atmosphere.

In 1909, H. J. Salisbury arranged for a copy to be made of Leonardo da Vinci's painting of the Last Supper and for this to be placed over the

Communion Table. The copier spent several months in Italy in the execution of this commission.

The Pulpit is built of several different kinds of marble; white marble from Carrera in Italy, gold marble from Sienna in Italy, Green marble from Tinos in the Aegean and a red polished local Radyr stone. It replaced the original oak pulpit in 1912.

In 1919, the brass Eagle lectern, given by the men and women who served in the Great War, was dedicated 'in Memory of their fallen comrades and in humble gratitude for their own return.'

In the 1950s the North Transept was adapted as a small Chapel with moveable seating. The Table was made by Ernest Moss from a redundant pew. The hassocks are from International House: they and the Lectern Fall were designed by Anne Butler and illustrate parables.

The flags of the uniformed organisations are kept in the Chapel and are paraded on the fourth Sunday of each month.

A plaque on the wall commemorates James Reed, aged 18, who was drowned when the Titanic sank. Given by his fellow scholars, it used to mark his place in the Sunday School.

In 1969, the Preacher's rostrum and Lectern, used originally by the Trinity Womens' Hour was placed in its present position during the Ministry of the Rev'd Arnold Morris to enable him to achieve closer contact with the Congregation.

The Cross on the Communion Table was given in memory of Catherine Frances Hosegood in 1949. There have always been flowers on the Communion Table during services, and these are now given by members to mark special anniversaries.

Some of the wood originally in the Church was pine: the Doors, the Communion Rail and the Screen at the back of the Church. Over the years, they have been replaced by oak, as has the Font given in 1922. These were all memorial gifts and were made by W.A. Clarke and Co. of Llandaff. In addition the Church has received many other memorial gifts which are in constant use.

The plaque on the north wall of the Chancel carries the names of those killed in the 1939-45 War and was given in memory of Graham Hosegood.

His father, A. W. Hosegood, Secretary of the Church for many years, thought that the Church had been sufficiently embellished and that the problem for the present and the future would be to maintain the Church. To encourage people to give gifts of money, he gave the plaques on the South Wall of the Chancel on which endowments are commemorated.

During 1988, a library for adults and children was created in the South Transept. On the wall of the Transept is a panel which previously hung in the Entrance Hall of International House: 'The World under our Roof' by Michael Edmunds.

The lighting fixtures, the heating system and the sound amplification system have been updated from time to time. The present arrangement includes a 'Loop system' for the hard of hearing.

In 1992 and 1993 a major programme of work on the Church was undertaken. The spire was rebuilt, stonework treated, rainwater goods repaired and the finials replaced. The Church became a Grade II Listing building in May 1993.

**The Ancillary Premises**

The Schoolroom, built in 1896, served as the Church for some years and, from time to time when the Church could not be used, has subsequently been used for the same purpose.

It consisted of a large, high, galleried hall, with small classrooms off, a Library and a Primary Room and Church Parlour above. It was entered by steep steps on the Stanwell Road side, through doors marked 'boys' and 'girls', and by a small door opening on to Woodland Place.

In 1905, The Woodland Institute in Woodland Place was purchased and used for Youth Work, and, in the daytime, by Llansannor School. Later, part was taken for a chapel keeper's house. With the developments on the main site, the remainder was used less and less and the whole was sold in 1974 to the Church in Wales.

After the end of the 1939-1945 War, the flourishing life of the Church, particularly in its Youth Work and Drama Group, revealed the inadequacy of the original Schoolroom and minor adaptations were made in 1946.

In 1965 extensive alterations were undertaken: a wide access from Woodland Place with a crush hall, staircase and wide passageway giving access to what came to be called 'Trinity Hall' was created, and a stage and proscenium were built. The whole formed a not inconsiderable 'little theatre' with a complete range of lighting equipment and raked auditorium when so used.

January 1970 marked the opening of the Trinity Day Centre. The single storey extension to the Hall was built on the forecourt facing Stanwell Road: a large room where meals could be served in the daytime and which was available for church use in the evenings and on Sundays. In addition, the passageway into the south porch of the Church was created so that the whole premises, Church and Hall, can be used as one.

The occasion of the building of this extension was used to update and increase the toilet facilities, to make the premises accessible to wheelchairs, and to create a kitchen in what had originally been the library.

By the 1980's, the Trinity Hall premises were in urgent need of renovation, and radical reconstruction of the interior was undertaken in 1986. By installing an additional floor, a large multi-purpose hall was created on the first floor, and a series of rooms of varying sizes on the ground floor, including storage space, kitchen and more lavatories. The crush hall, now foyer, was further increased in size, and an office, lift and prayer chapel, designed by a student from the Cardiff School of Design, open on to it. The Table – a carpenter's bench – and The Cross by Michael Edmonds from the Chapel at International House are presently in the foyer.

In 1992 and 1993 a second major programme of work was undertaken on the Trinity Hall premises. The slate roof was replaced, the north wall of the Hall rebuilt and the chimney stack taken down. Extensive dry rot was discovered under the floor in the entrance foyer and prayer chapel and this was treated. The Hall was listed as a Grade II building in May 1993.

# BIBLIOGRAPHY

## Penarth and District

Benjamin, E. Alwyn, *Penarth 1841-1871: A Glimpse of the Past.* Cowbridge: D. Brown and Sons Ltd. 1980.

Carradice, Phil, *Headlands School: in Camera* Quotes Ltd.: Buckingham, 1991.

Daunton, M. J., *Coal Metropolis Cardiff 1870-1914.* Leicester: Leicester University Press, 1977.

Gibbs, John Morel, *Morels of Cardiff: The History of a Family Shipping Firm.* Cardiff: National Museum of Wales, 1982.

Hilling, John B., *Cardiff and the Valleys.* London: Lund Humphries, 1973.

*Mate's Illustrated Guide to Penarth.* W. Mate and Sons Ltd. Bournemouth, 1903.

Moore, Patricia, *South Glamorgan. A County History.* Cowbridge: Stuart Williams, 1975.

Thorne, Ray, *Penarth. A History. Volume 1 and Volume 11 1975 and 1976.* Risca, Newport: Starling Press, 1976.

Tilney, Chyrstal, *A History of the Parish of Penarth with Lavernock.* Published by the author, 1988.

## Methodism

Brake, George Thompson, *Policy and Politics in British Methodism 1932-1982.* London: Edsall. 1984.

Chadwick, Owen, *Michael Ramsay: A Life.* London: Oxford University Press, 1991.

Currie, Robert, *Methodism Divided.* London: Faber and Faber, 1968.

Davies, Rupert, *Methodism.* Peterborough: Epworth Press, 1984.

Garlick, Kenneth, *Garlick's Methodist Registry.* London: Edsall 1983.

Gibbs, John Morel, *Methodist Residential Schools. A Conflict of Attitudes.* London: Board of Management for Methodist Residential Schools, 1989.

Jobson, Frederick J., *Chapel and School Architecture.* Facsimile reprint, Peterborough: Methodist Publishing House., 1850.

Maltby, W. Russell, *Obiter Dicta.* Epworth Press, 1932.

A History of the Methodist Church in Great Britain. Vol. 3, London: Epworth Press, 1983.


**Methodist Service and Hymn Books,** all published by the Methodist Publishing House, Peterborough.

*The Methodist Hymn Book.* (M.H.B.) 1933.

*The Methodist Service Book.* 1975.

*Hymns and Psalms.* (H. and P.) 1983.


**Trinity Minute Books – in chronological order:**

*Penarth and Barry Circuit Minute Book 1893-1930.*

*Penarth Circuit Sunday School Council Minute Book 1912-1943.*

*Trinity Trust Minute Book 1940-1976.*

*Trinity Leaders Meeting Minute Book 1947-1954.*

*Penarth and Barry Circuit Minute Book 1959-1965.*

*Penarth Circuit Finance and General Purposes Minute Book 1962-1976.*

*Trinity Finance Committee Minute Book 1965-1969.*

*Trinity Leaders Meeting Minute Book 1965-1970.*

*Penarth and Barry Circuit Minute Book 1966-1971.*

*Trinity Leaders Meeting Minute Book 1970-1982.*

*Penarth Circuit Meeting Minute Book 1972-1981.*

*Trinity Property Committee Minute Book 1974-1982.*

*Trinity Finance Committee Minute Book 1974-1982.*

*Trinity Church Council Minute Book 1983-1987.*

## Trinity Periodicals

*The Circuit Record 1914-1950* (incomplete), either in The National Library of Wales, Aberystwyth or the Glamorgan Archives, Cathays Park, Cardiff.

| *Contact.* | *Vol.1* | *1962-1970.* |
| | *Vol.2* | *1970-1979.* |
| | *Vol.3* | *1980-1991.* |
| | *Vol.4* | *1991-1993.* |

*Trinity Diamond Jubilee. 1951*

*Trinity 2000. 'Where Many Ways Meet'. 1986.*

## Records of other Churches

*Albert Road Methodist Church and Community Centre. Penarth: 1907-1991.*

*Cathays Methodist Church. Cardiff. Centenary Celebration: 1882-1982.*

*Porthkerry Road Methodist Church, Barry. Centenary Celebration: 1889-1989.*

# GLOSSARY

## A Note on Nomenclature

The Methodist system of church organisation and government has evolved from that established by John Wesley to meet the needs of his growing 'Movement' in the Eighteenth century, and is still to be found today in the Methodist Church in Britain and in other Methodist Churches around the World. Sizable parts of it, too, can be recognised in the national United or Uniting Churches that have developed in a number of countries. The Church has become progressively democratic, but there are still traces of clerical influence, stemming from Wesley himself.

The main elements are set out below.

The Society is the term used originally by Wesley to indicate groups of people who had joined with him. The term is now used to cover the group based on a local church; the church members.

Leaders or Stewards are the terms used to designate those appointed by the Society to have, with the Minister, care of the Society.

The Trustees were those who, until the Church was restructured in 1976, had legal responsibility for the administration of Methodist properties.

The Circuit is the group of local Methodist Churches, so grouped as to best serve local situations and to reflect changes in social and demographical factors. One of the ministers in the circuit is designated as Superintendent. Lay Circuit Stewards are appointed to have, with the Minister, the care of the Circuit.

The District Synod is the body in which the circuits in a particular area are grouped for administrative convenience and to provide a two-way channel of communication between the Conference and the circuits. It is presided over by a ministerial Chairman.

The Conference, which meets annually, is the supreme legislative body of the Methodist Church. The Pastoral Session, which is concerned almost entirely with ministerial matters, consists of 288 ministers, the great majority elected by the districts or Conference. They are joined by 288 lay representatives for the Representative Session, also elected. Ministers are stationed in their circuits by the Conference. The Conference is presided over by the President, always a minister, and the Vice President, a layman or laywoman; both are elected for one year.

The Connexion is the term used to describe those who were 'in connexion with Mr. Wesley.' It underlines the fact that all Methodists and all Methodist Churches are in connexion with each other in contrast to a system of independent groups.

Gibbs, Elizabeth, 32, 97, 103, 115
Gibbs, Gladys (née Morel), 31, 33-35, 64, 66-67, 97, 101-103, 106, 115, 119, 121
Gibbs, James, 9, 171-173
Gibbs, John Angel, 32, 64-67
Gibbs, John Angel Sen. and family, 31-32, 34, 97, 99, 102, 278
Gibbs, John Morel, 32, 78, 100-101, 104, 109-110, 112, 118, 124, 129, 131, 133, 149-150, 159, 161, 178, 183-184, 194, 216
Gibbs, John and Sheila's family, 101, 118, 140, 206
Gibbs, Sheila (née Newton), 110, 112, 114, 124, 133, 149, 161-162, 174-175, 177-178, 195, 214, 228
Gibbs, William, 32-33, 84-85, 97-99, 103
Gibbs, William Benjamin, 28, 32, 34
Girl Guides, 73, 78, 108, 110, 117, 125, 135, 201, 210, 213, 222, 280
Good, Jean, 9, 152
Gypsy Smith, 60

Hancock, Robert J., 34, 54
Harmer, Leslie and Anne, 213
Harris, Douglas and Sheila, 204
Hatton Evans, Ivor, 54, 75
Hatton Evans, Olive, 54, 71-72
Hibbert, Arthur and Maud, 34 57
Hinde family, 54
Hingley, Robert, 121-130
Hooper, Elaine (née Williams), Alan and family, 221

Hosegood, Arthur and family, 70, 78, 87, 115, 123, 167-168, 281
Hughes, Hugh Price, 41, 44

International House of South Wales, 139, 178-180, 184, 192-193, 207-209, 219-221, 235, 273-274, 282

James, Donald and family, 87, 110, 117, 123, 151, 152, 181, 209
James, Edward, Sheila and family, 205, 222
Jefferson, Derek, 127, 129, 219
Jenkin, H. J. and Mrs, 96
Jenkins, Frank, 52, 71, 88, 107, 126
Jewell, Albert and Gill, 232-240
Johnes, Huw and Anna, 188
Johnes, Geraint, 188, 192
Johns, Kelvin, 171-173
Johnston, J. J., 69-75, 76, 91-93
Junior Church, 168-170, 191, 203-204, 210-211, 223-224, 228, 237-238

Knighton, Anne (née Evans), 154-155, 218-219, 230, 241-247
Knighton, Donald, 88, 91, 118-119, 122, 128, 155, 218-219, 236, 245, 247, 273
Knighton, George and Evelyn, 70, 90, 107, 110, 126, 155, 219
Knighton, Mary, 87, 88, 101, 107-109, 113, 119, 122, 127, 129, 154, 219
Kreiger, John, 178

Newton, Herbert and Jess, 70, 86, 91, 95, 97, 99, 101, 102, 106, 115
Newton, Sheila, *and see Gibbs*, 69-70, 78, 95, 100, 104, 109

Occupations of Trinity Members, 82, 260-261
Organ, 55, 115, 126, 189, 226, 279
Owen, Edwin, 66
Owen, Mrs Wesley, 79

Pacifism, 63-64, 66, 100-101, 118
Parish, Arthur and Marie, 187-188
Parish, Elizabeth (Gillespie), 188, 192, 205
Parkes, James, 109-112
Parry, Joseph, 22
Pearce family, 54
Pearce, Mark Guy, 69
Pearson, Griffiths John, 62, 104
Pedwell, Janet and family, 237-238
Pegler, Percy and family, 76-85
Penarth and Barry Circuit, 28-29, 34, 66, 82, 89, 91-93, 109, 128, 133, 142
Penarth Circuit, 142, 159, 175, 203, 210, 214, 263-264
Penarth Council of Churches, 133, 178, 207, 214, 224-225, 238
Penarth House, 21, 31, 57, 178
Penarth Schools, 34, 35, 73, 77, 80, 188, 218, 244
Perks, Sir Robert, 44, 251
Pew Rents, 71, 81-82, 143-145, 167, 259, 265
Pickard, Ernest, 131-139

Play Group, 205, 224, 238
Player's Church, Tin Tabernacle, 26, 28, 35, 56, 278
Plymouth Windsor-Clive family, 14-19, 23, 25, 48, 248
Poley, June, 226
Ponsford, Howard and Olive, 156, 161, 165, 179, 189, 194, 202, 225, 232-233
Ponsford, David, 189
Pope, F. J., 63-64
Pratt, Bertha, 117
Pratt, L. H. Allen, 75, 86, 106, 115, 137
Pulpit, 57, 69, 280

Ramsey, Michael, 158, 163, 264-265
Reith, Tim, 238
Relationships with other Churches, 56, 78, 82, 104, 119, 126, 129, 133-134, 157-163, 178, 193-194, 201 211, 214, 218, 224-225, 228, 235, 238, 240-241, 248-249
Requisitioning of Premises, 116-117, 121-122
Restructuring, 175, 193, 203, 267-268
Roberts, Colin, 209
Roberts, Eileen *and see Chivers,* 73
Roberts, Stan and Bronwyn, 237

Saint Augustine's Church, 14, 23, 26, 56, 159
Saint Maeburne, 34, 80, 209, 265